SPORT AND CRIME

This is the first book to explore fully the connections between sport studies and criminology, opening up critical new frontiers in the study of sport and crime.

Rooted firmly in established critical criminological traditions, the book also employs insights from emerging theoretical frameworks such as cultural criminology, governmentality theory and critical security studies to make better sense of a range of transnational and contemporary cases, events and trends that reveal, in different ways, the crimes and harms that are present in sport. Empirically grounded, including case studies of the 2022 World Cup in Qatar and the Tokyo 2020 Olympic Games, it explores emerging themes in contemporary sport, including but not limited to corruption, doping, youth crime, terrorism, violence and transgression, and human rights abuses. *Sport and Crime* consciously pushes the boundaries of what might be considered the critical criminology of sport.

This is an essential text for any course on sport and crime, and invaluable reading for any student or researcher with an interest in the sociology of sport, sport development, sport policy, the politics of sport, critical criminology or socio-legal studies.

Peter Millward is Professor of Contemporary Sociology at Liverpool John Moores University, UK. His main research interests are in the areas of sport, social movements, cultural relational sociology and, here, critical approaches to understanding crime, criminality and harm. He has undertaken several research projects funded by the UKRI and European Commission. He is joint editor of the Routledge book series *Critical Research in Football* and serves on the editorial board of a number of internationally leading journals, including *Sociology*.

Jan Andre Lee Ludvigsen is Senior Lecturer in International Relations and Politics with Sociology at Liverpool John Moores University, UK. Broadly, his main research areas are within the social and political study of sport, and his research on sport mega-events, security, risk and fandom has been published in journals such as the *International Review for the Sociology of Sport*, *Journal of Consumer Culture*, *Leisure Studies* and *Journal of Sport and Social Issues*. He has also authored *Sport Mega-Events, Security and Covid-19: Securing the Football World* (Routledge, 2022).

Jonathan Sly is Lecturer in Applied Criminology at Canterbury Christ Church University, UK. His research interests focus on contemporary manifestations of aggressive masculinity. This includes sports-related violence and associated subcultures globally, subjective inter-personal violence and street culture in late-modern Britain, and the links between transgressive practices and social class in the contemporary era. He also has a broader academic interest in the social scientific analysis of crime and deviance, contemporary illicit substance markets and consumer culture, sport management and sports fandom, reflexive and biographical qualitative research methodologies, and critical debates and new directions in criminological theory.

Frontiers of Sport
Series editor
Alan Bairner
Loughborough University, UK

Sport is ubiquitous in the modern era. As such, it is engaged with by exponents of other academic disciplines and professional groups. This innovative series explores the close relationships that exist between sport and other disciplines and professions, and traces the theoretical and professional boundaries that they share. Each book in the series introduces the key themes, topics and debates that define a particular discipline and its engagement with sport – such as sport and sociology, or sport and politics – offering an invaluable overview for all students and scholars working in sport and each mainstream discipline.

Available in this series:

Sport and Sociology
Dominic Malcolm

Sport and Film
Seán Crosson

Sport and Architecture
Benjamin S. Flowers

Sport and Crime
Towards a Critical Criminology of Sport
Peter Millward, Jan Andre Lee Ludvigsen and Jonathan Sly

For more information about this series, please visit: www.routledge.com/Frontiers-of-Sport/book-series/FOSP

SPORT AND CRIME

Towards a Critical Criminology of Sport

Peter Millward, Jan Andre Lee Ludvigsen and Jonathan Sly

Routledge
Taylor & Francis Group

LONDON AND NEW YORK

Cover Image: © Getty Images

First published 2023
by Routledge
4 Park Square, Milton Park, Abingdon, Oxon OX14 4RN

and by Routledge
605 Third Avenue, New York, NY 10158

Routledge is an imprint of the Taylor & Francis Group, an informa business

© 2023 Peter Millward, Jan Andre Lee Ludvigsen and Jonathan Sly

The right of Peter Millward, Jan Andre Lee Ludvigsen and Jonathan Sly to be identified as authors of this work has been asserted in accordance with sections 77 and 78 of the Copyright, Designs and Patents Act 1988.

All rights reserved. No part of this book may be reprinted or reproduced or utilised in any form or by any electronic, mechanical, or other means, now known or hereafter invented, including photocopying and recording, or in any information storage or retrieval system, without permission in writing from the publishers.

Trademark notice: Product or corporate names may be trademarks or registered trademarks, and are used only for identification and explanation without intent to infringe.

British Library Cataloguing-in-Publication Data
A catalogue record for this book is available from the British Library

Library of Congress Cataloging-in-Publication Data
A catalog record for this book has been requested

ISBN: 978-1-032-23324-6 (hbk)
ISBN: 978-1-032-23322-2 (pbk)
ISBN: 978-1-003-27679-1 (ebk)

DOI: 10.4324/9781003276791

Typeset in Bembo
by Apex CoVantage, LLC

CONTENTS

Acknowledgements   *vi*

1   Introduction   1

2   Sport and the Critical Criminological Imagination   13

3   Sport, Corruption and White-Collar 'Criminality': Crimes of the Powerful (1)   41

4   Governing Young People and Communities through Sport   77

5   Modes of Security, Governance and Surveillance in Sport   93

6   Cultural Criminology, Sport and Transgression   123

7   Sport and Social Harms – Qatar and World Cup 2022 in Focus: Crimes of the Powerful (2)   144

8   Conclusion: (Even) Further Towards a Critical Criminology of Sport   179

Index   *189*

ACKNOWLEDGEMENTS

Undoubtedly, there are a number of people that we want to acknowledge, who have been important sources of support and guidance in the process of writing this book.

Collectively, we first wish to acknowledge the Series Editor of the Frontiers of Sport book series, Alan Bairner, for his support throughout the various stages of this book project. Then, we also wish to thank Simon Whitmore and Rebecca Connor at Routledge for their constant guidance and help over the last years.

Since Pete co-wrote his last book, *Collective Action and Football Fandom* (2018, with Jamie Cleland, Mark Doidge and Paul Widdop), he and Anna have welcomed their second child, Jack Richard Millward (in 2019). Pete dedicates this book to Jack and wishes to thank Anna and Layla for their constant patience with a 'Dad and the Lad' combination running around the family home creating chaos. Sometimes utter chaos. On an academic level, Pete developed the idea for this book some years before its publication with colleagues and friends, Laura Kelly and Emma Poulton. That version of *Sport and Crime* never managed to see the light of day but served as an inspiration to this text and so enormous thanks are due to Laura and Emma. He would also like to place on record his appreciation to co-authors Jan and Jon for collegiality, friendship and support in writing this version of the book. Thanks, as always, are due to members of 'The Football Collective'. Jon would like to acknowledge the co-authors for their encouragement and patience.

Jan wishes to dedicate this book to his family who he can always rely on for true support and encouragement. He also wishes to thank Jodie Hodgson for her support, advice and patience during the writing stages of this book. He also forwards a special thanks to other friends, colleagues or research collaborators. This includes, of course, not only Peter and Jon but also Dan Feather, Joe Moran, Jack Sugden, André Keil, Dave Webber, Mark Turner, Matthew Hill, David Tyrer, Dan Parnell, John Hayton, Chris Allen and Lizz Peatfield.

Finally, whilst we'd like to emphasise that any errors are entirely those of the authors, we remain hopeful and confident that *Sport and Crime: Towards a Critical Criminology of Sport* will represent an important addition to its fields.

1
INTRODUCTION

Sport, Crime and Criminology: Introducing a Complex Relationship

It is now well-established that sport matters in the social world (Dunning, 1999; Morgan, 2006). Indeed, George Orwell (1945) described serious sport as 'war minus the shooting'. For Orwell, international sport was conflictual and packed with hatred, violence, jealousy and disregard for all rules. Whereas this seems to suggest that sport matters for many of the 'wrong' reasons, we can currently see the social scientific study of sport has steadily progressed into new avenues and experienced the rise of new academic subdisciplines (Malcolm, 2012). For example, the sociology of sport was recently described as a 'burgeoning subdiscipline' of the twenty-first century (Tian and Wise, 2020) and had previously been dubbed the 'liveliest and most fruitful' of all sport's academic subdisciplines (Dunning, 2004: 17). It must be emphasised that this has not always been the case. Giulianotti and Brownell (2012: 211) highlight how sport, despite its importance in modern public life, has 'tended to be treated as an insufficiently "serious" subject for scholars in the social sciences, arts, and humanities'. Now, however, it is highly regular to speak of a sociology of sport (Dunning, 2004; Malcolm, 2012), sport geography (Bale, 2003), sport history (Mandell, 1984), sport law (Parrish, 2003; Thornton, 2011), the politics of sport (Allison, 1986, 2004), the political sociology of sport (Gilchrist et al., 2015) and physical cultural studies (Silk and Andrews, 2011).

A distinctive, energetic and burgeoning *criminology of sport* has, notwithstanding, remained underdeveloped, and perhaps somewhat conflated *with* the mentioned subdisciplines of the sociology of sport or sport law. That is *not* to say, however, that scholars have not noticed or realised the sheer potential for a distinctive criminology of sport (Groombridge, 2017; Corteen, 2018; Meek, 2013; Nichols, 2010) – or that academics have outright failed to tackle, either theoretically or empirically,

DOI: 10.4324/9781003276791-1

the manifold of issues related to crime, social control, punishment or harm that occur within, throughout or via sport (Samatas, 2007; Kelly, 2011; Kennedy and Silva, 2020). Though, as Finley (2013) asserts, criminological research exploring sport has primarily done so in relation to 'crimes' committed by athletes or fans. To be sure, we argue that whereas the 'crimes' of sport have been critically zoomed in on by researchers, such explorations have too seldom applied critical criminological theoretical lenses – a challenge we explicitly pick up and correct in this book.

Preceding our book, Nic Groombridge's (2017) *Sports Criminology: A Critical Criminology of Sports and Games* marked an important moment. In his monograph, Groombridge provides the first critical criminological perspective of sport. Throughout his work, contemporary criminological issues situated in sport – including crime prevention, criminal justice and social control – are explored through cases of, inter alia, boxing, motorsport and football. Importantly, his main intention is to 'say something to and about criminology more generally' (p. 155). Brisman (2019) reviews *Sports Criminology: A Critical Criminology of Sports and Games* and concludes that it 'seem[s] more like an opening bell or a starting pistol' than the development of a field' (p. 384). He further argued that 'Groombridge comes across in this chapter [Chapter One of the text] as a father wanting acknowledgment of paternity without the responsibilities of child-rearing' (p. 373). We offer a much warmer reception, but clearly there is space to theme and understand discussions according to critical criminological themes, to stretch the concepts and add value to them using examples from sport, as we do here. A key value of Groombridge's (2017) contribution lies in its creation of a momentum for an emerging field. And, as he states, his book sought to do exactly that; 'to encourage more engagement' (p. 12) in the field. Adding to this, Corteen (2018) proposed a critical criminology of professional wrestling and sports entertainment. She argues that this would form a part of 'sports criminology – *a very new area* of exploration within critical criminology' (p. 149, emphasis added). Furthermore, Jump's (2020) *The Criminology of Boxing, Violence and Desistance* represents another important, yet recent contribution in the field. The momentum that clearly has been built up, we seek to tie into, capitalise on and boost further by bringing together the social study of sport with critical criminology. In that sense, *Sport and Crime: Towards a Critical Criminology of Sport* makes an important and timely contribution to a field that arguably has the potential to be both lively and fruitful as a subdiscipline (cf. Dunning, 2004), which is powerfully demonstrated by recent the contributions mentioned earlier.

As Groombridge (2017) notes in relation to the earlier literature, criminological issues in sport have typically been approached from a sociology of deviance perspective. Within the prior work, he specifically outlines the work of Atkinson and Young (2008) and Blackshaw and Crabbe (2004) as two contributions that have 'come close to sports criminology' (Groombridge, 2017: 7). Indeed, in the preface of *Deviance and Social Control in Sport* (2008), Atkinson and Young do reflect on a longstanding 'frustration' over the 'missed opportunities to develop and expand sociological understandings of sport deviance through cross-fertilization between these two subdisciplines' (p. vii), referring to the sociology of sport and criminology.

Atkinson and Young argue that, throughout the 'subfield criminology, deviance, and social control, sport is rarely considered seriously, despite the many and varied controversies, corruptions, and illegalities *out there*' (ibid., original emphasis). Primarily concerned with 'deviance' in sport, Atkinson and Young made important advances towards a criminology of sport, with their use of criminological perspectives as applied to deviant sport communities, deviant athletic bodies and the popular mediation of sport-related deviance. However, they do not necessarily intend to advance the criminology of sport as a field itself. Rather, they help us understand how the theoretical tools from criminology clearly can assist the sociology of sport. Meanwhile, Blackshaw and Crabbe (2004) remain principally concerned with the consumption of sport that can be seen as 'deviant'. The core of their argument is captured by their statement that:

> Our somewhat depressing point is that in the age of consumer capitalism, when those experiences come into contact with celebrity, they become commodity forms which are presented performatively, glamorised and, like the prospect of weapons of mass destruction, sexed up for our consumption.
>
> *(p. 182)*

Thus, Crabbe and Blackshaw present a central plank that parallels 'deviance' in sport to consumption, mediatisation and 'moral panics' (Cohen, 2002; Critcher, 2002).

Ultimately, a bridge-building between sport and critical criminology, as well as theoretical refreshment exercises have been called for by scholars positioned within the two disciplines (Atkinson and Young, 2008; Armstrong and Hodges-Ramon, 2015; Corteen, 2018). Furthermore, within the academic spheres, we can also observe that sport have come to feature in, for instance, special sections of criminological journals (see *Criminal Justice Matters*, 2012, 88(1), 14–33, for a subsection on 'sports and 'harm'). Meanwhile, London's housing for the 2012 Summer Olympics was in the spotlight of the *British Criminological Association*'s summer newsletter (see Millie et al., 2012).

So, there seems to be a general acceptance that there is a powerful and dynamic link between 'sport' and 'criminology'. Notwithstanding, it may still be argued that scholarly investigations into 'crime', 'social justice', 'social control', 'deviance' and 'harm', when examined through sport, tend to feature in outlets whose aims and scopes are chiefly oriented towards the sociology of sport. For example, to date, there is – to the best of our knowledge – still not an international journal fully dedicated to the criminology of sport and, arguably, the social scientific area of Criminology has not been made the most of in the academic study of sport, whether that is grassroots or elite sport. Indeed, a scan of key journals such as the *British Journal of Criminology, Criminology & Criminal Justice, Theoretical Criminology, Critical Criminology* and *Crime, Media, Culture* also confirms that sport, with some important exceptions (e.g. Stott et al., 2012; McBride, 2020), has been often ignored despite its criminological relevance.

Even though the relative infancy of the criminology of sports may suggest otherwise; it is important to emphasise that the relationship between 'sport' and 'crime' is not exclusive to, or a product of the twenty-first century. It must, therefore, be placed in a socio-historical frame. Further, this complex relationship is inherently *broad*, given the manifold of existing definitions of both 'sport' and 'crime' and the disciplinary developments of criminology (Chapter 2). For example, sport has been a site for deviant acts of 'terrorism' (Cleland, 2019; Atkinson and Young, 2008), football-related violence and 'hooliganism' (Pearson, 2012), athletes breaking the law (see Lamothe and Barbie, 2020), doping (Moston and Engelberg, 2021; Yar, 2014) and corruption (Boykoff, 2016; Jennings, 2011; Sugden and Tomlinson, 2017; Numerato, 2016). Thus, sport, Armstrong and Hodges-Ramon (2015) write, has become a *nexus* for criminal activity and incidents.

Often, such incidents and behaviours have attracted widespread media and public attention, and subsequent policy or criminal justice responses. For example, in the 1980s, the then British Prime Minister, Margaret Thatcher, waged a 'war' on football 'hooliganism' (*The Independent*, 2016). Meanwhile, the post-9/11 global 'war on terror' epoch has massively impacted 'security' and 'surveillance' complexes at sport stadia and mega-events around the globe (Giulianotti and Klauser, 2010). Sport, hence, has commonly found itself at the very heart of political or state responses to 'crime' and 'criminal' or 'deviant' behaviours found on both the 'inside' and 'outside' of sport. Moreover, in recent years, the controversial and dubious practices of sport governing bodies, including the International Olympic Committee (IOC) and *Fédération Internationale de Football Association* (FIFA), have been subject to increased attention, as episodes of systematic bribery and corruption have been uncovered in the bidding processes for some sport mega-events (Boykoff, 2016).

Despite this, it is still our contention that the 'crime-sport' nexus is not – and must not be approached as – synonymous with 'high-profile' cases, exceptional and catastrophic disasters or behaviours that often generate sensationalist headlines. Indeed, Groombridge (2017: 12), who encourages more engagement with criminological issues in sport, notes that:

> That engagement goes beyond football hooliganism and athlete deviance. It can move from the criminalisation of kids playing street games, to events on pitch, into board rooms and on to the exclusive hotels favoured by international sports associations when deciding the venue for the next sporting mega-event and back to the dreams and merchandise sold to those street kids.

Ultimately, what we see here is that 'crime' or 'deviance' in sport also relates to far more 'mundane' and 'lower-profile' acts. The socio-spatial boundaries of 'crime' and 'deviance' in sport are far-reaching and diffuse. It may relate to criminalised, alternative lifestyle choices of sport and leisure, risk-taking and underground subcultures (Chapter 6). For example, between 1978 and 1989, the use, sale and ownership of skateboards were – by law – banned in Norway. For more than a decade, skateboards were seen as a public menace, and it was not until 1989 that skateboarding was finally decriminalised in Norway. The skateboarding ban had subsequently led skateboarders to set up secret ramps to avoid the attention of law enforcements (Olympic Channel, 2020). This sheds a light on how sport may be a site wherein risk cultures and subcultures can emerge (Giulianotti, 2009) as a response or resistance to regulatory practices or laws and modern life more generally (Chapter 6). Moreover, sport can provide a platform for resistance or social justice movements on local, national and transnational levels (Boykoff, 2020; Scraton, 2016). Boykoff's (2020) recent study of socialist anti-Olympic activists in Los Angeles and Tokyo demonstrates this exactly. Essentially, it can be suggested that Carrabine et al.'s (2020) insistence that 'criminology' can have multiple meanings is accurately encapsulated by sport and, fundamentally, sport provides new fields for a critical criminological investigation and imagination, because the relationship between 'crime' and 'sport' is so *diffuse*, *contested* and *broad*.

This book advances the critical criminology of sport. Central to the critical criminological understanding is societies' power relations, and how the 'powerful' create, administer and enforce laws that the 'less powerful' are subjected to and regulated by (Corteen, 2018). This, again, causes or perpetuates inequality, social injustice and harms. Thus, advancing the critical criminology of sport, we will adapt critical criminological approaches to the study of a wide array of different sports, sporting structures and institutions, and cultures in sport. These sporting practices, structures and cultures can all reveal, or express wider power relations found in the modern world, we argue.

Ultimately, as the next section highlights, we are mainly concerned with how theories of critical criminology can assist, nuance or extend the social scientific understanding of 'crime', 'deviance' and 'criminality' in sport. From a social scientific standpoint, this is both timely and important for at least four key reasons. First, as has been discussed, scholars have over the recent years proved the potential of and encouraged more scholarly work in this area (Groombridge, 2017; Atkinson and Young, 2008; Corteen, 2018). As such, a basic yet concurrently indispensable starting point for this book is that we respond to and reflect on these proposals for further research in the field.

Second, as Francis (2012: 15) argues, 'sport is and always will be harmful . . . because of the rivalries it generates, the competitive element that it embodies and the close physical contact that involvement in it often demands'. Such argument speaks to the continued importance of studying an *ongoing* – possibly *eternal* – criminological issue. If sport will always be 'harmful', as Francis suggests, then social researchers must consequently be alive to this and seek to understand and critically engage with the social worlds and structures that allow for such 'harms' to (re)circulate and preserve over time. Such a commitment also lies at the very core of this book.

Third, as elite sport's commercial drive and neoliberal underpinnings continue to expand globally, so do the (un)intended and (in)visible consequences of this perpetuate. Indeed, we examine this, for example, in the case of the Qatar 2022

World Cup's construction projects (see Chapter 7), which according to *The Guardian* (2021) has caused thousands of deaths and harm to migrant workers hired to construct the new World Cup stadiums. The 'harms', generated through sport thus, do not merely impact those *directly involved* in the athletic side or dimensions of sport. Similarly, the efforts to 'secure' sport mega-events, in the post-9/11 context (Chapter 5), have proved to exclude and marginalise certain social groups, like local and homeless youth, and local residents of different host cities (Kennelly, 2015; Boykoff, 2020). As such, the 'harms' and apparatuses of 'social control' that emerge and, indeed, co-exist within sport cut right across the wider society and do not always make distinctions between 'sporting' and 'non-sporting' settings, people or social groups. Hence, the 'crimes of sport' exceed sporting spheres and collectively call for criminological investigation.

Fourth, as Chapter 2 discusses, the several meanings of critical criminology have become increasingly diffuse and subject to continual development and revision. As such, a prudent question to ask may be 'what exactly is critical criminology?' Broadly, critical criminology can be seen as a theory of understanding criminality and criminalisation, an academic discipline and an ideas-based movement, as we discuss in Chapter 2. One of the fundamental pillars of critical criminology includes a commitment to critically approach the power relations and the narratives of the 'powerful' surrounding 'crime' or 'criminalisation'. Yet as Corteen (2018: 138) reminds us, '[n]o standard definition of critical criminology exists; rather various branches of critical criminologies co-exist'.

This remains important and, in that sense, we endeavour to capture this. And, by using sport as a novel entry point, we feel that we thereby partake in the wider critical criminological (re)imagination and co-existence, by shedding a light on one very important area of criminology – that is, *sport* – which has been left largely under-appreciated and under-theorised from a critical criminological standpoint, with some important exceptions (Groombridge, 2017; Atkinson and Young, 2008). As Groombridge (2017: 157) rightfully concludes, '[d]rug use, fraud, bribery and international law and policing are the stuff of modern sport, and so need criminological examination'. This is a succinct argument which we agree with upon proceeding. And, in that sense, we simultaneously subscribe to an idea that whilst criminological approaches can be made the most of to improve the social scientific sensemaking of sport, it concurrently possesses the ability to reveal wider trends speaking to 'crime', 'harm', 'social justice' and 'social control', and indeed the shortcomings of the criminal justice system (see e.g. Scraton, 2004).

Aims and Rationales of This Book

This section will address this book's key aims and rationales. Our aims must, however, be viewed in context of the previous discussion which sets the scene and agenda for advancing the criminology of sport further and for adding to the scholarly contributions of Groombridge (2017), Jump (2020), Atkinson and Young (2008) and Blackshaw and Crabbe (2004). Our first and most central aim in this book is, fundamentally, to showcase the wide yet under-utilised repertoire of critical criminological approaches to the social study of sport. Our goal is to show exactly why the application of criminological theory is at the forefront of sport in the present-day and thereby make an important contribution to the existing literature.

However, there is little uniformity in the theoretical approaches of criminological research, and our master perspectives throughout this text are taken from the critical criminological branch and the range of critical perspectives that could be positioned under this banner. The conceptual basis of many of the approaches we will draw upon can be traced back to the work of Taylor et al. (1973, 1975) and borrow a range of conflict perspectives from sociology – including Marxism, Feminism, Left Realism and Critical Theory – to argue that the genesis of 'crime' and the nature of 'justice' are based within a complex structure of class and status inequalities.

Law, punishment and mechanisms of social control are part of a system of social inequality and serve to produce and perpetuate it. Critical criminologists recognise a range of inequalities that are reinforced through criminalisation and typically seek to challenge them. In this book, we will do this in the context of sport. To do this, we will also draw on other useful critical concepts and approaches, including zemiology, which extends the previous analyses to consider crime as a form of 'social harm' that must be understood in the context of local, national and global political economy; (post) Foucauldian governmentality studies, which provide a different set of critical tools for analysing ways of thinking about, and techniques for securing, the 'conduct of conduct' within, but also beyond, the state; and cultural criminology, which explores how cultural forces interweave with crime and crime control, conceptualised as cultural products that carry multiple meanings

Thereby, we apply ideas new to sport in the form of current criminological theories to empirical examples and case studies that are novel to criminology. Ultimately, the key rationale behind this aim is attached to an underlying but important idea that *if* the frontiers of 'sport' and 'criminology' – both separately and in tandem – are to be advanced, then ideas have to emerge from outside the existing intellectual boundaries. Simultaneously, our application of current criminological perspectives also allows for rethinking exercises of cases and examples in sport that may have been explored by researchers, but that is yet to be criminologically analysed.

Our second key aim is intertwined with the first aim but must be seen as ambitious by itself. With this book, we seek to add to the field with a burgeoning research agenda. Indeed, we have already touched upon our intention to add to the recent vibrancy in this subfield and utilise the aforementioned momentum that has been created over the last few years. As such, our main arguments also feed into this emerging research agenda which we ignite. Whilst we seek to showcase the several critical criminological theories that may be applied to sport, there are still a range of other theoretical perspectives and tools within critical criminology that can be applied to new sporting contexts, cases and controversies. These will be highlighted throughout, but mainly in our final chapter (Chapter 8). Here, we outline research agendas speaking to green and feminist criminologies of sports, and emerging questions in light of the catastrophic COVID-19 pandemic.

In that sense, we also aim to encourage social scientists to make full use of the broad spectrum of critical criminological theoretical and conceptual tools in their future investigations into the broad spectrum of sport and sporting practices. Crucially, as Stubbs (2008) submits, further developments within critical criminology are likely to be influenced by inter-disciplinary work. Fruitful and constructive conversations with other disciplines indeed remain vital and, in that respect, our emerging research agenda (Chapter 8) is inter-disciplinary by its very nature and directed at academics and students possessing an interest in 'crime' or 'sport' or, of course, the intersections between the two.

Structure of the Book: A Summary

In this book, we argue that the application of critical criminological theories should be located at the frontiers of sport. Therefore, throughout this book, we use established and emerging theoretical frameworks and apply these to different areas of contemporary sporting practices that warrant further examination, debate or revisitation. The book advances to fill the gaps in the literature between 'criminology' and 'sport' and is divided into eight main chapters including this introduction chapter. In each chapter, we apply a critical criminological lens and therefore, Chapter 2 seeks to provide an overview of the key developments within critical criminology. It discusses the foundations of critical criminology and maps the contours of critical criminology as a school of thought, a mobilisation and as a social theory that allows for advancing the study of 'crime', 'criminal activity' and 'criminal behaviour' within and through sport.

Then, Chapter 3 examines 'white-collar crime' and the 'crimes of the powerful' (Croall, 2001; Whyte, 2009) in elite sport's highly commercialised contexts. Here, we deploy Sutherland's (1939) concept of 'white-collar crime' and explore how this is manifested in sport. Drawing largely upon the pioneering and investigative work of Jennings (2011), Sugden and Tomlinson (1998, 2003) and Boykoff (2016, 2020), this chapter's focus is on how the practices of sport's governing bodies, such as IOC and FIFA, can assist in understanding of corruption and 'white-collar crime' in sport. So, this chapter explores the intersections between networks of powerful elites, corporate sponsorships and cases of bribery, including the 2015 FIFA corruption case.

Youth programmes involving sport form part of the crime reduction strategies in several countries. Hence, Chapter 4 explores the connections between sports-based interventions (SBIs) and 'crime'. Whilst it is often (optimistically) assumed that sport presents an 'effective' crime reduction tool which can deter 'anti-social behaviour' or 'criminal activity' (Coalter, 2007), this chapter critically challenges this notion utilising some of Foucault's ideas around governmentality. This chapter reviews the existing literature on SBI's effectiveness and critically analyses SBIs in relation to wider strategies of governance (Kelly, 2011) and social control (Spaaij,

2009). This chapter argues that isolated cases of 'success' exist but extends existing views holding that SBIs and existing policies may, in fact, work to govern young people and their communities, reproduce social inequalities and categorisations that are masqueraded behind the façade of sport's alleged 'positive' social and individual impacts.

Chapter 5 is concerned with 'security' and surveillance' in sport. We position these broad concepts as modes of governance and social control. We specifically explore how post-9/11 security developments have intensified sport mega-events' securitised environments. Here, we draw upon insights from Critical Security Studies (CSS) which advocate the position of individuals as referent objects for 'security' rather than the state (Wyn Jones, 1999). This chapter explores how sport mega-event 'security' and 'surveillance' practices and technologies may remain in communities, post-event, as so-called 'security legacies'. Further, as concerned with the meaning of 'security' at sport mega-events, we argue that this cannot equate with the exercise of influence by the 'powerful' actors involved in a sport mega-event's securitisation, like the police, authorities, security agencies or sport governing bodies, on less 'powerful' populations like fans or residents of host cities. Finally, this chapter explores three typologies of surveillance in sport, with a particular focus on the surveillance of athletic bodies and performances vis-à-vis drug testing and policies.

In Chapter 6, we explore the multiple meanings of crime within the present-day Western society, as we employ cultural criminology to understand 'transgression' in sport. Following Ferrell et al. (2015), we outline how critical criminology may be applied to sports such as mixed martial arts, bare-knuckle boxing and other 'extreme sports', and the presentations of these behaviours in popular culture. We also revisit the closely related theory of 'edgework' and its relevance in sport and leisure contexts. This chapter thus positions transgression in sport within late-modernity's changes within consumption and culture.

Chapter 7 critically investigates the case of the 2022 FIFA World Cup to be staged in Qatar. Since 2010, the 2022 World Cup has been surrounded by controversy (Millward, 2017). Indeed, a recent *The Guardian* (2021) report suggested that over 6,500 migrant workers from India, Pakistan, Nepal, Bangladesh and Sri Lanka had died since 2010 in relation to the event's stadium projects. In this context, this chapter draws upon the critical criminological 'social harm' perspective (see Hillyard et al., 2004; Hillyard and Tombs, 2007). This perspective is synthesised with conceptual insights from 'relational sociology' (Crossley, 2012). Hence, in relation to the 2022 World Cup's stadium constructions, these insights are used to explore the themes of responsibility, mistreatment and harm with regard to migrant workers. Our emerging argument here is that the narratives of migrant construction workers in Qatar exemplify the social harms that are experienced in contemporary sport.

Finally, Chapter 8 ties together the book's themes and key arguments. It addresses how the stated aims of this book are accomplished through a summary of the book. We also provide a timely and emerging research agenda which can assist the continual development of the 'criminology of sport' as an academic field. Essentially, we argue that other criminological theories can – and should – be applied to the diverse field of sport. As we argue, this book's themes and recent events, including the COVID-19 pandemic, have demonstrated exactly why the application of criminological theory is and will remain at the frontier of sport. In the present day, researchers therefore face an important but potentially rewarding challenge in bringing the social study of 'sport' and 'crime' *even* closer on both theoretical and empirical levels.

References

Allison, L. (1986) *The Politics of Sports*, Manchester: Manchester University Press.
Allison, L. (2004) *The Global Politics of Sport: The Role of Global Institutions in Sport*, London: Routledge.
Armstrong, G. and Hodges-Ramon, L. (2015) 'Sport and crime', *Oxford Handbooks Online*: 1–24.
Atkinson, M. and Young, K. (2008) *Deviance and Social Control in Sports*, Champaign, IL: Human Kinetics.
Bale, J. (2003) *Sports Geography*, New York: Routledge.
Blackshaw, T. and Crabbe, T. (2004) *New Perspectives on Sport and 'Deviance': Consumption, Performativity and Social Control*, London: Routledge.
Boykoff, J. (2016) *Power Games: A Political History of the Olympics*, London: Verso.
Boykoff, J. (2020) *NOlympians: Inside the Fight Against Capitalist Mega-Sports in Los Angeles, Tokyo & Beyond*, Novia Scotia: Fernwood Publishing.
Brisman, A. (2019) '"Are you serious?": Sports criminology: A critical criminology of sport and games: A review', *Critical Criminology* 27: 373–392.
Carrabine, E., Cox, A., Cox, P., Crowhurst, I., Di Ronco, A., Fussey, P., Sergi, A., South, N., Thiel, D. and Turton, J. (2020) *Criminology: A Sociological Introduction*, Abingdon: Routledge.
Cleland, J. (2019) 'Sports fandom in the risk society: Analyzing perceptions and experiences of risk, security and terrorism at elite sports events', *Sociology of Sport Journal* 36(2): 144–151.
Coalter, F. (2007) *A Wider Social Role for Sport: Who's Keeping the Score?* London: Routledge.
Cohen, S. (2002) *Folk Devils and Moral Panics*, London: Routledge.
Corteen, K.M. (2018) 'A critical criminology of professional wrestling and sports entertainment', *The Popular Culture Studies Journal* 6(1): 138–154.
Criminal Justice Matters. (2012) 88(1): 14–33.
Critcher, C. (2002) 'Media, government and moral panic: The politics of paedophilia in Britain 2000–1', *Journalism Studies* 3(4): 521–535.
Croall, H. (2001) *Understanding White Collar Crime*, Maidenhead: McGraw-Hill Education.
Crossley, N. (2012) *Towards Relational Sociology*, Abingdon: Routledge.
Dunning, E. (1999) *Sport Matters*, London: Routledge.
Dunning, E. (2004) 'Sociology of sport in the balance: Critical reflections on some recent and more enduring trends', *Sport in Society* 7(1): 1–24.
Ferrell, J., Hayward, K. and Young, J. (2015) *Cultural Criminology: An Invitation*, London: Sage.
Finley, L. (2013) 'Examining state and state-corporate crime surrounding major sporting events', *Contemporary Justice Review* 16(2): 228–250.

Francis, P. (2012) 'Sport and harm: Peter Francis introduces the themed section for this issue', *Criminal Justice Matters* 88(1): 14–15.

Gilchrist, P., Holden, R. and Millward, P. (2015) 'Special section introduction: The political sociologies of sport', *Sociological Research Online* 20(2): 141–144.

Giulianotti, R. (2009) 'Risk and sport: An analysis of sociological theories and research agendas', *Sociology of Sport Journal* 26(4): 540–556.

Giulianotti, R. and Brownell, S. (2012) Olympic and world sport: Making transnational society?' *The British Journal of Sociology* 63: 199–215.

Giulianotti, R. and Klauser, F. (2010) 'Security governance and sport mega-events: Toward an interdisciplinary research agenda', *Journal of Sport and Social Issues* 34(1): 49–61.

Groombridge, N. (2017) *Sports Criminology: A Critical Criminology of Sports and Games*, Bristol: Policy Press.

The Guardian. (2021) 'Revealed: 6,500 migrant workers have died in Qatar since world cup awarded', available from: www.theguardian.com/global-development/2021/feb/23/revealed-migrant-worker-deaths-qatar-fifa-world-cup-2022 [accessed 10/2021].

Hillyard, P., Pantazis, C., Tombs, S. and Gordon, D. (eds.) (2004) *Beyond Criminology? Taking Harm Seriously*, London: Pluto Press.

Hillyard, P. and Tombs, S. (2007) 'From "crime" to social harm?' *Crime, Law and Social Change* 48(1–2): 9–25.

The Independent. (2016) 'Margaret Thatcher's government thought football fans so violent she set up a "war cabinet"', available from: www.independent.co.uk/news/uk/politics/margaret-thatcher-s-government-thought-football-fans-so-violent-she-set-war-cabinet-a6883226.html [accessed 10/2021].

Jennings, A. (2011) 'Investigating corruption in corporate sport: The IOC and FIFA', *International Review for the Sociology of Sport* 46(4): 387–398.

Jump, D. (2020) *The Criminology of Boxing, Violence and Desistance*, Bristol: Bristol University Press.

Kelly, L. (2011) ' "Social inclusion" through sports-based interventions?' *Critical Social Policy* 31(1): 126–150.

Kennedy, L. and Silva, D. (2020) ' "Discipline that hurts": Punitive logics and governance in sport', *Punishment and Society* 22(5): 658–680.

Kennelly, J. (2015) ' "You're making our city look bad": Olympic security, neoliberal urbanization, and homeless youth', *Ethnography* 16(1): 3–24.

Lamothe, J.C. and Barbie, D.J. (eds.) (2020) *Athletes Breaking Bad: Essays on Transgressive Sports Figures*, Jefferson, NC: McFarland.

Malcolm, D. (2012) *Sport and Sociology*, London: Routledge.

Mandell, R.D. (1984) *Sport: A Cultural History*, New York: Columbia University Press.

McBride, M. (2020) 'Tackling offensive behaviour in Scottish football: A how (not) to guide to developing criminal justice policy?' *Criminology & Criminal Justice*: 1–19.

Meek, R. (2013) *Sport in Prison: Exploring the Role of Physical Activity in Correctional Settings*, London: Routledge.

Millie, A., Harris, C. and Gelsthorpe, L. (eds.) (2012) *British Society of Criminology Newsletter* 70: 1–20.

Millward, P. (2017) 'World cup 2022 and Qatar's construction projects: Relational power in networks and relational responsibilities to migrant workers', *Current Sociology* 65(5): 756–776.

Morgan, W.J. (2006) *Why Sports Morally Matter*, New York/London: Routledge.

Moston, S. and Engelberg, T. (2021) *Detecting Doping in Sport*, Abingdon: Routledge.

Nichols, G. (2010) *Sport and Crime Reduction: The Role of Sports in Tackling Youth Crime*, London: Routledge.

Numerato, D. (2016) 'Corruption and public secrecy: An ethnography of football match-fixing', *Current Sociology* 64(5): 699–717.
Olympic Channel. (2020) 'Foul play: The time Norway banned skateboarding', available from: www.olympicchannel.com/en/stories/features/detail/when-norway-banned-skateboarding/ [accessed 10/2021].
Orwell, G. (1945) 'The sporting spirit', *Tribune*, 14 December.
Parrish, R. (2003) *Sports Law and Policy in the European Union*, Manchester/New York: Manchester University Press.
Pearson, G. (2012) *An Ethnography of English Football Fans: Cans, Cops and Carnival*, Manchester: Manchester University Press.
Samatas, M. (2007) 'Security and surveillance in the Athens 2004 Olympics: Some lessons from a troubled story', *International Criminal Justice Review* 17(3): 220–238.
Scraton, P. (2004) '4 death on the terraces: The contexts and injustices of the 1989 Hillsborough disaster', *Soccer & Society* 5(2): 183–200.
Scraton, P. (2016) *Hillsborough: The Truth*, London: Random House.
Silk, M.L. and Andrews, D.L. (2011) 'Toward a physical cultural studies', *Sociology of Sport Journal* 28(1): 4–35.
Spaaij, R. (2009) 'Sport as a vehicle for social mobility and regulation of disadvantaged urban youth: Lessons from Rotterdam', *International Review for the Sociology of Sport* 44(2–3): 247–264.
Stott, C., Hoggett, J. and Pearson, G. (2012) '"Keeping the peace" social identity, procedural justice and the policing of football crowds', *The British Journal of Criminology* 52(2): 381–399.
Stubbs, J. (2008) 'Critical criminological research', *The Critical Criminology Companion* (Eds. T. Anthony and C. Cunneen), Sydney: Hawkins Press, pp. 6–17.
Sugden, J. and Tomlinson, A. (1998) *FIFA and the Contest for World Football: Who Rules the People's Game?* Cambridge: Polity Press.
Sugden, J. and Tomlinson, A. (2003) *Badfellas: FIFA Family at War*, London: Mainstream.
Sugden, J. and Tomlinson, A. (2017) *Football, Corruption and Lies: Revisiting 'Badfellas, the Book FIFA Tried to Ban*, London: Routledge.
Sutherland, E. (1939) 'The white-collar criminal', 52nd American Sociological Association Conference, 27 December.
Taylor, I., Walton, P. and Young, J. (1973) *The New Criminology: For a Social Theory of Deviance*, London: Routledge & Kegan Paul Books.
Taylor, I., Walton, P. and Young, J. (eds.) (1975) *Critical Criminology*, London: Routledge & Kegan Paul Books.
Thornton, P.K. (2011) *Sports Law*, Sudbury, MA: Jones and Bartlett Publishers.
Tian, E. and Wise, N. (2020) 'An Atlantic divide? Mapping the knowledge domain of European and North American-based sociology of sport, 2008–2018', *International Review for the Sociology of Sport* 55(8): 1029–1055.
Whyte, D. (2009) 'Paradoxes of regulation', *Regulating the Illicit Market in Antiquities* (Eds. P. Green and S. MacKenzie), London: Hart, pp. 159–177.
Wyn Jones, R. (1999) *Security, Strategy, and Critical Theory*, London: Lynne Rienner.
Yar, M. (2014) *Crime, Deviance and Doping: Fallen Sports Stars, Autobiography and the Management of Stigma*, Basingstoke: Palgrave MacMillan.

2
SPORT AND THE CRITICAL CRIMINOLOGICAL IMAGINATION

Introduction

Carrabine et al. (2020: 3) argue that 'criminology has many meanings'. Despite Young (2011a: 252) claiming 'critical criminology is the criminology of late modernity', Carrabine et al.'s point can certainly be extended to the understanding of critical criminology, which has changed meaning, or at least proliferated in that meaning, since it first emerged in the UK in the late 1960s. Briefly summarised, critical criminology can be seen as first, a theory of understanding criminality and criminalisation second, a branch of an academic discipline (Tierney, 2009; Walklate, 2007) and third, an ideas-based form of collective action that railed against previously established ways of understanding crime and deviance (Ruggiero, 2021).

Taylor et al.'s *The New Criminology* (1973) and *Critical Criminology* (1975) shaped the original school of critical criminology. Broadly described, the first waves of critical theory of criminology posit that crime is defined by the ruling class, who directly proscribe criminality upon the majority – who are therefore 'kept under control'. The ruling class can be located within the state legislators or those in privileged market positions (for instance, banks and other moneylenders) but are few when counted against the masses that they control and – potentially – criminalise. The critical theory of criminology is therefore shaped by (neo) Marxist and other conflict understandings of society and tends to be more concerned with violations of 'social harm' (Hillyard et al., 2004; Canning and Tombs, 2021) than with criminal lawbreaking. Later, some variations of the theory of critical criminology underwent a left realist revision, changing the terms of reference from an explicitly (neo) Marxist understanding to introduce some ideas of human agency. In many senses, critical criminology – as a school of thought or a range of theory – can be 'anti-[conventional] criminology' (Carlen, 2002; Ruggiero, 2021). This chapter gives an overview of the development of critical criminology in its manifestations as

DOI: 10.4324/9781003276791-2

i) a school of thought, ii) a form of collective action and iii) a paradigm of ideas in which issues and studies of 'crime' and 'criminal' activity in sport can be discussed.

The Emergence of Critical Criminology

Polletta (2006) argues that bouts of collective action are set against narratives that report injustice and suggest that a (socially subjective) 'fairer' world can emerge from the mobilisation. A narrative that we do not wish to disrupt has been widely told about roots of British critical criminology that can be traced back to the 1968 National Deviancy Conference (hereon NDC), held at York University (see Carlen, 2002; Jefferson, 2021; Mooney, 2011, 2019; Pavlich and Brannigan, 2007; Young, 2011a). This narrative offers a group of scholars who sought to collaborate to develop a 'fairer' way of understanding crime and criminality than 'official' and Home Office analysis (Ruggiero, 2021). The conference marked a radical breakaway from the (Third) National Conference of Teaching and Research on Criminology at the University of Cambridge by an 'embryo [of] criminologists in their last months of graduate research or in the very first months of teaching' (Rock, 1988: 190). The aim of the group was to conceive a disciplinary field that understood crime primarily through the lens of social justice rather than conventional law and order that dominated 'official' criminology. These aims were born from 'feelings towards official criminology [which] ranged from distrust at its orientation towards administrative needs and impatience with its highly empirical, anti-theoretical bias, to simply a mild lack of interest in the sort of studies that were being conducted' (Cohen, 1973: 8).

O'Brien and Yar (2008) state that understanding that crime is tied to social structures and circumstances is the central tenet of the critical criminology that emerged from the group. This means that what 'crime' is depends on the historical, political, cultural and economic conditions within a society at a given point in time. Furthermore, they state that according to the theory of critical criminology, there is no necessary link between crime and social responses to it (O'Brien and Yar, 2008). Accordingly, deviancies such as 'street crime' are often high on the 'public agenda' (defined by the media, politicians and criminal justice agencies) and yet fraud – which generates significantly higher net economic losses – is far less likely to become the object of such campaigns. Therefore, the discrepancy between social responses to these crimes is a function of the political and economic forces that set the overall crime agenda. The theoretical roots of the original group of critical criminologists lay in a fusion of (neo) Marxist ideas with deviancy theory that had recently emerged in the universities of (predominantly) East coast cities in the United States (see Ferrell et al., 2015). This development had two philosophical variants: first, subcultural theory – particularly that of Albert Cohen and Richard Cloward, who had been influenced by Robert Merton and labelling theorists including Howard Becker – which allowed a focus on both the 'deviant' action and the reactions it. Second, the conflict theory roots of those in the critical criminological paradigm assume that 'crime' has a material base and those in positions of material power have the authority to label those actions that are not amenable to their cultural codes as 'criminal'. As such, 'the law' protects the wealthy and powerful of society. These ideas sat comfortably amongst a group of similar young scholars – who were led by Stuart Hall – that grew from the University of Birmingham's Centre for Contemporary Cultural Studies (hereon CCCS). The CCCS' ideas blended Gramscian neo-Marxism with a new cultural sociology to critically look at the social problems that were said to be evident in Britain at the time.

The critical criminological pioneers from the 1968 NDC conference were Stanley (Stan) Cohen, Wesley (Kit) Carson, Mary McIntosh, David Downes, William (Jock) Young, Paul Rock and Ian Taylor. All apart from Mary McIntosh reached a professorial rank in the following years. The group quickly forged connections to the critical social work scholar, and now *BBC Radio 4* host of the 'Thinking Aloud' programme, Laurie Taylor as well as those at CCCS. In describing the forging of collective ideas of the group, Stan Cohen recounts:

> Official criminology was regarded with attitudes ranging from ideological condemnation to a certain measure of boredom. But being a sociologist – often isolated in a small department – was not enough to get away from criminology: some sort of separate subculture had to be carved out within the sociological world. So, ostensibly for these reasons (although this account sounds suspiciously like colour-supplement history), seven of us met in July 1968, fittingly enough in Cambridge in the middle of the Third National Conference of Teaching and Research, organised by the Institute [of Criminology] and opened by the Home Secretary. We decided to form a group to provide some sort of intellectual support for each other to cope with collective problems of identity.
>
> *Cohen (1981: 194)*

Similarly, Ken Plummer who was outside the immediate group but whose work clearly connected with their ideas remembered in his eulogy to mark Stan Cohen's passing in 2013:

> In July 1968 a few young sociologists met to discuss their disillusionment with criminology and the orthodoxies of sociological approaches to it. Subsequently, termly conferences were organised at the University of York between September 1998 and 1973 attracting some 1,300 people. . . . These were the conferences of young radicals: youthful, exuberant, fun loving and intellectually alive.
>
> *Plummer (2013a)*

However, Leon Radzinowicz, who represented the Institute for Criminology at Cambridge University in 1968, later recounted the formation of the NDC group in rather different terms:

> In the middle of the Third National [Criminology] Conference, taking place in Cambridge in July 1968, a group of seven young social scientists and

criminologists, participants of the Conference, met secretly and decided to establish an independent 'National Deviancy Conference' and soon afterwards they duly met in York. At the time, it reminded me a little of naughty schoolboys, playing a nasty game on their stern headmaster. It was not necessary to go 'underground' because we were not in any way opposed to discussing new approaches to the sociology of deviance . . . Although not invited to their conference in York I asked one of my senior colleagues in the Institute to go there as an observer. My attitude was by no means hostile or patronizing. As I stated at the time, movements in ideas, like life in general, often lead to seeming unexpectedly baffling results. Those were the years of dissent, protest and ferment in the United States with their unmistakable echoes in Britain. They affected not only the ways people acted, but also their thinking on many matters relating to social life and its reinterpretations. But it was also a reaction to some extent inevitable and to some extent misguided of the new generation of British criminologists against what appeared to be the stolid establishment of Criminology as personified by the Cambridge Institute and probably also by its first Director.

(Radzinowicz, 1999: 229)

One of the immediate aims of the 'young radicals' (Plummer, 2013a) or 'naughty schoolboys' (Radzinowicz, 1999: 299, perhaps highlighting the gendered nature in which the 'official' academic group understood the world in 1968) was to establish a regular platform to 'intellectually support each other' (Cohen, 1981: 194). Here, scholars could critically discuss official criminological approaches and develop a stronger sociological platform to discuss ideas of 'crime', 'deviance' and 'criminality'. As hinted at by Radzinowicz, it seems that not all within the established criminological circles welcomed the development of the group, even if they claimed not to be 'hostile or patronizing'. Indeed, Radzinowicz (1999) notes the space to critically discuss scholarly ideas emerged when Laurie Taylor's host institution of York University provided the first of a flurry of 13 conferences that the group convened between 1968 and 1973. In 1974, the group formalised this arrangement with the establishment of the European Group for the Study of Deviance and Control – a collective that exists in the contemporary era (Scott, 2016). At the sessions, Young (2011a: 252) records the group discussing theoretical and methodological challenges to the critical study of 'crime' and deviance alongside an analysis of some of the 'criminological' issues that they thought to be pertinent. For instance, Jock Young (1968) discussed the deviancy of recreational drug use, Stuart Hall (1968) analysed the rise of 'hippy' culture and Paul Willis (1972) offered insights into motorcycle subcultures (alongside Dick Hebdige and Mike Featherstone providing other papers on subcultures, see Young, 2011a: 252). Peter Sedgewick and Jeff Coulter discussed anti-psychiatry, and Ken Plummer contributed to debates with Mary McIntosh on 'deviant' sexualities (Young, 2011a: 252–253). However, most interestingly in the context of this book, Ian Taylor developed one of the first social scientific accounts in the understanding of football 'hooliganism' and working-class culture. He later elaborated these ideas in chapters provided for edited collections of the emerging 'Sociology of Sport' by Eric Dunning (Taylor, 1971a) and 'deviancy' by Cohen (Taylor, 1971b), the former of which was developing with a Norbert Elias' inspired 'figurational' framework. Yet, since then – and particularly after Ian Taylor (1991) wrote his last piece on football hooliganism – sport appears to have slipped off the critical criminological agenda until Groombridge's (2017) book *Sports Criminology* and the increase of activity it gave rise to. In this book, we make further moves to bring it back.

The Sociological Imagination and the Emergence of Critical Criminology

Beyond their conflict-centred theoretical orientations, the critical criminologists were clearly influenced by C. Wright Mills' (2005 [1959]) *The Sociological Imagination*, as testified by Jock Young (2011b) coining *The Criminological Imagination* over 40 years after the initial NDC meeting, alongside more recent researchers in the field, such as Barton et al. (2007: 2), calling for an 'expansion of the criminological imagination'. Mills (2005 [1959]) argued that sociological inquiry is the result of a coming together of individual biography and wider social historical trend, whereby the 'personal [often] becomes the political' in social research. To those ends, it is useful to explore the historical location of the emergence of critical criminology and the personal biographies of the seven original protagonists.

The period in which the NDC was developed is popularly remembered as a year in which social movements emerged from several universities across the world (van Swaaningen, 1997: 74). These protests impacted the world in profound ways. McAdam (1982) records that the 1960s marked an era in which young people across the Western world became more aware of potentially oppressive powers of 'social structures' (including the state, the law and the economy) and the levels of discrimination experienced by groups who had been obviously disadvantaged (such as those from lower social classes, women, homosexuals, ethnic minorities, etc.) and largely blamed for any emerging social ills. The expansion of higher education meant that more students were entering the university system from less elevated social backgrounds and politicising academia to understand inequality in new ways. Indeed, 'many of those involved in the NDC and the development of critical criminology came from such backgrounds and were the first members of their families to go into higher education' (Mooney, 2011: 16). More specifically, the year of the first NDC – 1968 – is significant because it marked the Tet offensive in Vietnam, which fuelled student-led anti-war protest movements across the world (but especially in the United States) and the French student protests in May of that year which sparked violent clashes with the police 'especially caught the imagination of the founders of the NDC and was the focus of much discussion at the inaugural conference held later that year' (Mooney, 2011: 16). As Young (2011a: 252) argued, critical criminology emerged 'at the cusp of change', inspired by 'a world where oppressive relationships of class, age, gender and ethnicity became heightened and evident (in that historical order)'.

18 Critical Criminological Imagination

Following C. Wright Mills' methodology for the interrogation of public issues with the sociological imagination takes us to explore the biographies of the seven original critical criminologists and the intersection of the 1960s as a period of social change. On such involvement, Jock Young points out:

> My own involvement in it [NDC] was initially reluctant to say the least. It was a time when we regarded people with 9 to 5 jobs as complete failures, lived in communes and regarded the 'straight' world with complete disdain. I was living in Notting Hill where [the rock band] Pink Floyd played weekly at the local parish hall, Jimi Hendrix was at Middle Earth and there was poetry in the streets. Academic conferences were not exactly where it was at. I was persuaded to go to the first NDC in York in 1968. I remember Mike Brake – later to be well known for his books on youth culture (Brake, 1980, 1985) – saying to me the evening we arrived, 'What *are* [original emphasis] doing here, man? Let's get out quick and get to Leeds where there's much better clubs.' We stayed all the same and the next day I gave my first academic paper, 'The Role of Police as Amplifiers of Deviancy, Negotiators of Reality and Translators of fantasy' (1971a). A pretentious title but it still captures for me a constant theme of the way in which powerful forces in society create demons out of illusions which then, through stigma and oppression, take on a reality of their own.
>
> *Young (2011a: 252)*

So, who was Jock Young in 1968 and who did he become? How did his personal biography help to shape the contours of critical criminology? Young was born in Midlothian, Scotland in 1942, but moved to Aldershot – a middle-class Hampshire town that is well known for its army base – when he was 5 years old (Hayward, 2010). From the quote provided by Young we learn that by 1968 was living in Notting Hill. In that period, it was not the affluent area of London that it is today, rather it had a reputation for breeding criminal behaviour and its Victorian terraced houses were largely run down, providing poor living conditions for its residents. Young was not what might be thought of when describing the 'typical' academic rather, his

> mates [were] drug dealers, junkies and a burglar on the run, the underground and the underworld firmly entwined [and he] was fascinated by the nascent hippie culture, the interface of bohemian, West Indian and ne'er-do-well life, the strange pantomime of police and drug users, the extraordinary venom, the repulsion and attraction that such an innocuous drug like cannabis and such a quiescent subculture evoked.
>
> *(2011a: 246)*

His research reflected his life, drawing empathy with petty criminals in *The Drugtakers* (1971) which was described by Hayward (2010: 262) as documenting 'the flinty social interactions that surrounded the control of drugs in his neighbourhood, paying particular attention to the extraordinary moral panics that frequently bubbled up in their wake'. Until his passing in 2013, Jock Young was Distinguished Professor of Criminal Justice at the City University of New York, but his research contribution is typically characterised by a longstanding opposition to middle-class cultural conformity and the ideologies associated with state power and imperialism, which Hayward (2010) argues is likely to stretch back to his upbringing in military-focussed Aldershot.

The work of Stan Cohen is honoured in Downes et al.'s (2007) edited collection *Crime, Social Control and Human Rights* which draws together chapters which explore his biography, seminal views on the theorisation of 'moral panics' (see Cohen, 2011 [1972]) and issues of social control. Indeed, when discussing the intersection of Cohen's work, views and personal life, the editors of the text claim:

> Stan Cohen was at an important stage committed to the view that it was difficult to disentangle the personal and biographical from the professional and intellectual. He told his friend and sometime collaborator, Laurie Taylor, that he had for a long while been 'sold on the 60s idea that you could integrate every part of your life: the idea that your soul, your teaching, writing, political activity could all be harmonised into a single whole' (Taylor, 2004). He later modified that view, calling it a 'kitsch theoretical synthesis' and saying that it should be replaced by no more than a linkage joining the 'private/personal with the political/public' (Cohen, 2003: 2–3). But the biographical and intellectual did converge in his own life in several interesting ways. He would use himself and his circumstances reflexively as materials.
>
> *Downes et al. (2007: xiix)*

Stan Cohen passed away in 2013 – aged 70 years old – after suffering from Parkinson's disease (Downes, 2013; Taylor, 2013). He was born into a Jewish family in Johannesburg and trained as a social worker during the apartheid in his home country, before moving to the UK in 1963 to study for a PhD at the London School of Economics (hereon LSE). This led to him taking jobs in London, Durham and Essex, before emigrating to Israel in 1980 and then returning to London in 1994 (Downes et al., 2007: xxiii). Taylor (2013) argues that his concern with media overreaction informed *Folk Devils and Moral Panics* (2011 [1972]), his influential study of the 1960s skirmishes between the youth subcultures of 'mods' and 'rockers', which grew from his doctoral study (Downes, 2013; Findlay, 2010). Cohen and his wife were longstanding critics of the Israel government's treatment of Palestinians (Downes, 2013). Taylor (2013) suggests that this concern led him into active conflict with the apartheid regime in his native South Africa which led him – during his time at the Hebrew University of Jerusalem (1981–95) – to lead a major inquiry into the Israeli army's use of torture in the occupied territories, and this concern led him to play a central role in the establishment in 2000 of the

Centre for the Study of Human Rights at the LSE (see also Hutter, 2013), as well as his *States of Denial* monograph (2000), evidencing the importance of his biography to his work.

At the LSE, Stan Cohen's colleague was David Downes who experienced a long career at the institution. Downes was born in 1938 in Sheffield and, as an undergraduate, read Modern History at Keble College (Oxford) before moving to carry out research at LSE after initially applying to the university to study social work (Newburn and Rock, 2009: 2). In 1966, Downes published *The Delinquent Solution* which presented a study of crime that was associated with the nature of subcultures *and* trailblazing the rise of the NDC by 2 years. Tierney (2009: 72) records Downes' book as 'the most theoretically sophisticated sociological study of youth crime then available [and . . .] arrived at a time when sociological criminology was poised to develop very significantly in Britain', suggesting that 'looking back from the vantage point of today to the time when Downes's book was published, the lack of sociological research on crime seems remarkable'. Wider testimony to Downes' work is recorded in *The Politics of Crime Control: Essays in Honour of David Downes* that Tim Newburn and Paul Rock edited in 2009. This collection is made up of 11 essays, including contributions by Stan Cohen as well influential critical criminologists from subsequent intellectual waves including Dick Hobbs, Robert Reiner, Frances Heidensohn and Newburn. Paul Rock did not contribute to the collection but worked with Cohen and Downes at the LSE after studying as an undergraduate at the institution. After gaining his PhD from Nuffield College (in 1970), he returned to LSE, eventually becoming Professor of Social Institutions. He has worked closely with Downes and – amongst other work – co-authored *Understanding Deviance: A Guide to the Sociology of Crime and Rule-Breaking* (2011) with him.

A fifth founding member was Kit Carson (born in 1940 and passed away in 2019, Haines and Whyte, 2019). Carson's work is honoured in Brannigan and Pavlich's (2007) edited collection *Governance and Regulation in Social Life: Essays in Honour of W.G. Carson*. This body of work includes a chapter by Paul Rock and broadly reflects Carson's research interests in the fields of white-collar crime, policing, disaster management and occupational health and safety. His working career took him to roles at the University of Auckland and La Trobe University. Mary McIntosh (born in 1936 and died in 2013) was the sixth founding member of the British-based critical criminology group in 1968. Peta Steel (2013) described her as 'a strong, caring women . . . who was the daughter of socialist parents. Her brother Andrew McIntosh would become a Labour peer, and leader of the Labour Party on the Greater London Council'. Her career took her to Oxford University, the University of California, Berkeley – where she was 'deported after being arrested following a protest against the House Un-American Activities Committee' (Steele, 2013) – the Home Office Research Unit, where she was a research officer, the University of Leicester, Borough Polytechnic and the University of Essex, where she stayed for over 20 years, before a post-retirement voluntary position at the Citizens Advice Bureau in North London.

McIntosh was an active member of the Women's Liberation Movement, the Gay Liberation Front and the Communist Party and her principal research interests in challenging the orthodox 'deviancy' of (homo) sexuality alongside a broad interest in critical criminology. Plummer (2013b) points out that in 1968 – the year in which the NDC was founded – 'The Homosexual Role' was published, which became the foundational argument for the contemporary sociology of homosexuality. This chapter challenged the view that homosexuality was a clinical pathology and argued that same-sex relations shifted in meaning and practice according to historical and cultural circumstances. McIntosh also developed a critique of family life, publishing *The Anti-Social Family* in 1982 (with Michèle Barrett). This book argued against the normative ideology of the nuclear family, suggesting that it excluded and marginalised many people. Her activist connections were evident in her work that called for changes in social policy to benefit women by reducing their dependence on a 'male breadwinner', thus advocating the legal and financial independence of women.

Ian Taylor was the seventh member of the group, and it is his work which draws the closest connections between sport and critical criminology, as evidenced by Jock Young's (2001) description of him as working 'prolifically in the fields of criminology, politics, urban studies, sport and popular culture. He was a polymath, writing on a wide array of subjects, including soccer hooliganism, gun control, the Hillsborough disaster, glam rock and money laundering'. Taylor died of cancer at the age of 56 (born in 1944, died in 2001); he was educated at Durham and Cambridge Universities before acquiring his first academic post at the University of Bradford. Taylor spent much of his working life in Canada and Australia before returning to England and the University of Salford in 1989, before returning to Durham University in 1998 as the Principal of Van Mildert College (Darby, 2002).

Walklate (2000) argued that Ian Taylor's final monograph, *Crime in Context*, was his 'magnum opus'. Indeed, the book won the American Society of Criminology's award for the best book published in 1999 (Gruneau, 2002). This highlights the gap between the sociological understandings of crime and sport, despite Taylor contributing to both fields. To be sure, for sociologists of sport, Taylor's main intellectual contributions were his two attempts to understand the reasons for football fan 'disorder' across his career. Both of his theories were influential in the sociology of sport, hemming into Groombridge's (2017: 12) call for a sports criminology beyond football hooliganism and athletic deviance, such as drug-taking. Giulianotti (1999: 41) argued that Taylor's two approaches represented 'an explanatory somersault on football', given that he 'had begun with the idea that hooligans were popular "resistance fighters", but then abandoned this in the 1980s, to define them as serious social menaces'. This change of position reflects Taylor's theoretical interests and assumptions at the given points in his career as ideas within the emerging critical criminology moved and reshaped. In Taylor's first account (1971a, 1971b), which emerged from the first NDC papers, he argued that football hooliganism – largely defined as pitch invasions – where the working-class 'subcultural rump's' response to the perceived loss of the game to the profit-driven leisure industry

(Taylor, 1971a, 1971b, 1984: 10). In this account, his approach is distinctly Marxist, focussing upon traditional fans' alienation from the increasingly commercialising game as they seek a return to the era of 'participatory democracy', when he believed that fans saw football clubs as truly community organisations (Taylor, 1971a, 1971b). Taylor clearly understood hooliganism to come in two (perhaps inter-linked) forms: pitch invasions and fights between rival fan groups. In the (unclearly specified) participatory democracy era (Taylor refers to both the abolition of the football players' maximum wage in 1961 and post-war counter-urbanisation as key transition points), fans followed an unwritten rule that pitch invasions would not occur because supporters believed that the ground was 'theirs' and the turf was sacred. However, in the post-participatory democratic era, supporters' alienation meant that intrusions on to the field of play became more common. Also, with rising player salaries, football club directors' pursuit of more affluent fans and the public address system playing popular music (rather than on-the-pitch performances from the local brass band) unhinging the club from the local working-class community, the subcultural rump sought to maintain football's role in the 'working-class weekend' (Taylor, 1976). One of the most common ways to show this resistance was to exaggerate their working-class – often aggressive – masculine values and engage in 'hooligan' (fan violence) encounters (1971a, 1971b, 1976). Of course, Taylor was alive to the fact that the original members of alienated working-class 'hooligan' element may not still commit such offences, but the argument is made that younger 'hooligans' are socialised within the working-class cultures and internalise the disaffected rump's values. So, Taylor saw one form of hooliganism, as a behaviour defined as criminal and deviant by the ruling classes, arising out of a discontentment at the trajectory football had taken away from its most committed fans. By the 1980s, Taylor (1987) had changed tack as he saw additional causes of football violence, pointing out that the policies and ideology of the New Right government in Britain contributed to an aggression which became manifest in predominantly working-class activities – such as football support. This reflected the wider proliferations and modifications to the critical criminological line of argument at that point.

Taylor (1989) attempted to fuse the two accounts together in his attempt to analyse the events that unfolded during 1989's Hillsborough disaster in which 97 Liverpool F.C. fans lost their lives. Taylor knew the Hillsborough football stadium well, given that it was the home ground of the team he supported – Sheffield Wednesday F.C. – and it seemed likely to have provided site at which the anecdotal evidence that informed the emergence of his Marxist attempts to explain the phenomena of football hooliganism was collected. However, he appears to have misunderstood – partially accepting the false narratives that the mainstream print media reported that were associated to the disaster (perhaps accounted for by him working in Canada at the time) – by presenting that a combination of fans' alienation from football's increasingly commercialised conditions, including spiralling player wages and entrance ticket prices, and supporters' frustrations born from the politics of the New Right government caused the disaster. Later, more thorough accounts strongly disputed such claims (see Scraton, 2016). Indeed, more critical stories – which instead placed blame on to the organisation of policing and security matters – became accepted as the government's official narrative after 23 years of sustained protests by fan groups in 2012 (Conn, 2012), although senior police officers were ultimately found not guilty of charges they faced including gross negligence manslaughter (Conn, 2019).

Taylor appeared to accept this error of analysis in future years, as noted by his former PhD student (and now eminent Professor) Anthony King (2002: 82) who pointed out that despite the strong connections between his research on masculine fan cultures in football and the Hillsborough article (1989), Taylor never encouraged him to read the piece. The possibility of attempting to analyse the particular – a named football disaster – without meaningful data demonstrates the potential limits of a theory that is without empirical reality.

Taylor's work arguably provides the greatest substantive connection to our aim of this book, by discussing and analysing criminality in sport using a critical criminological perspective. But our claims are grounded within substantive practice. However, the insights gained from the other scholars and those that followed in the School are also important, and it is for these reasons that we now turn to the contributions from the group in *The New Criminology* (Taylor et al., 1973) and *Critical Criminology* (Taylor et al., 1975), alongside more recent updates of the theory.

The First Wave of Theory: *The New Criminology* and *Critical Criminology*

Explaining the genesis of the first wave of critical criminology, Rock (1988: 191) offers:

> In 1973, the Marxist exegetists, Taylor, Walton and Young, pointed to the hidden politics of bourgeois criminology (Taylor et al., 1973). In 1977, the feminist Carol Smart listed the patriarchal attitudes which buttressed criminology (Smart, 1977). And almost everybody professed to recoil from positivism (Platt, 1975). In effect, the new generation were refracting and amplifying wider debates, bringing into criminology the definitional quarrels and developments of sociology. Within that rather tumultuous jostling for space, encouraged and displayed in the books of the 1970s, there may well have been a purposeful exaggeration of conflict.

Indeed, Watts et al. (2008: 71) point out that sceptics or critics of 'official criminology' (including Edwin Sutherland, whose work on white-collar crime is discussed in Chapter 3) predate the rise of the NDC. However, as suggested earlier, the 1960s and 1970s were marked by the scale and seriousness with which various 'radicals' questioned the dominant consensus in criminology. Broadly, scholars such as Matza (2017 [1960]), Becker (1963) and Cicourel (2017 [1968]) worried about the problems involved in doing a criminology that claimed to 'objective' – trying to identify general rule 'causes of criminal behaviour' which ignored the complexity and the interpreted character of human activity and preferred to draw upon 'symbolic interactionist' traditions in US sociology in developing their critique of the orthodoxy. Crucially, these critics vehemently rejected the conventional assumption that crime was an objective fact enabling the collection of masses of *empirical* data as a basis for explanatory theory. Moving beyond criticism, they proposed some new ways of studying 'crime'. In the UK, the critical criminological community grew, principally utilising Marxist ideas through the NDC, and the first notable published output was *The New Criminology: For a Social Theory of Deviance*, written by Ian Taylor, Paul Walton[1] and Jock Young in 1973.

The first part of *The New Criminology* emphasises a reinterpretation of the history of criminological thought. O'Brien and Yar (2008) suggest that this was intended to reveal how the development of modern criminological theory's view of crime – in its forms, motivations and effects – had been trapped in a 'conventional' account. Taylor et al. (1973: 263) argued that this account had deflected attention 'away from a structural analysis of the forces conducive to crime and disorder' (ibid.: 263) and had failed to grasp 'crime as human action, as reaction to positions held in an antagonistic social structure, but also as action taken to resolve those antagonisms' (ibid.: 236). In *The New Criminology*'s account, 'crime' is not the callous or greedy act of predatory individuals but a consequence of the contradictory circumstances in which (especially poor) people find themselves. The book carried the aim of creating 'a fully social theory' of crime and deviance (Taylor et al., 1973: 3). Whether it achieved its goal is open to some debate: for instance, Payne et al. (1981: 105) described it as the 'major manifesto of NDC Marxism'[2] but Cowling (2008: 108) claimed that it 'says surprisingly little about a new way of understanding criminology'. As Rock argues, the book gave birth to a new – Marxist-influenced – way of understanding 'crime and criminality' in which they sought to build upon the symbolic interactionists critiques by placing this within a conflict theory perspective to try to examine the dynamics of society as a whole. Hence, the aim of creating 'a fully social theory' of crime and deviance was born (Mooney, 2011). Alongside the Marxist assumptions about the economic base largely controlling individual behaviour, *The New Criminology* made two sizable methodological and philosophical contributions to understanding crime which clearly broke from the official approaches. First, it attacked positivist approaches to criminology (and more broadly, social science) and particularly emphasised how the criminal justice system was fundamentally flawed in its selection and labelling of actions as 'criminal', particularly drawing attention to how the crimes of the working class are more easily detected than those of the more powerful groups in society. Indeed, on this point, Gouldner (1973: x) commented – in the book's foreword – that it is 'made thoroughly clear' that the study of criminology should involve 'the critical understanding of both the larger society and of the broadest social theory; it is not the study of some marginal exotic or esoteric group, be they criminals or criminologists'. Second, Taylor et al. (1973) clearly argued that it is important for theory to be sociologically imagined by being placed in its wider social and historical context. This means that 'crime' labelling and detection are historically contingent – what was 'criminal' or 'not criminal' in 1973 might be different in 1873 or even 2022 – and that the events of the present period are crucial if we are to fully comprehend the nature of crime and the reaction to it.

The New Criminology vehemently criticises classicism and positivism – the then-dominant criminological theories – by taking issue with theories that a) set the individual apart from society and b) fail to provide a sense of historical context. The major 'adversary' it identifies is the establishment criminology – which the NDC groups were mobilised against – because they see it as first, endorsing a positivistic explanation for crime and, second, uncritically presenting 'criminality' as the result of social or personal pathologies, thus advocating correctionalism through criminal sanctions and/or rehabilitation rather than looking towards its 'root causes' that are often found within relationships to the economy or the state (Muncie, 1998: 221). The concluding chapter of *The New Criminology* turns away from critiquing the major theories and practices of criminology to setting in transit an attempt to produce a critical paradigm for understanding 'crime' and 'criminality'. They argue that this is premised on seven ideas – and the connections between them – that emerged from their critique of the state of criminological knowledge in 1973. These will now be described.

First, Taylor et al. (1973: 270) argued that a theory of understanding 'crime' and 'criminality' must be able to place the deviant act in terms of its wider structural origin and called for the development of a 'political economy of crime' to emerge. They suggested that this must consider intermediate structures such as ecological areas, subcultural location and the distribution of opportunities to commit 'crime' but that the state and the economy which create inequalities of wealth, power and authority should be prioritised in any analysis. Individual issues should be evaluated in the emergent theory but in the context of understanding that people are not atomised and cut off from structural concerns. Second, they argued that the immediate origins of the deviant act be analysed, in 'a *social psychology of crime*' which recognises that men 'may *consciously* choose the deviant road, as the one solution to the problems posed by existence in a contradictory society' (Taylor et al., 1973: 271). This means that

> an adequately social theory of deviance must be able to explain the different events, experiences or structural developments that precipitate the deviant act [and] explain the different ways in which structural demands are interpreted, reacted against, or used by men at different levels in the social structure, in such a way that an essentially deviant choice is made.
>
> *(Taylor et al., 1973: 271)*

As such, the people may choose to commit 'crime' but these choices are conditioned by their place in the social structure. Third, they argued that the theory must take into account the 'real *social dynamics* surrounding the actual acts'

(Taylor et al., 1973: 272) and look at the 'criminal' act itself, as many people choose to engage in particular – 'criminal' – solutions to their problems, without being able to carry them out. Therefore, a social theory of deviance should explain the relationship between beliefs and action and optimum 'rationality' that social actors chose and the behaviours they actually carry through. For instance, they argue that a working-class adolescent, who has been confronted with blockage of opportunity and with problems of status frustration, who is alienated from the kind of existence offered out to him in contemporary society, may want to engage in hedonistic activities – that might include finding immediate pleasure through the use of alcohol, drugs or in extensive sexual activities – or s/he may choose to reject the society that s/he feels has rejected him/her by committing acts of vandalism. Thus, crime – in the case of Taylor's (1971a, 1971b) account, football hooliganism – might be a subjectively desirable solution to a social problem. Fourth, they call for the 'immediate origins of social reaction' to be taken into account in a '*social psychology of social reaction*' that is 'an account of the contingencies and the conditions which are crucial to the decision to act against the deviant' (Taylor et al., 1973: 272). By this, they mean that 'criminal' act may be is the product of close personal relationships – including their reactions – such as 'an adolescent's attempt to win acceptance as "cool" or "tough" in a subculture of delinquency, or from a businessman's attempt to show ability as a sharp practitioner' (ibid: 272). Carrying out this behaviour may encourage a member of the actor's family or peer group to refer him/her to an external 'expert' because that behaviour is seen to 'be odd', which may result in the criminalisation (or medicalisation) of that individual. Thus, there is a degree of choice on the part of the social audience that defines the labelling of the action as 'criminal' (or 'ill') – it may be thought that the behaviour *is* odd, but a decision is made to 'keep it in the family'; or it may be thought that although the individual *has* been acting suspiciously or has been behaving illegally, it would be too troublesome to involve the police. Thus, what is reported to the authorities who label an act as 'criminal' is partially subject to the reaction of the audience who experiences it. As such, large-scale 'social harms' may not be criminalised (Canning and Tombs, 2021).

Fifth, Taylor et al. (1973) argued that the 'wider origins of deviant reaction' need to be taken into account to develop '*a political economy of social reaction*' (ibid: 274). Thus, they mean that the social reaction of others to the 'criminal' act, including those who are both those involved in legitimate activity and those engaged in rule-breaking activity, need to be analysed according to their position in the social structure. Sixth, Taylor et al. (1973: 275) stated that 'the outcome of the social reaction on [the] deviant's further action' must be interrogated. Therefore, they suggested that deviants should be understood as having some degree of consciousness of what to expect in the event of apprehension and reaction to their actions. They argued that this meant that a

> fully social explanation of the outcome of social reaction to the further actions of the apprehended deviant, therefore, would be one in which the

deviant actor is always endowed with some degree of consciousness about the likelihood and consequences of reaction against him, and in which his subsequent decisions are developed from that initial degree of consciousness.

(ibid.: 276)

Thus, the social reaction to the act of deviancy may shape further actions. Finally – and seventh – Taylor et al.'s 'fully social theory' of crime, criminality and deviancy involves observing 'the nature of the deviant process as a whole' (ibid.: 276). This means that the six earlier stated requirements 'must not be treated simply as essential factors all of which need to be present (in invariant fashion) if the theory is to be social' but '[r]ather it is that these formal requirements must all appear in the theory, as they do in the real world, in a complex, dialectical relationship to one another' (ibid.: 277), meaning that the social scientist must not ignore any of the outlined steps in analysis to understand criminality, but that not all have to yield answers for a 'new' criminological theory to be useful in an analysis of social problems.

Taylor, Walton and Young followed up *The New Criminology* with an edited collection, *Critical Criminology* (1975) in which Cowling (2008: 115) argues that their 'ideas emerge more clearly'. Cowling suggests that this clarity is most obviously provided in the opening two chapters of the collection. The first of these, 'Critical Criminology in Britain: Review and Prospects' is by the three editors. In the piece, the authors argue that deviant actions should be examined in terms of their meaningfulness to the deviant actor, taking seriously his/her vocabularies of motive, rather than – as in official criminological narratives – explaining them away as a form of pathology. They follow Alvin Gouldner by favouring a 'psychedelic culture' which rejects the central values of industrial society such as moneymaking, achievement, routine economic roles and the inhibition of expression but encourages each individual to do his/her own thing. As such, they argue that society contains a range of alternative realities that are all authentic and should not be easily labelled 'deviant' or criminalised. Thus, the criminology which goes with this orientation is anti-utilitarian and concentrates on victimless crimes, with methodology that is less concerned with replicating the empirical method of the natural sciences but is intuitive (see Cowling, 2008: 116). Taylor et al. (1975: 30) argue that their radical theory could expose the double standards of ruling groups (and their interests) and that the motivation for doing this should be to demonstrate the 'institutionalised, regular and widespread' deviancy amongst the powerful, a result of the structural position that they hold, rather than necessarily being about a wider moral appeal.

The second chapter in the collection is also by Jock Young and is titled 'Working-Class Criminology' (1975). Young begins the piece by listing the major features of official and orthodox, 'scientific' criminology before going on to describe the critical alternative. Essentially, in their theory the deviant is a rational, conscious actor, who is free of the determinants of past events and physical or psychic disturbance and may exist in a homogenous and normatively consistent subculture. He elaborates that their theory has less interest in utilitarian crimes and instead centres upon expressive deviancy, such as marijuana use and prostitution rather than burglary and murder.

The book is extended by a further six chapters, offered by Tony Platt (on 'Prospects for a radical criminology in the USA'), Herman Schwendinger and Julie Schwendinger, Geoff Pearson (on 'Misfit sociology'), William J. Chambliss, Richard Quinney and Paul Q. Hirst. In the latter chapter, Hirst (1975: 204) took issue with the Marxist roots of critical criminology, by arguing that 'there is no "Marxist theory of deviance", either in existence, or which can be developed within orthodox Marxism'.

The two texts proved to be influential but were not immune from criticism, which came in several forms. First, there is the argument that the insights offered in the books – particularly *The New Criminology* – are spectacularly underdeveloped. For instance, Cowling (2008: 108) argues that *The New Criminology* 'says surprisingly little about a new way of understanding criminology. It reads more like an unusually critical criminological theory textbook', whilst Watts et al. (2008: 81) make a similar criticism by stating '[a]s for the substantive claim to have outlined a "new criminology", their proposal amounted to a few pages of abstracted and often incoherent theorizing about crime'. Sumner (1994: 291) suggested that arguments made in the books were overdrawn with critiques of other works ill-developed and premised on 'straw man' characterisations. In essence, he argues that the call for the abandonment of all prior conceptions of crime and deviance was nothing but a parody of the complexity of crime and deviance. As such, Watts et al. (2008: 81) describe *The New Criminology* as 'a book with very serious weaknesses'. A second objection to the work was that the new/critical criminology had gone too far in the relativism of reality and 'real crime' that came from it. To elaborate, some suggested that attempts to 'relativise' crime and deviance destroyed its basis of social scientific inquiry (see Sumner, 1994; Watts et al., 2008). Third, the work continued to be ignored by the criminological mainstream: as a bout of collective action, it was not very successful in altering the way in which legal systems, or even those more conservative schools of criminology, dealt with the 'problem of crime'. As such, Cohen (1998) regretted this 'isolation' when reflecting upon the impact of critical criminology 20 years after the rise of the NDC. Fourth, the premise of challenging power injustices in the criminal justice system became accepted by many feminist criminologists, but Smart (1977, 1997) and Walklate (2013) used the theoretical and political assumptions of feminism to show how – despite Mary McIntosh's membership in the original NDC group – Taylor et al. (1973, 1975) continued to render women as invisible to 'malestream' criminology (see Carrabine et al., 2020: 85). On top of these points, some of the most powerful criticisms came from within the group, as the meaning of critical criminology became more diffuse.

The Second Wave of Theory: Critical Criminology's Turn to Left Realism

As Hil (2002) writes:

> Following publication of *The New Criminology* there emerged two distinct bodies of critical reaction. First, those from within the left-leaning side of the

discipline who attacked the book . . . (see Downes and Rock, 1979). Second, in the wake of New Right politics, a reinvigorated breed of administrative criminologists scoffed at what seemed the crass idealism of radical criminology. From the early 1980s onwards, administrative criminologists focused increasingly on the plight of victims, situational and environmental crime prevention and community-based programs.

By the mid-1970s, the group conferences began to be held less regularly, and its members began to work on their own branches of 'critical criminology'. As such its meaning became increasingly diffuse. Ross (2011: 1) argued that the (sub)discipline 'matured into a diverse body of work', but Barak (1998: 34) stated that he did not 'believe that its current usage has any specific meaning beyond the generic convenience of providing organizational and social identity for its adherents'. As Hil notes, by the late 1970s, David Downes and Paul Rock had forcibly moved towards symbolic interactionism as a response to the neo-Marxist roots of critical criminology as evidenced by their edited collection, *Deviant Interpretations* (1979). However, at the final NDC conference – held in 1979 – Jock Young coined the term 'left idealism' to refer to the first wave of critical criminology and began to give preference to a second wave of 'left realism' critical criminology. This showed a clear fracture in the group's previous theoretical unity (Mooney, 2011). Also in 1979, Margaret Thatcher became Prime Minister of Britain with an administration of the radical – and new – right. Her Conservative Party government aimed to advance the UK as a market society whilst reducing the strength of the welfare state. Mooney (2019) argued that the crime rate subsequently rose, and the critical criminological foundations earlier outlined by the NDC group and their collaborators, with respect to social exclusions caused by class and poverty, and led to the emergence of left realism.

A key weakness of the radical critical criminological approach of *The New Criminology* and *Critical Criminology* was that the theory failed to adequately explain individual criminal and deviant behaviour because of its overriding interest in the way power and class functioned to define crime and enforce law (Hayward, 2010). Without accounting for this, the theory left itself open to criticisms of 'romanticising criminals' as revolutionaries that were resisting the oppressive capitalist structures – as was the case in Taylor's (1971a, 1971b) original explanatory accounts of football hooliganism (however defined). Watts et al. (2008) suggest that this criticism was advanced by Geoffrey Pearson (1975) who referred to himself as a 'left realist' in his chapter in Taylor et al.'s *Critical Criminology*. These points were taken on board by Taylor and Young, especially when it became apparent that the working classes were disproportionately experiencing spikes in crime, further substantiating the view that radical criminology was 'not taking crime seriously' (Lea and Young, 1984; Lea, 1986). Thus, according to Mooney (2011), the revised critical criminology of left realism sought to listen to the concerns of ordinary people to reclaim the politics of crime and disorder from the political right. Like the first wave of critical criminology, left realism continued to be set against 'official' criminology – by then the Home Office's new administrative criminology – which had also altered to describe the fear of crime as more of a problem than crime itself. As the left realist implies, it uses discourses and categories of 'power' – like 'class', 'exclusion' and 'oppression' – to challenge the politics of conventional criminology whilst insisting that crime remains an objectively real problem that need not be deconstructed. Thus, in *What Is to Be Done about Law and Order?* (Lea and Young, 1984) and *Law and Order: Arguments for Socialism* (Taylor, 1981), the emerging theory of left realism aimed to portray the 'reality' of crime as experienced in poor neighbourhoods, challenging those – quite arguably as they did in Taylor et al. (1973, 1975) – who minimised the deviancy of working-class crime and placed emphasis on the crimes of the ruling class, such as the police, corporations and state agencies.

The left realism of Lea and Young (1984) and Taylor (1981) did not abandon all (neo) Marxist ideas from the first wave of critical criminological theory. Indeed, left realists agree with radical theorists by arguing that 'crime is a reaction to an unjust society' (Lea and Young, 1984: 45). However, left realists do not believe that the criminal should not be blamed for responding to inequality with offending behaviour. This analysis carried favour with those who were looking for a more policy-orientated and 'impact' centred approach to understanding crime and tended to focus on both ends of the social structure. On this, Hayward (2010: 264) argued:

> When set out in such straightforward terms, left realism appears highly attractive. Viewing crime as an 'amalgam' of many 'interacting elements' (e.g. the victim, the public, the police and other agencies of social control, the legal rules of criminal law, the criminal act, and the offender) allowed left realists to consider such issues as multiple victimisation, multi-agency co-operation, progressive crime prevention, even street lighting – all things that previously had largely been ignored by radical criminologists in favour of the overarching goal of revolutionary sociopolitical transformation.

By the time Ian Taylor (1982, 1984, 1987, 1989, 1991) returned to sport to give his work on football hooliganism a left realist revision, Frosdick and Marsh (2016) point out that he had become unseated in providing the most widely drawn upon theory in describing/explaining the subcultural violence by Marsh et al.'s (1978) 'ethogenic' approach, whilst the figurational sociologists emanating from Leicester University were busily drawing up their framework that would become dominant for at least a decade afterwards (see Dunning et al., 1988; Murphy et al., 1990; Williams et al., 1992 [1984]). Taylor's (1987) article drew upon the labelling theories that were largely embraced in the first wave of critical criminological theory to make clear that the 'blame' for the Bradford fire disaster (1985), in which 57 fans died, was not the fault of the 'working-class' supporters who could be conflated as 'hooligans' but was, in fact, an accident that was caused by inappropriate facilities and – most specifically – a wooden stand with a tarmac roof that accidentally caught alight by a cigarette. However, in his description of the Heysel disaster, in which 39 supporters died because of combination of unsafe provisions and fan disorder, he discussed the agency of football fans in creating a potentially violent and exclusive culture (Taylor, 1987). In Taylor's 1982 chapter, he claimed that the growth of football-related violence from its original identification as a serious social problem in 1960s Britain to its status in the 1980s as a contemporary manifestation of racism and gang warfare was socially located within 'real' state and economic relations. He argued that during the mid-to-late 1970s football violence became a working-class youth expression or displacement of real accelerating economic anxieties into a ritual form of aggression against the imagined sources of such anxiety, giving rise to nationalism, regionalism, xenophobia, racism and general intolerance (Taylor, 1982). By 1991, Taylor was echoing Young's (1981: 206) pledge to 'think seriously about crime' by 'taking Hillsborough seriously' (Taylor, 1991) with a left realist account of the disaster. However, in all of his post-*Law and Order* (1982) accounts, human agency was more important than in his original discussions. To be sure, he argued that social locations were important in shaping behaviours but that supporters had choice to actively resist the commercialisation of football for democratic reasons or create violent and exclusive cultures (although it is unclear why he saw such actions as a straight choice). He interpreted his task as mediating between these two positions, adopting an ultimately ambiguous critical position that neither dismissed nor vindicated football fans, producing a left realist account of football hooliganism.

Like the first wave of critical criminology, the left realist splinter of the theory also drew criticisms, many of which came from within the radical school of criminology that Taylor, Young and their colleagues originally spawned. These critiques came from at least three directions. First, Sim (1987) strongly attacked left realism arguing that the accounts put forward did not explore the 'real' roots of the 'criminality' which lay in the wider capitalist system. Thus, whilst Lea and Young (1984) acknowledged that inequality might spawn behaviour that becomes criminalised, Sim (1987) argues that they did not interrogate these ideas strongly enough and instead seemed happy for the individuals who have been labelled as a 'criminal' to be described as a deviant. Second, Hillyard et al. (2004), followed by Barton et al. (2007) and Canning and Tombs (2021), clearly articulated a range of arguments that confluence through stating that the left realist approach – much like right realist approaches – mainly ignores the crimes of more powerful groups in society, and instead has a sharp focus on street crime (see also Coleman, 2012 [2004]). Third, Carlen (2002) argued that left realist criminology uncritically accepts the establishment's definitions of 'crime', 'criminality' and – by implication – 'deviancy'. She argues that criminology should challenge the ways in which underreported crimes against women operate, and therefore there should be a much greater stress on issues of domestic violence. Other feminist criminological theorists, such as Smart (1989), have also been critical of left realism in its tackling both of female criminal behaviour and of its failure to explain crimes that are traditionally seen as targeting women, such as rape. The shift towards left realism did not spell the end of the first wave of critical criminological theory which continued to view crime through the lens of capitalist social divisions. However, the shift did cause – or at least reflect – a clear division within the critical criminological school, leading Barak (1998) to question the extent to which a unified theory continued to exist. If it continued to exist, it certainly proliferated in subsequent decades.

Summary: Sport and Critical Criminology in the Twenty-First Century

Walton and Young (1998) opened the door to critical debate on criminological issues in the twenty-first century with the publication of their edited collection, *The New Criminology Revisited*. The text featured separate chapters by Taylor, Walton and Young as well as contributions by ten other scholars. The engagement with the theory for critical criminological analysis that was outlined in the final chapter of *The New Criminology* was strangely downplayed across the collection with many contributions turning towards the critiques of the pre-1973 discourses of criminality within criminology as key features of the more recent text. Indeed, Walton (1998: 6) stated that in the 'debate over the impact and importance of *The New Criminology*, it is probable that too much attention was paid to the nature of its tentative general theory of crime' and turned his chapter to emphasise 'the importance of realist criminology' (1999: 11) rather than the radical roots of the original text. Young (1998: 24) was keener to engage with the theory, giving a brief reminder of its constitutive parts before arguing that 'there is very little that one would find fault with today'. Stan Cohen (1998) disagreed, finding four major faults with the radical theory. He argued that the first wave of radical critical criminology had first, an incorrect analysis by stating that it should not have demystified 'the crime problem as the product of media myth, moral panics, faulty categorization or false consciousness' but that crime should 'be acknowledged as a problem for the powerless, who are often its targets' (ibid.: 105). Second, he suggested that the theory too easily reduced the criminal justice system and 'criminality' as a 'mere reflection of class interest' when the reality was more complex (ibid.: 106). Third, Cohen (p. 106) thought that the approach was too harsh on 'the traditional causal questions of positivism' which he recognised did not mean reviving psychological determinism but did invite a discussion about the connection between 'crime' and 'criminality' and variables such as 'poverty, deprivation, racism, social disorganisation, unemployment, loss of community and the power of gender'. Finally, Cohen found problems with the original radical criminology's abandonment of 'the discourse of the old criminology and to try and construct an alternative with its own problematic', as he was argued that the ideas in *The New Criminology* isolated themselves by failing to make the theory 'politically relevant by operating on the same terrain that conservatives and technocrats have appropriated' (Cohen, 1998: 106).

Young marched through the door that was opened by *The New Criminology Revisited* by publishing *The Exclusive Society* (1999), *The Vertigo of Late Modernity* (2007) and *The Criminological Imagination* (2011b) in the subsequent years. All shared a general disdain for a positivist approach to understanding crime, a belief that the roots of crime and criminality lay in the power relations of society, but all were ambiguous in not rendering the role of human agency to be meaningless. Indeed, in all three texts, Young (1999, 2007, 2011b) reconnects debates around criminalisation to socio-economic marginalisation. As such, he strongly rejects the claims to 'remoralise' a dysfunctional 'underclass' by punitive sanctions (defined in social, legal and economic terms). The trilogy's scope and aims seemed like a rallying call to critical criminologists, however, by the twenty-first century the 'meaning' of critical criminology had altered: the movement changed, the school splintered and the theory more diffuse. Importantly, this led Ross (2011: 10) to argue that critical criminology has no 'single definition'.

There is great debate in research into 'collective actions' about what a mobilisation's 'success' might constitute (Giugni, 1998). For Rochon and Mazmanian (1993) incorporation into the power structures is a desirable outcome for a protest. Paul Rock and David Downes had appeared to move away from the radical wave of critical criminology by the late 1970s but were part of the original group of protagonists that challenged official discourses of crime. In 2009, the *British Society of Criminology Newsletter* announced their incorporation into the state with the news that they (with Tim Newburn) had been commissioned by the government to write an 'official history of the Criminal Justice System' (Rock, 2009: 16). Hil (2002) argued that 'critical criminologists have always been fearful of losing their critical edge if absorbed into the agendas of reform and correction' but this signified that two of the original group had effectively *become* the official narrative of the Criminal Justice System – a move that could signify either the success of the original group (they had conquered the official narratives) or its failure (the official narratives had conquered them). The substantive feature of critical criminological thought still sought to call into question the legitimacy of the state's powers of social control and challenged the inequalities created in the advanced capitalist system (see Barton et al., 2007; Carrington and Hogg, 2011; Hillyard et al., 2004) but the original movement had changed. Similarly, the school of critical criminology had arguably fallen away since the final NDC conference of 1979, despite the continued development of the European Group for the Study of Deviance and Control. However, in 2011, contemporary critical criminologists Simon Winlow and Rowland Atkinson held an event at the University of York, in which the original contributors of Jock Young, Stan Cohen and Tony Jefferson attended alongside younger researchers. In the spirit of the forerunner events, the conference gave rise to an edited collection: *New Directions in Crime and Deviancy* (2012).

However, our book is principally focussed on the theories of critical criminology and their potential for understanding 'crime', 'deviance' and 'criminality' in sport. It is certain that – reflecting the movement and the school – the theory of critical criminology has changed since the first NDC in 1968, the publication of *The New Criminology* in 1973 and the rise of the left realist revision in the early 1980s. DeKeseredy and Dragiewicz (2018: 25–59) attempted to draw together the state of the nation of twenty-first century proliferations of critical criminological theory and argued that at least seven varieties had emerged: feminism (see Collins, 2021; DeKeseredy and Schwartz, 2009; Ogle and Batton, 2009), masculinity theories (see DeKeseredy and

Schwartz, 2005; Messerschmidt and Tomsen, 2018), left realism (see DeKeseredy and Schwartz, 2018; Wacquant, 2008), peacemaking criminology (see Fuller, 2003; Pepinsky, 2013), postmodern criminology (see Arrigo, 2019), cultural criminology (see Ferrell, 2003; O'Neill and Seal, 2012) and convict criminology (see Ross and Richards, 2003). This list excludes other social issues in which critical criminology-inspired work has been used to analyse – such as hate crime (see Perry, 2003) – whilst emergent critical theories such as zemiology, that is, the study of social harm (Hillyard et al., 2004; Canning and Tombs, 2021) and victimology, as the study of victimisation and the relationships between victims, offenders and the criminal justice system (Mawby and Walklate, 1994) can be added to that list. Critical criminology has *no* single meaning in the twenty-first century, apart from a unity of looking to the transgressive features of 'crime', 'criminalisation' and 'deviance' that are beyond official narratives of the criminal justice system. And how has sport been used as a site to explore critical criminological issues in the twenty-first century? The answer is marginally, if at all. Ian Taylor, who was the only member of the original group to discuss any dimension of sport died prematurely in 2001, but King (2002: 86) argued that if he had lived 'it is unlikely that he would ever have returned to the sociology of football' as his thoughts had turned elsewhere. Beyond Taylor, engagements with sport are few and far between, which is why Groombridge's (2017) intervention into the field was so important in prompting new debate. Garland and Treadwell (2010), Ayres and Treadwell (2012), Hopkins and Treadwell (2014) and Stott et al. (2012) have followed Taylor in publishing about football 'hooliganism' in ways that could be viewed as encompassing some of the critical criminological ideas, but Groombridge (2017: 12) is correct to assert that it and athletic deviance have dominated whatever debate has existed. Crime, deviance and criminality – in multiple forms – are found in more areas than football hooliganism in sport, and we answer Groombridge's call in this book, by following two aims: first, to shed further light on the transgressive understanding of 'crime', 'criminality' and 'deviance' in sport by using published sociology of sport material and reanalysing it using critical criminological frameworks and second, to consider how those frameworks can be further developed by using the case evidence emerging from sport. This quest begins in the next chapter which employs the range of critical criminological theories on corruption and, specifically, white-collar crime to look at business and management practices that have developed in the *Fédération Internationale de Football Association* (FIFA) and the International Olympic Committee (IOC).

Notes

1 Paul Walton is not referred to in the original group of NDC critical criminologists but played a key role in the formation of the ideas in the school, given his co-authorship and co-editorship of *The New Criminology* and *Critical Criminology*. He became Professor of Communications at Thames Valley University after previously working at Goldsmiths and University of Wales College.
2 The authors directly acknowledge the book as a 'product of discussions and developments in and around the National Deviancy Conference' (Taylor et al., 1973: xv).

References

Arrigo, B.A. (2019) 'Postmodern criminology on race, class, and gender', *Race, Gender, and Class in Criminology the Intersections* (Eds. M.D. Schwartz and D. Milanovic), Abingdon: Routledge, pp. 73–89.

Ayres, T.C. and Treadwell, J. (2012) 'Bars, drugs and football thugs: Alcohol, cocaine use and violence in the night time economy among English football firms', *Criminology & Criminal Justice* 12(1): 83–100.

Barak, G. (1998) *Integrative Criminology*, Aldershot: Ashgate.

Barton, A., Corteen, K., Scott, D. and Whyte D. (2007) 'Introduction: Developing a criminological imagination', *Expanding the Criminological Imagination: Critical Readings in Criminology* (Eds. A. Barton, K. Corteen, D. Scott and D. Whyte), Cullompton: Willan Publishing, pp. 1–14.

Becker, H.S. (1963) *Outsiders; Studies in the Sociology of Deviance*, London: Free Press.

Brake, M. (1980) *The Sociology of Youth Culture and Youth Subcultures: Sex and Drugs and Rock'n'Roll?* Abingdon: Routledge.

Brake, M. (1985) *Comparative Youth Culture: The Sociology of Youth Cultures and Youth Subcultures in America, Britain and Canada*, Abingdon: Routledge.

Brannigan, A. and Pavlich, G. (eds.) (2007) *Governance and Regulation in Social Life: Essays in Honour of WG Carson*, Abingdon: Routledge.

Canning, V. and Tombs, S. (2021) *From Social Harm to Zemiology: A Critical Introduction*, Abingdon: Routledge.

Carlen, P. (2002) 'Controlling measures', *Criminal Justice* 2(2): 155–172.

Carrabine, E., Cox, A., Cox, P., Crowhurst, I., Di Ronco, A., Fussey, P., Sergi, A., South, N., Thiel, D. and Turton, J. (2020) *Criminology: A Sociological Introduction*, Abingdon: Routledge.

Carrington, K. and Hogg, R. (2011) 'Critical criminologies: An introduction', *Critical Criminology: Issues, Debates and Challenges* (Eds. K. Carrington and R. Hogg), Abingdon: Routledge.

Cicourel, A.V. (2017 [1968]) *The Social Organization of Juvenile Justice*, Abingdon: Routledge.

Cohen, S. (ed.) (1973) *Images of Deviance*, London: Penguin.

Cohen, S. (1981) 'Footprints in the sand: A further report on criminology and the sociology of deviance in Britain', *Against Criminology* (Eds. S. Cohen), Oxford: Transaction Books.

Cohen, S. (1998) 'Intellectual scepticism and political commitment: The case of radical criminology', *The New Criminology Revisited* (Eds. P. Walton and J. Young), London: Palgrave Macmillan.

Cohen, S. (2000) *States of Denial*, Cambridge: Polity Press.

Cohen, S. (2003) 'Response to public orator by professor Stanley Cohen, University of Essex, 9 July 2003, cited in: Downes, D., Rock, P., Chinkin, C. and Gearty, C. (eds.) (2007) *Crime, Social Control and Human Rights: From Moral Panics to States of Denial, Essays in Honour of Stanley Cohen*, Abingdon: Routledge.

Cohen, S. (2011 [1972]) *Folk Devils and Moral Panics*, Abingdon: Routledge.

Coleman, R. (2012 [2004]) *Reclaiming the Streets*, Abingdon: Routledge.

Collins, V.E. (2021) 'Looking to critical criminology to centre gender and violence against women in state crime studies', *The Howard Journal of Crime and Justice* 60(3): 370–387.

Conn, D. (2012) 'Hillsborough disaster: The truth', *The Guardian*, 12 September, available from: www.guardian.co.uk/football/2012/sep/12/hillsborough-disaster-police-coverup-revealed [accessed 11/2021].

Conn, D. (2019) 'Hillsborough: David Duckenfield found not guilty of manslaughter', *The Guardian*, 28 November, available from: www.theguardian.com/uk-news/2019/nov/28/hillsborough-david-duckenfield-verdict [accessed 11/2021].

Cowling, M. (2008) *Marxism and Criminological Theory: A Critique and a Toolkit*, Basingstoke: Palgrave.
Darby, P. (2002) 'Ian Taylor, 11 March 1944–19 January 2001', *Soccer and Society* 3(1): 97–80.
DeKeseredy, W.S. and Dragiewicz, M. (2018) 'Introduction: Critical criminology', *Routledge Handbook of Critical Criminology* (Eds. DeKeseredy, W.S. and M. Dragiewicz), Abingdon: Routledge.
DeKeseredy, W.S. and Schwartz, M.D. (2005) 'Masculinities and interpersonal violence', *Handbook of Studies on Men and Masculinities* (Eds. M.S. Kimmel, J. Hearn and R.W. Connell), London: Sage.
DeKeseredy, W.S. and Schwartz, M.D. (2009) *Dangerous Exits: Escaping Abusive Relationships in Rural America*, New Brunswick, NJ: Rutgers University Press.
DeKeseredy, W.S. and Schwartz, M.D. (2018) 'Left realism: A new look', *Routledge Handbook of Critical Criminology* (Eds. W.S. DeKeseredy and M. Dragiewicz), Abingdon: Routledge.
Downes, D. (1966) *The Delinquent Solution*, London: Routledge and Kegan Paul.
Downes, D. (2013) 'Stanley Cohen: Distinguished criminologist', *The Independent*, 24 February, available from: www.independent.co.uk/news/obituaries/stanley-cohen-distinguished-criminologist-8508645.html [accessed 11/2021].
Downes, D. and Rock, P. (1979) *Deviant Interpretations: Problems in Criminological Theory*, New York: Barnes and Noble.
Downes, D. and Rock, P. (2011) *Understanding Deviance: A Guide to the Sociology of Crime and Rule-Breaking*, Oxford: Oxford University Press.
Downes, D., Rock, P., Chinkin, C. and Gearty, C. (eds.) (2007) *Crime, Social Control and Human Rights: From Moral Panics to States of Denial, Essays in Honour of Stanley Cohen*, Abingdon: Routledge.
Dunning, E., Murphy, P. and Williams, J. (1988) *The Roots of Football Hooliganism: An Historical and Sociological Study*, London: Routledge & Kegan Paul.
Ferrell, J. (2003) 'Cultural criminology', *Criminological Perspectives: Essential Readings* (Eds. E. McLaughlin, J. Muncie and G. Hughes), London: Sage.
Ferrell, J., Hayward, K. and Young, J. (2015) *Cultural Criminology: An Invitation*, London: Sage.
Findlay, M. (2010) 'Stanley Cohen', *Fifty Key Thinkers in Criminology* (Eds. K. Hayward, S. Maruna and J. Mooney), Abingdon: Routledge.
Frosdick, S. and Marsh, P. (2016 [2005]) *Football Hooliganism*, Abingdon: Routledge.
Fuller, J. (2003) 'Peacemaking criminology', *Controversies in Critical Criminology* (Eds. M. Schwartz and S.E. Hatty), Abingdon: Routledge.
Garland, J. and Treadwell, J. (2010) ' "No surrender to the Taliban!" Football Hooliganism, Islamophobia and the rise of the English defence league', *Papers from the British Criminology Conference* 10: 19–35.
Gouldner, A. (1973) 'Foreword', *The New Criminology: For a Social Theory of Deviance* (Eds. I. Taylor, P. Walton and J. Young), London: Routledge & Kegan Paul Books.
Groombridge, N. (2017) *Sports Criminology: A Critical Criminology of Sports and Games*, Bristol: Policy Press.
Gruneau, R. (2002) 'Just one of the lads: Remembering Ian Taylor', *Soccer & Society* 3(1): 88–92.
Giugni, M.G. (1998) 'The outcomes of social movements: A review of the literature', *Annual Review of Sociology* 24: 371–393.
Giulianotti, R. (1999) *Football: A Sociology of the Global Game*, Cambridge: Polity Press.
Haines, F. and Whyte, D. (2019) 'Obituary – Kit Carson', *British Society of Criminology Newsletter* 84: 37–38.

Hall, S. (1968) 'The hippies: An American "moment"', *Centre for Contemporary Cultural Studies Papers*, University of Birmingham, available from: http://epapers.bham.ac.uk/3336/1/Hall_1968_SOP16.pdf [accessed 11/2021].
Hayward, K.J. (2010) 'Opening the lens: Cultural criminology and the image', *Framing Crime: Cultural Criminology and The Image* (Eds. K.J. Hayward and M. Presdee), Abingdon: Routledge.
Hil, R. (2002) 'Facing change: New directions for critical criminology in the early new millennium?' *Western Criminology Review. Artículo en Internet*, available from: https://westerncriminology.org/documents/WCR/v03n2/hil/hil.html [accessed 11/2021].
Hillyard, P., Pantazis, C., Tombs, S. and Gordon, D. (eds.) (2004) *Beyond Criminology: Taking Harm Seriously*, London: Pluto.
Hirst, P.Q. (1975) 'Radical deviancy theory and Marxism', *Critical Criminology* (Eds. I. Taylor, P. Walton and J. Young), London: Routledge & Kegan Paul Books.
Hopkins, M. and Treadwell, J. (eds.) (2014) *Football Hooliganism, Fan Behaviour and Crime: Contemporary Issues*, Basingstoke: Palgrave MacMillan.
Hutter, B. (2013) 'Stan Cohen', *LSE Blogs*, 8 January, available from: https://blogs.lse.ac.uk/condolences/2013/01/08/stancohen/ [accessed 11/2021].
Jefferson, T. (2021) *Stuart Hall, Conjunctural Analysis and Cultural Criminology: A Missed Moment*, Basingstoke: Palgrave MacMillan.
King, A. (2002) 'Ian Taylor: A personal contemplation', *Soccer & Society* 3(1): 81–87.
Lea, J. (1986) 'Towards social prevention', *Middlesex Polytechnic Centre for Criminology Working Paper*, November 1986.
Lea, J. and Young, J. (1984) *What Is to Be Done About Law and Order?* London: Penguin.
Marsh, P., Rosser, E. and Harré, R. (1978) *The Rules of Disorder*, London: Routledge and Kegan Paul Books.
McAdam, D. (1982) *Political Process and the Origins of Black Insurgency*, Chicago: University of Chicago Press.
Mills, C.W. (2005 [1959]) *The Sociological Imagination*, Oxford: Oxford University Press.
Mooney, J. (2011) 'Finding a political voice: The emergence of critical criminology in Britain', *The Handbook of Critical Criminology* (Eds. W. DeKeseredy and M. Dragiewicz), London: Routledge, pp. 13–31.
Muncie, J. (1998) 'Reassessing competing paradigms in criminological theory', *The New Criminology Revisited* (Eds. P. Walton and J. Young), London: Palgrave Macmillan.
Murphy, P.J., Williams, J. and Dunning, E. (1990) *Football on Trial: Spectator Violence and Development in the Football World*, London: Routledge.
Newburn, T. and Rock, P. (eds.) (2009) *The Politics of Crime Control: Essays in Honour of David Downes*, Oxford: Oxford University Press.
O'Brien, M. and Yar, M. (2008) *Criminology: The Key Concepts*, Abingdon: Routledge.
Ogle, R.S. and Batton, C. (2009) 'Revisiting patriarchy: Its conceptualization and operationalization in criminology', *Critical Criminology* 17(3): 159–182.
O'Neill, M. and Seal, L. (2012) *Transgressive Imaginations: Crime, Deviance and Culture*, London: Palgrave Macmillan.
Matza, D. (2017 [1960]). *Becoming Deviant*, Abingdon: Routledge.
Mawby, R. and Walklate, S. (1994) *Critical Victimology: International Perspectives*, London: Sage.
Messerschmidt, J.W. and Tomsen, S. (2018) 'Masculinities and crime', *Routledge Handbook of Critical Criminology* (Eds. W.S. DeKeseredy and M. Dragiewicz), Abingdon: Routledge.
Mooney, J. (2019) *The Theoretical Foundations of Criminology: Place, Time and Context*, Abingdon: Routledge.

Pavlich, G. and Brannigan, A. (2007) 'The shift from crime to governance in the sociology of law', *Governance and Regulation in Social Life: Essays in Honour of WG Carson* (Eds. A. Brannigan and G. Pavlich), Abingdon: Routledge.

Payne, G., Dingwall, R., Payne, J. and Carter, M. (1981) *Sociology and Social Research*, London: Routledge.

Pearson, G. (1975) 'Misfit sociology and the politics of socialization', *Critical Criminology* (Eds. I. Taylor, P. Walton and J. Young), London: Routledge & Kegan Paul Books.

Pepinsky, H. (2013) 'Peacemaking criminology', *Critical Criminology* 21(3): 319–339.

Perry, B. (2003) 'Where do we go from here? Researching hate crime', *Internet Journal of Criminology* 3: 45–47.

Platt, T. (1975) 'Prospects for a radical criminology in the USA', *Critical Criminology* (Eds. I. Taylor, P. Walton and J. Young), London: Routledge & Kegan Paul Books.

Plummer, K. (2013a) 'Inspirations: The national deviancy conference', *Ken Plummer Blog*, 8 February, available from: https://kenplummer.com/2013/02/08/inspirations-the-national-deviancy-conference/ [accessed 11/2021].

Plummer, K. (2013b) 'Inspiration and in memoriam: Mary McIntosh', *Ken Plummer Blog*, 8 January, available from: https://kenplummer.com/2013/01/08/inspiration-and-in-memoriam-mary-mcintosh/ [accessed 11/2021].

Polletta, F. (2006) *It Was Like a Fever: Storytelling in Protest and Politics*, Chicago: University of Chicago Press.

Radzinowicz, L. (1999) *Adventures in Criminology*, Abingdon: Routledge.

Rochon, T.R. and Mazmanian, D.A. (1993) 'Social movements and the policy process', *The Annals of the American Academy of Political and Social Science* 528(1): 75–87.

Rock, P. (1988) 'The present state of criminology in Britain', *The British Journal of Criminology* 28(2): 58–69.

Rock, P. (2009) 'Writing an official history of the criminal justice system', *British Society of Criminology Newsletter* 63: 16, available from: www.britsoccrim.org/wp-content/uploads/2016/04/bscn-63-2009-Rock.pdf [accessed 11/2021].

Ross, J.I. (2011) 'Cutting the edge: Where have we been and where are we going?' *Cutting the Edge* (2nd Edition) (Eds. J.I. Ross), London: Transaction Publishers.

Ross, J.I. and Richards, S.C. (2003) *Convict Criminology*, Belmont, CA: Wadsworth/Thomson Learning.

Ruggiero, V. (2021) *Critical Criminology Today: Counter-Hegemonic Essays*, Abingdon: Routledge.

Scott, D. (2016) 'Prologue', *Emancipatory Politics and Praxis: An Anthology of Essays Written for the European Group for the Study of Deviance and Social Control, 2013–16* (Eds. D. Scott), London: EG Press.

Scraton, P. (2016) *Hillsborough: The Truth*, London: Mainstream Publishing.

Sim, J. (1987) 'Repressing the living dead: Penal policy and the Peterhead demonstration', *Critical Social Policy* 7: 68–72.

Smart, C. (1977) 'Criminological theory: Its ideology and implications concerning women', *British Journal of Sociology* 28(1): 89–100.

Smart, C. (1989) *Feminism and the Power of Law*, London: Routledge.

Smart, C. (1997) *Law, Crime and Sexuality: Essays in Feminism*, London: Sage.

Steele, P. (2013) 'Mary McIntosh: Sociologist, writer and pioneer in the feminist and gay movements', *The Independent*, 21 February, available from: www.independent.co.uk/news/obituaries/mary-mcintosh-sociologist-writer-and-pioneer-feminist-and-gay-movements-8505638.html [accessed 11/2021].

Stott, C., Hoggett, J. and Pearson, G. (2012) "Keeping the peace' social identity, procedural justice and the policing of football crowds', *The British Journal of Criminology* 52(2): 381–399.

Sumner, C. (1994) *The Sociology of Deviance: An Obituary*, Maidenhead: Open University Press.

Taylor, I. (1971a) 'Football mad: A speculative sociology of soccer hooliganism', *The Sociology of Sport: A Selection of Readings* (Eds. E. Dunning), London: Frank Cass, pp. 352–377.

Taylor, I. (1971b) 'Soccer consciousness and soccer hooliganism', *Images of Deviance* (Eds. S. Cohen, 1973), London: Penguin.

Taylor, I. (1976) 'Spectator violence around football: The rise and fall of the "working class weekend"', *Research Papers in Physical Education* 4: 4–9.

Taylor, I. (1981) *Law and Order: Arguments for Socialism*, London: Palgrave McMillan.

Taylor, I. (1982) 'On the sports violence question: Soccer hooliganism revisited', *Sport, Culture and Ideology* (Eds. J. Hargreaves), London: Routledge and Kegan Paul.

Taylor, I. (1984) 'Professional sport and the recession: The case of British soccer', *International Review for the Sociology of Sport* 19: 7–30.

Taylor, I. (1987) 'Putting the boot into a working class sport: British soccer after Bradford and Brussels', *Sociology of Sport Journal* 4: 171–191.

Taylor, I. (1989) 'Hillsborough, 15 April 1989: Some personal contemplations', *New Left Review* 177: 104–120.

Taylor, I. (1991) 'English football in the 1990s: Taking Hillsborough seriously?' *British Football and Social Change: Getting into Europe* (Eds. J. Williams and S. Wagg), Leicester: Leicester University Press.

Taylor, I., Walton, P. and Young, J. (1973) *The New Criminology: For a Social Theory of Deviance*, London: Routledge & Kegan Paul Books.

Taylor, I., Walton, P. and Young, J. (eds.) (1975) *Critical Criminology*, London: Routledge & Kegan Paul Books.

Taylor, L. (2004) 'The other side of the street', *Social Justice* 32(2): 82–88.

Taylor, L. (2013) 'Stan Cohen obituary', *The Guardian*, 23 January, available from: www.theguardian.com/education/2013/jan/23/stanley-cohen [accessed 11/2021].

Tierney, J. (2009) *Key Perspectives in Criminology*, Maidenhead: McGraw-Hill Education.

Van Swaaningen, R. (1997) *Critical Criminology: Visions from Europe*, London: Sage.

Wacquant, L. (2008) *Urban Outcasts: A Comparative Sociology of Advanced Marginality*, Bristol: Polity Press.

Walklate, S. (2000) 'Ian Taylor's crime in context: A critical criminology of market societies: Book review', *Sociological Research Online* 5(2), available from: www.socresonline.org.uk/5/2/taylor.html [accessed 11/2021].

Walklate, S. (2007) *Understanding Criminology: Current Theoretical Debates*, Maidenhead: McGraw-Hill Education.

Walklate, S. (2013) *Gender, Crime and Criminal Justice*, Abingdon: Routledge.

Walton, P. (1998) 'Big science: Dystopia and utopia – establishment and new criminology revisited', *The New Criminology Revisited* (Eds. P. Walton and J. Young), London: Palgrave Macmillan, pp. 1–13.

Walton, P. and Young, J. (Eds.) (1998) *The New Criminology Revisited*, London: Palgrave Macmillan.

Watts, R., Bessant, J. and Hil, R. (2008) *International Criminology: A Critical Introduction*, Abingdon: Routledge.

Winlow, S. and Atkinson, R. (eds.) (2012) *New Directions in Crime and Deviancy*, Abingdon: Routledge.

Williams, J., Dunning, E. and Murphy, P. (1992 [1984]) *Hooligans Abroad: The Control of English Fans in Continental Europe*, London: Routledge.
Willis, P. (1972) 'A motorbike subculture', 9th National Deviancy Conference, January.
Young, J. (1968) 'The role of the police as amplifiers of deviance, negotiators of reality and translators of phantasy', 1st National Deviancy Conference, November.
Young, J. (1971) *The Drugtakers: The Social Meaning of Drug Use*, London: Paladin Press.
Young, J. (1975) 'Working-class criminology', *Critical Criminology* (Eds. I. Taylor, P. Walton and J. Young), London: Routledge & Kegan Paul Books.
Young, J. (1981) 'Thinking seriously about crime: Some models of criminology', *Crime and Society: Readings in History and Theory* (Eds. M. Fitzgerald, G. McLennan and J. Pawson), London: Routledge & Kegan Paul.
Young, J. (1998) 'Breaking Windows: Situating the New Criminology', *The New Criminology Revisited* (Eds. P. Walton and J. Young), London: Palgrave Macmillan.
Young, J. (1999) *The Exclusive Society*, London: Sage.
Young, J. (2001) 'Ian Taylor: Sociologist pioneering radical approaches to the study of crime, sport and popular culture', *The Guardian*, 24 January, available from: www.theguardian.com/news/2001/jan/24/guardianobituaries2 [accessed 11/2021].
Young, J. (2007) *The Vertigo of Late Modernity*, London: Sage.
Young, J. (2011a) 'Critical criminology in the twenty-first century: Critique, irony and always the unfinished', *Critical Criminology: Issues, Debates and Challenges* (Eds. K. Carrington and R. Hogg), Abingdon: Routledge.
Young, J. (2011b) *The Criminological Imagination*, Cambridge: Polity Press.

3
SPORT, CORRUPTION AND WHITE-COLLAR 'CRIMINALITY'

Crimes of the Powerful (1)

Introduction

Two broad discourses to understand 'crimes of the powerful' exist in the academic press. The first focusses on 'wrongdoings' – as either 'criminal' or 'immoral' acts – of those in strong market and/or political positions who distort the landscape in which they work to leverage subjectively favourable positions for themselves in neoliberal and emerging economies whilst the second, which we address in Chapter 7, explores those in influential positions who create or fail to protect lay citizens from 'social harm' (see Canning and Tombs, 2021; Carson, 1970a, 1970b, 1974, 1979, 1980a, 1980b, 1982, 1985a, 1985b; Hillyard et al., 2004; Tombs and Whyte, 2003; Whyte, 2009). In this chapter, we examine 'white-collar criminality' as 'crimes of the powerful' in the exploration of those acts carried out by organising bodies in the governance of sports, most notably the International Olympic Committee (IOC) and the *Fédération Internationale de Football Association* (FIFA).

Hagan (1998: 101) argues that white-collar crime 'is probably the most widely used criminological concept' since it was first introduced by Edwin Sutherland in his '*The White-Collar Criminal*' address to the *American Sociological Association* (1939). Sutherland (1949: 9) broadly saw the act as 'a crime committed by a person of respectability and high social status in the course of his occupation', thus encompassing a range of different actions. Sutherland (1940: 2) argued that white-collar crime 'can be found in every occupation, as can be discovered readily in casual conversation with a representative of an occupation by asking him [sic], 'What crooked practices are found in your occupation?' Sugden and Tomlinson (1999: 389) argue that those in positions of authority in sport often 'have much to show off, but even more to hide' but their 'crooked practices' – like in other spheres of society – are often difficult to uncover. The British investigative journalist Andrew Jennings' vignette exemplifies these challenges in speaking truth to power:

> I'm a criminal. Yes, I'm a convicted criminal. And this is my crime. A court in Lausanne, in Switzerland, ruled in 1994 that I had shown 'a deep contempt towards the International Olympic Committee [IOC], its president and its members, criticizing their personalities, their behaviour and their management. I was guilty of telling lies for profit'. I got a five-day suspended jail sentence from that court.
>
> I'm a criminal because I wrote a book that told the truth. A book that revealed Juan Antonio Samaranch was a loyal Franco fascist for 37 years – I've recently found a picture of him doing his favourite right-arm exercise. Here he is [displays photograph], fourth from the right. Doesn't he look smart? Here he is . . . in 1974.
>
> He was an IOC vice-president then. Six years later they made him President. And I revealed that IOC members took bribes. And they did. It's all true.
>
> But they're not the criminals. I am. And, what's more, the IOC banned me. I was banned from their press conferences, from covering their meetings, from doing my job as a reporter. And if you think they're beginning to sound a little heavy-handed, a little, shall we say, on the totalitarian side, then get this: they illegally got hold of my phone records, identified some of my contacts. And *then* they used *their* police contacts to try to dig dirt on my friends. This is true! Samaranch personally called a Spanish police chief to get some dirt on my friend and fellow journalist Jaume Riexach. At least, that's what Samaranch *tried* to do. Instead he got a little muddled and by mistake called Jaume's number and started talking to Jaume as if he were the chief of police. Jaume had to tell him, Look, Mr President, you've made a mistake . . . I know it sounds like something the Marx Brothers dreamed up, but it's not. This is the real world of sport. These people have real power and the money to do as they want, and here's how they're using it.
>
> Samaranch and his IOC were not the only ones. Now, it's happening with FIFA. I published a truth about FIFA. I said that President Sepp Blatter pays himself a secret bonus. They banned me. I carried on publishing. Their agents stole my phone records. They identified people they thought might be my contacts and tried to intimidate them. I carried on. They used FIFA funds to attack me with their lawyers. And on, and on. And don't forget, these people are supposed to be running *sports* events. That's their *job*, isn't it?
>
> *Jennings (2011: 388–389)*

Andrew Jennings passed away on 8 January 2022. This chapter would not be possible without his work on the IOC and FIFA but such is challenge of exposing white-collar criminality, he was not hugely well known. In this chapter, we use his work, and other critical scholars to probe the underlying politics of the issues alluded to in the previous quote, most notably analysing them – and in turn extending – the theories offered by Edwin Sutherland on white-collar crime and differential association. To begin this discussion, we outline white-collar crime as a critical criminology.

White-Collar Crime as a Critical Criminology

There are clear definitional issues when discussing white-collar crime and – situated in the various matrices of power in society – difficult questions to answer when asking 'whose side are we are?' in our analysis of it (Becker, 1967). Indeed, in the context of sport there are also philosophical questions to ask about whether 'rule-breaking' constitutes the deviant act, or as Slapper and Tombs (1999) query, whether such acts must be criminalised through national or international legal systems to be thought of as falling within the gaze of 'criminology'? Given Slapper and Tombs' (1999) question, notwithstanding that most legal systems are nationally defined, 'white-collar crime' does not exist as a single action in most systems. Rather, 'white-collar crime' might be a series of other actions, such as bribery, insider trading, embezzlement, money laundering, identity theft and copyright infringement/forgery (see Croall, 2001: 5). For this reason, precise definitions of 'white-collar crime' are difficult to conceptualise: Gerber and Jensen (2007: xi) state that there 'are almost as many definitions of the term white-collar crime, as there are researchers that have addressed the topic' arguing that it becomes a 'residual category' in which 'much of what does not fit into "traditional criminology" is subsumed under this category' (Gerber and Jensen, 2007: xii).

Edwin Sutherland (1939) was not the first social scientist to discuss the crimes carried out by the 'powerful'. Rather, Edward A. Ross (1909) – described by Rafter (2009) as an early pioneer of 'criminology' – discussed the 'criminaloid' concept, describing businessmen who carried out harmful activities under a public mask of respectability, 30 years earlier. Indeed, Braithwaite (1985) points out that Sutherland was influenced by Willem Bonger's *Criminality and Economic Conditions* (1916) which argued that capitalism had developed a society composed of egoistic individuals and called for an understanding of 'criminality' that took into account both 'crime on the streets' and 'crime in the suites'. But Sutherland was important in a breakaway from established criminological positions which uncritically blamed factors such as poverty, broken homes and stigmatised personalities for creating 'crime'. Criminal acts were, in fact, also committed by those from wealthy and powerful positions, secure home lives and of 'sound' minds. Lawbreakers might be positioned in middle-class professions, socially located away from the poor who are more likely to get caught and thus, 'criminalised'. Ten years after he introduced the concept of 'white-collar crime' to the academic field, Sutherland published *White-Collar Crime* (1949). Although a fear of libel action meant that his publisher screened out many of the details in his research until 1983, this monograph documented the crimes carried out by 70 of the largest private investment companies and 15 public utility corporations in the United States. Sutherland's main call (1939, 1949, 1983) was for researchers to question existing power relationships by expanding their focus to include the analysis of criminal and unethical behaviours by upper class, or 'respectable', offenders. In doing so, he principally drew upon a theory of 'differential association' (Sutherland, 1974), which forcibly departed from the pathological and biologically deterministic perspectives, instead of generating answers through social explanations. By pushing forward the theory of differential association, Sutherland (1974) makes nine key points. First, criminal behaviour – like other forms of behaviour – is learned. Second, this process of learning is social and accrued through processes of communication and interaction with others. Third, personal communication is the most important form of interaction in this learning process. As such, behaviours tend to be learned through groups rather than through the media. Fourth, this learning process may be complicated but usually include processes of developing the techniques to commit the crime (which may range in complexity) and also a socialisation of the specific directions of motives and attitudes. In other words, learned understandings of how and why actors commit crimes are necessary. Fifth, the specific direction of such motives and desires is learned through the group's cultural definitions of specific legal codes (or elements of them) as favourable or unfavourable. Sixth, individuals may engage in criminal behaviour through repeated exposure and thus individual internalisation of definitions that are favourable to violations of law. However, seventh, differential association may vary in its intensity, frequency and duration and sit relative to the social bonds within the group, or in other words, the value and contact with those in positions of subcultural influence. Eighth, the learning of criminal behaviours is conditioned through (anticipated) rewards, set against (anticipated) punishments. Finally, ninth, criminality may arise from expressions of general needs and values but they do not determine such behaviours as non-criminal actions may also be expressions of identical needs.

That Sutherland sought to analyse those crimes that were committed by 'respectable' offenders has been widely applauded and facilitated further discussion to develop in this area (Braithwaite, 1985; Friedrichs et al., 2017; Haines, 2020; Simpson, 2019; Whyte, 2007). As discussed in Chapter 2, Taylor et al. (1973, 1975) deepened this position with their first steps into 'critical criminology' (Downes and Rock, 2011: 243). Further, Lilly et al. (2018: 261) point out that within

> a few short years [of Taylor et al.'s *The New Criminology*], a spate of books appeared carrying titles such as *Crimes of the Powerful* (Pearce, 1976), '*Illegal But Not Criminal*': *Business Crime in America* (Conklin, 1977), *Corporate Crime* (Clinard and Yeager, 1980), *Corporate Crime in the Pharmaceutical Industry* (Braithwaite, 1984), *Wayward Capitalists* (Shapiro, 1984), and *The Criminal Elite* (Coleman, 1985).

The study of white-collar crime was proliferating although this also produced ambiguities in the definition of 'white-collar crime'. Indeed in 1996, *The National White-Collar Crime Center: Training and Research Institute* held a workshop titled 'Definitional Dilemma: Can and Should There Be a Universal Definition of White-Collar Crime?' in West Virginia and advanced the following definition:

> Illegal or unethical acts that violate fiduciary responsibility or public trust, committed by an individual or organization, usually during the course of legitimate occupational activity, by persons of high or respectable social status for personal or organizational gain.
>
> Helmkamp et al. (1996: 351)

This definition appears uncontroversial but the extent to which it adds precision is questionable: previously Shapiro (1984) had asked if it should characterise actions or actors, types of offense or types of offenders or a social location of a 'deviant' (or deviant behaviour) and Croall (2001: 6–7) asked similar questions two decades after Shapiro and 5 years later than *The National White-Collar Crime Center: Training and Research Institute*'s workshop. Measuring its prevalence is equally challenging as Croall (2001) points out that such acts are largely 'undetected and underreported, few [white-collar "criminals"] are prosecuted and victim surveys are necessarily limited. Even where victims are aware of some harm, it may be too trivial to consider reporting' (ibid: 22).

Blackshaw and Crabbe (2004: 29–31) engage ideas about white-collar crime and sport, largely borrowing from Sutherland's ideas but within a Marxian framework. We extend Blackshaw and Crabbe (2004: 30), who draw a distinction between owners/managers and participants/spectators in our analysis, by offering that there are three broad areas which white-collar 'criminality' might operate in the context of sport. First, there are those white-collar criminal actions, defined by set of nationally or internationally prescribed judicial laws which are 'illegal'. Such actions may include an elite manager or club owner's tax evasion or money laundering, for example, in March 2020, HM Revenue & Customs (HMRC) was investigating the tax affairs of 330 footballers, 55 clubs and 80 agents and confirmed it had recovered £396m from the industry since 2015 (Homer, 2020). This is 'white-collar crime'.[1] Second, each sport has its own set of rules, as defined by its governing body. Breaking rules may not be illegal in the eyes of judicial processes but are prohibited by governing bodies. Such actions may include, for instance, an organisation that might have majority shareholdings in two teams that could play each other, potentially distorting conventional views of 'fair play' and thereby breaking Union of European Football Associations (hereon UEFA's) 'Integrity of the UEFA Club Competition: Independence of the Clubs' rule that was brought into action in 1998 (see Breuer, 2019). This is 'white-collar rule-breaking' – actions that are 'against the rules' but not 'against the law'. Third, sports are imbued with their own sets of cultural values and politics or, expressed in another way; its various stakeholders make decisions about what is 'morally' or 'ethically' right (McNamee and Parry, 2002). Simon

(2006) advanced the term 'elite deviance' to include 'unethical acts' intentionally committed by those in white-collar positions, and this is applicable to sport. For example, in some sports, there has been resistance from supporter groups about the application of practices from the wider world of business (such as leveraged buy-outs) that are deemed 'acceptable' in sports in other cultures across the world (see, for instance, Millward, 2011, 2013). Borrowing from Simon (2006), these acts are 'white-collar deviant'. The next section will advance this chapter by looking at the emergence of a group of influential sports administrators who worked in tandem with Adidas entrepreneur, Horst Dassler.

Horst Dassler and 'The Club'

Brooks et al. (2013: 5–6) point out that 'white-collar criminality' and 'corruption' describe a wide range of actions in sport, including bribery, collusion, conflicts of interest, embezzlement, extortion, cronyism, fraud, lobbying and money laundering. Notwithstanding detection issues, the legality of these actions is changeable across temporal and spatial locations. The Olympic Games have provided the site in which large numbers of articles exploring 'white-collar crime' and 'corruption' have been published. Research on this theme has ranged from vote-rigging in the decision-making processes (Philippou, 2021) to athletes illegitimately stealing competitive advantage in performance (Hanstad et al., 2008). Andrew Jennings' work (2009, 2012, 2014, 2016; Jennings and Simson, 1992; Simson and Jennings, 1992) on various elements of white-collar crime, corruption and, in particular, bribery, gift giving and outcome fixing in relation to the IOC and FIFA has been instructive to our analysis. As a starting point to this, Jennings identifies an association of decision-makers and influential sponsors that he refers to as 'the Club'. Sutherland (1940: 3) described white-collar criminality as 'what Al Capone called "the legitimate rackets"'. This reference offers little precision to a definition of white-collar criminality but chimes with the bonds and associations of influential actors involved in the governance of a number of sports competitions, specifically including the IOC and FIFA, from the second half of the twentieth century onwards (Simson and Jennings, 1992).

The root of 'the Club' lies with the Dassler brothers, Adi and Rudolf Dassler who were cobblers based in the German town of Herzogenaurach. In the 1920s, they formed a small shoe company, Gebrüder Dassler. Adi Dassler produced football and running shoes that were simultaneously lighter and sturdier than their competitors and older brother Rudolf chiefly marketed the products. At the time, Smit (2007, 2008) states Adolf Hitler was in the political ascendancy, becoming leader of the *Nationalsozialistische Deutsche Arbeiterpartei* in 1921. Once he was democratically elected as chancellor in 1933, Hitler aided the growth Dassler brothers' business (Smit, 2007). By the 1936 Berlin Olympics, German athletes were wearing the Dasslers' sports shoes. Smit (2007, 2008) states that these Games shaped Adi Dassler's theory that recruiting athletes who generated excitement helped build a 'brand'. The Dassler's befriended coaches to encourage their players to wear the company's complementary sportswear rather than paying for endorsements. In the post-War years, Adi and Rudolf's relationship soured and the Gebrüder Dassler enterprise fell apart. In the aftermath, Rudolf set up Puma and Adi also developed a new name for his shoes, Adidas.

Horst Dassler was Adi's son. In his early adulthood, Horst moved to Alsace to set up a French division of Adidas, designed to specifically account for that national market (Bose, 2012). Smit (2007) suggests that Horst Dassler shadowed other companies to hide some product lines from his father. However, he learned from his father that befriending influential sports officials, including those in charge of the Olympics, could yield commercial results (Smit, 2007, 2008). He knew that athletes' endorsements of his products were important in capturing the markets of ordinary citizens in the wealthy countries of North America and Western Europe. In a successful attempt to forge these connections, Horst Dassler created 'the Club', which was made up of aspiring sports bureaucrats that displayed skills from the business and legal worlds and facilitated their movement into key roles in organisations by offering financial support and political favours (Simson and Jennings, 1992). Dassler would keep this association together through enticing 'promising' members into the group, rewarding them for actions that benefitted Adidas and also making them fearful of reporting their 'dirt' of deviant recriminations to the wider world. Thus, the Club was built based on reward and fear (Jennings, 2011).

Patrick Nally helped Dassler establish the Club. Yallop (2011: 138) describes Nally as 'a public relations and marketing man' who, 'in the late 1960s teamed upon with sports commentator Peter West'. Yallop (2011: 138) informs us that Nally and West 'formed a company with the principal aim of exploiting sport commercially' through pioneering in corporate event sponsorship. With specific reference to FIFA, Doidge (2014) argues that the transformation of practices towards explicit commercialism that members of the Club and – its successor – ISL ushered in reflect global neo-processes that were deepening in the wider society from the 1970s. He further suggests that such global institutions lack accountability to any singular national or supranational authority, and this means that personal contacts can be exploited offering increased potential for corrupt and nepotistic practices to grow. However, when the Club first began to grasp control over elite sport is less clear: IOC and, according to Simson and Jennings (1992), Club member, Dick Pound suggests that Dassler's involvement only came with the IOC Commission for New Sources of Finance in 1982 but the clear suggestion from Jennings is that, behind the scenes, the sportswear entrepreneur's influence was felt before then. Obtaining sports sponsorship is not usually illegal, and such actions normally comply with the IOC and FIFA's 'normal' rules although it shifted the events from the domain of 'sporting' to 'sporting' and commercial'. This practice is now normalised but in the 1960s Avery Brundage and Lord Exeter, then the presidents of the IOC and the International Amateur Athletics Federation President, thought it to be morally 'wrong': it was 'white-collar deviancy'.

Jennings (2009: 391) called the Club a 'front' for Dassler's interests and pointed out that immediately before the 1992 summer Olympic Games, 'the Club's' core members met to celebrate Dassler's life after he had passed away 5 years earlier (see also Simson and Jennings, 1992). Those people in attendance at the remembrance meeting included IOC President Juan Antonio Samaranch, FIFA President and IOC Committee member João Havelange, President of the IAAF Primo Nebiolo, ANOC's (Association of National Olympic Committees) President Mario Vazquez Rana, the World Taekwondo Federation's President Dr. Un Yong Kim, President of WADA (World Anti-Doping Agency) Dick Pound and Robert H. Helmick (President of the United States Olympic Committee between 1985 and 1991 but had resigned because of media reports that alleged that he had been a paid consultant to the organisations that were doing business with the committee and other sporting bodies). Simson and Jennings (1992) point out that other members of the Club included Russia's Vitaly Smirnov and Marat Gramov; Romania's Alexandru Siperco; Czechoslovakia's Vladimir Cernusak; Mongolian Shagdarjav Magvan; Poland's Wolzimierz Reczek; Bulgaria's Ivan Slavkov and Gunther Heinze from the former East Germany. Effectively, the Club was made up of those in influential positions at the IOC, FIFA, International Sport Federations and National Olympic Committees. Some, like Nally, initially thought that their actions were 'good for sport' but by the 1980s his position was changing:

> I was getting to the point where I was finding it difficult to know which side I was on. Was I on the side of the corporate sponsors who were shovelling out their money to improve their image? Was I on the side of the international federations who were spending all of that money? Or was I on the side of Horst Dassler who was exploiting it all for Adidas' benefit?
> *Patrick Nally (quoted in Simson and Jennings, 1992: 23)*

Patrick Nally left the Club in because of this dilemma in 1982 (Simson and Jennings, 1992: 101). Dassler led the remaining members of the Club in forming the Swiss-based International Sports and Leisure Marketing (ISL) that became responsible for marketing and publicity arrangements of the men's World Cup (World Cup) throughout the 1980s and 1990s. ISL collapsed in 2001 with debts of £153m but 7 years later, following a prolonged investigation by Swiss prosecutors, six former ISL executives were accused of a series of charges including fraud, embezzlement and the falsification of documents (Bond, 2008). Jennings (2008) points out that Jean-Marie Weber – whose job description at ISL was 'cultivating relationships' – was amongst the six. In essence, members of Dassler's 'Club' worked together to protect the mutual interests of actors in the network and yield their collective influence across the world, for instance, by 'supporting' each other and wielding influence behind the scenes in governing body elections.

Juan Antonio Samaranch and the International Olympic Committee

Juan Antonio Samaranch and his actions as IOC president are central to Jennings' analysis of governance at the sporting body. Samaranch was unbroken in his 21 years of service in the presidential role (1980–2001), making him the second longest serving president of the IOC. Additionally, he had been an IOC member since 1966. Just before he left presidential office, his son, Juan Antonio Junior, was admitted to the IOC. After Samaranch stepped down from office, he took an Honorary President for Life title from the International Olympic Committee until he passed away in 2010. Miller (1992) records that Samaranch was conscripted into the Republican armed forces during the Spanish Civil War (in 1938) but escaped by fleeing to France. He returned one later and studied at the IESE Business School in Barcelona, before engaging in a short-lived career in sports journalism and then serving on the municipal government of Barcelona, with responsibility for sports (1955–1962). From 1967 to 1971, this role grew into serving as a national delegate as minister for sports and then was president of the governing council for the Province of Barcelona (1973–1977). Miller (1992) notes that in the years immediately before he assumed IOC Presidency, Samaranch was appointed as Spanish ambassador to the Soviet Union and Mongolia (in 1977), combining this role with IOC vice-presidency (1974–1978). Jennings adds to this by suggesting that Samaranch copied an authoritarian leadership style from Franco; for instance, by trying to control the facilities and resources competitors might have access to in elections, as well as attempting to control the press and ideological apparatus to suit his arguments (Simson and Jennings, 1992: 72–73; Jennings, 2012). During Samaranch's time as IOC President, he oversaw six summer Olympic Games and five winter Olympics. He was also President during the voting for the hosting of six summer and six winter Olympic Games closing all of them, bar those held in Atlanta, Georgia in 1996, with the declaration that they had been 'the best ever' (Jennings, 2000). The first three summer Olympic Games Samaranch oversaw experienced boycotts (in 1980, 1984 and 1988), largely reflecting the ongoing Cold War of the period. The American-led boycott of the 1980 Moscow summer Games was not good for the public perception and popularity of the Olympic movement. However, Samaranch convinced his fellow-IOC members in his pre-election pledge that he would lead the movement away from this controversy. To deliver this promise, he utilised help from Dassler.

Christian Janette played a crucial role in connecting Samaranch and Dassler. Janette and Samaranch were associates after they had worked together in the organisation of 1972 summer Olympic Games in Munich. Shortly afterwards, Janette was recruited by Horst Dassler in recognition of his work in the delivery of this mega-event. In an interview with Jennings, Janette stated:

> In 1974 Samaranch knew that I was working with Horst Dassler and he told me that he would be interested to meet him and he invited us to Barcelona. At that time, he was Governor of Catalonia and we spent two or three days there and then it started. I knew then Samaranch would like to be President. Horst liked him and later they became good friends.
> *(Simson and Jennings, 1992: 76; Jennings, 2012)*

Dassler held influence in athletics across the world through his 'political team' which included John Boulter (in Europe), Professor Anwar Chowdhry (in Asia), Bobby Naidoo (in English-speaking African countries) and Colonel Hassine Mamouda (in French-speaking African countries), whilst Dassler and João Havelange held strong influence in Central and South America (Simson and Jennings, 1992: 32). Christian Janette helped to manipulate sporting power in USSR, which was targeted by Adidas because its athletes were amongst the global Olympic elite (Simson and Jennings, 1992: 34). In each of these areas of the world, Dassler would assist the federations in the ways that would most easily sway favour – perhaps through money or through sports equipment – and, according to Janette, Dassler 'would get the credit from the federation and that would put him in a very strong position' (quoted in Simson and Jennings, 1992: 35). Whether Dassler was guilty of 'bribes' or just provided 'gifts' to federations that were developing their sporting infrastructures is debatable.

The Eastern Bloc associations were targeted as potential presidential election winners for Samaranch after João Havelange had helped him gather support in Latin America, Africa and Asia. There were two ways in which Samaranch targeted votes from The Soviet Union. First, whilst campaigning, he served as Spanish ambassador to the Soviet Union and Mongolia (overlapping his role of IOC vice-president by 1 year). Gulko et al. (2010: 48) suggest that whilst he was in this role, the KGB had recruited Samaranch as a secret agent and, in return, they had promised him 'the presidency of the International Olympic Committee – through the votes of the USSR and the other socialist countries'. Second, Simson and Jennings (1992) argue that Dassler established trade links to East Europe and knew the officials who were organising the 1980 summer Olympics in Moscow. With the skills backing that Dassler, the Club and Adidas could offer, Samaranch had strong support in helping the Russians master sponsorship arrangements and organisational issues. This placed him in a favourable position. Yet, there was to be one final turn of events as in December 1979, the Russian Red Army moved into Afghanistan. The American response was to order boycott of the 1980 Moscow summer Olympic Games, and the post-Franco Spanish government wanted its Olympic Association to follow. Resultantly, Samaranch 'called in . . . every old favour' from the Spanish Olympic committee and the country competed in Moscow (Simson and Jennings, 1992: 83). With the Soviet Union's support guaranteed, Samaranch won his presidency election beating – amongst others – the Swiss Marc Hodler, to the role. From there on, Christian Janette reflected that Samaranch 'never did anything without advice from Horst Dassler, probably because he wanted to run the IOC as Horst Dassler ran Adidas' (Jennings, 2012: 468). Havelange's role is political role in the Club intriguing. When Havelange displaced Sir Stanley Rous as FIFA president in 1974 (see Sugden and Tomlinson, 1998a, 1998b, 1999, 2003, 2017; Tomlinson, 2014), he promised to expand the World Cup finals from 16 to 24 teams. However, Simson and Jennings (1992: 82) point out that Spain had taken the 1982 competition on the basis that it would be composed of 16 teams which would not fulfil Havelange's election promise. In Spain, there were doubts it could financially afford to deliver the infrastructure for another eight national football teams and their fans. Dassler provided extra finance for the event – in return for further influence over FIFA – and Samaranch played a political role by working with the Spanish organising committee. This resource was raised through Patrick Nally sourcing corporate sponsorship. Havelange's debt was that he would help to gather support for Samaranch's IOC presidential election campaign.

Miller's (1992) narrative of Samaranch's life shows his IOC presidential period to be a success by every measure. Although the 1984 summer Olympic Game, held in Los Angeles, were boycotted by Soviet bloc countries, Miller points out that the number of IOC participating member nations grew during every tournament under his stewardship. Miller (1992) documents that Samaranch was awarded the city's first Peace Prize to document his work after the 1988 Seoul summer Olympic Games. In the biography, Miller (1992) particularly focusses on a story that during Samaranch's presidency, the IOC was rescued from the financial crisis of the 1970s, drawing upon new sponsorship and television broadcasting deals that generated increasing levels of revenue. Jennings (2012) points out that many of these deals were facilitated through Dassler and 'the Club'. Indeed, Jennings (2012) reports that Dassler authored an article in the 1980 edition of the IOC's journal which stated that the organisation should reform to become an institution 'composed of representatives of sport and industry'. Effectively, he openly called for the commodification of the Olympics, re-orientating its values towards business in many of the similar ways that he had made Adidas a global brand.

The commodification of the Olympics added informal levels of soft governance to the organisation – sponsors and television markets – potentially changing the dynamics of its competitions. Indeed, Boykoff (2016: 117) suggests that: 'Today the Olympic Games are an enormous sports, media and marketing juggernaut, a top-tier athletic festival awash in corporate cash'. Hill (1996) suggests that Pierre de Coubertin, the founder of the IOC, established an Olympic spirit that was removed from external pressures, such as those developed through commercialism. This spirit was based upon competition over triumph and each athlete bidding to be best that s/he can be. Alternative readings of the Olympic movement might suggest that this spirit had partly ebbed away long before Samaranch became IOC president but the competition being shaped by sponsors and television markets marks a form of white-collar deviancy but not rule-breaking or criminality. Still, despite this, the idea of the ongoing Olympic spirit, alluding to sport that is free of commercialisation, continues to be rolled out immediately prior to all events (see *BBC*, 2012 for an example of this). Against this backdrop, however, Boykoff's (2016) political and historical account of the Olympics shows the Games have become increasingly commercialised since the 1970s and have come to characterise what he calls 'celebration capitalism', as defined by public-private commercial partnerships that are masqueraded under the banner of 'festivity' and 'celebration'.

The Games' commercialism can be viewed in two different ways. First, it may add a veneer of public accountability as corruption and cheating cannot be seen to take place in the Olympic Games; a failure to uphold this can create pressures to 'reform' the organisation, as happened in the aftermath of the Salt Lake City scandal. However, second, the impact on sponsors and television markets on the practices of the Olympic Games can be more pernicious. To elaborate, brands want to be associated with champions that are – in de Coubertin's Olympic spirit – 'Citius, Altius, Fortius' (or 'Faster, Higher, Stronger') and television audiences want to see events that demonstrate such aptitudes. Pressure to break Olympic records – to be faster, higher or stronger than earlier champions – is intense and felt by athletes, but it is the IOC who ultimately must deliver this to the public. As such, Yallop (2011) suggests a culture of 'not looking too hard' for performance-enhancing drugs may have developed. In either case, Jennings (2012) argues that Dassler had long recognised the latent marketability of the Olympic Games. However, he decided that, in an era where Nally was exploiting television broadcasts across the world, if ISL could act on behalf of the IOC, he could sell the sponsorship rights to a number of global brands – such as Coca-Cola, Visa, Kodak and Panasonic – across the world, significantly more revenue would be generated for the organisation and, in turn, his own agency. ISL's right to act on behalf of the IOC had come through behind-the-scenes agreements between the IOC (explicitly including those that belonged to the Club) and ISL rather than not coming from a transparent and competitive tender process. In many cases, the 'brokerage' involved the same individual representing both sides of the agreement. Samaranch (on behalf of the IOC) and Dassler (on behalf of ISL) signed The Olympic Partners (TOP) contract in May 1985. This agreement gave ISL a 20 per cent share of sales of 'the Olympic rings' to sponsors and broadcasters. The legality of these actions is complex but may be regarded as a form of 'white-collar deviancy'. However, the IOC increased its profitability, and subsequently details of the agreement were not reported to the public. The IOC's share of the new funds was utilised to pay athletes and other delegates' expenses, covering these costs for the first time. This act of wealth and generosity possibly further encouraged a culture of 'gift giving' that grew in the organisation and rose to the public's attention with the Salt Lake City games scandal.

The scandal around the Salt Lake City (Utah) winter Olympic Games formed a watershed moment in sensitising the public to some of the white-collar 'criminality', 'rule-breaking' and 'deviance' issues that had allegedly been carried out in various forms in the preceding years (Simson and Jennings, 1992; Jennings, 2000, 2011). The Salt Lake City Olympic Committee (SLCOC) had unsuccessfully bid to host winter Olympic Games for almost 30 years before, on 16 June 1995, it was announced to be the host city for the 2002 event. Rios et al. (2013: 4) suggest that SLCOC officials – including Tom Welch and David Johnson – who were playing leading roles in bidding for the event had changed lobbying tactics after noticing other potential host cities giving gifts in their campaigning. So, in 1989, they provided their first nominal 'gifts' to IOC members in the form of letter openers. Two years later, they began aggressively campaigning for the right to host the 2002 winter Olympic Games, and a decision was made to do 'whatever it took to win the bid'; this included using money to win votes (Rios et al., 2013: 4).

The legal position of taking gifts is unclear and temporally changeable. However, under IOC rules at that point, members were prohibited from accepting gifts worth more than $150 (USD). Valuing the level of gifts is difficult when the giver and the receiver have a vested interest in not disclosing the full details of any personal transaction. However, many took SLCOC gifts that were reasonably judged to be above this level in the form of cash, college places, the hire of paid sex workers and items as diverse as hip replacement operations, cosmetic surgery and musical instruments (Jennings, 2011: 392). Boykoff (2016: 151) also provides us with a glimpse into the nature of the gifts, writing that the 'committee also ran a full-blown scholarship program for IOC family members', whilst IOC voters making site visits in Utah were gifted 'free shotguns, skis, clothing, video games, hunting trips, shopping sprees, tickets to NBA basketball games, and even a $525 violin' (p. 152). Indeed, from 1991 to 1995, the SLCOC unofficially spent $1.2m [USD] on IOC members and their families (Jennings, 2000). Rios et al. (2013: 4) point out that the SLOC's payment for scholarships was uncovered in 1995 in Ernst and Young's audit of their records. The scandal became public 3 years later when a report emerged that showed a letter indicating the SLOC was paying an IOC member's child's school tuition fees. Swiss IOC member, Marc Hodler – who had recently served as the group's vice-president and was then heading a coordination committee overseeing the Salt Lake City games – alleged that a network of IOC members had taken bribes throughout the bidding process for the 1996 summer Olympic Games that were held in Atlanta (Georgia). Once this story became public, the SLCOC was under investigation along with the IOC and Tom Welch resigned from his position. The IOC, the USOC, the SLOC and – tellingly – the United States Department of Justice held 'independent investigations', with the IOC panel chaired by Dick Pound who had been a long-time associate of Samaranch.

The United States Department of Justice charged Johnson and Welch with Racketeer Influenced and Corrupt Organizations Act violations. Bribery cases against them went to trial in October 2003 but they were acquitted of 15 felony counts because of lack of evidence. Rios et al. (2013: 4) point out that amongst the SLCOC defence was the argument that its actions were merely replicating what other host cities had previously carried out – effectively, that the practice of bidding to host such events had normalised a culture of bribery and gift giving. A major impact of the allegations was that the discourse of corruption in the IOC became widely reported in the press. As a result, some corporate sponsors threatened to withdraw their sponsorships from the 2000 Sydney Summer Olympics (Jennings, 2000) and so the IOC Executive Board announced plans to overhaul the way cities bid to host games; these suggestions were firmed up by the reform sub-committee IOC 2000 Commission. Headlining these changes was the expulsion/forced resignation of six IOC members with ongoing investigations continuing into other others for taking bribes, gifts and scholarships from the organisers of the 2002 Salt Lake City Winter Olympic Games. The six members of the IOC were immediately voted to be expelled: Agustin Arroyo (Ecuador), Zein El Abdin Ahmed Abdel

Gadir (Sudan), Jean-Claude Ganga (Congo Republic), Lamine Keita (Mali), Sergio Santander (Chile) and Paul Wallwork (Samoa) (Siddons, 1999). Amongst those that were under investigation in January 1999 were 'Club' members Dr. Un Yong Kim and Vitaly Smirnov, along with Ivory Coast's Louis Guirandou-N'Diaye. Dutch IOC member Anton Geesink was also given a warning over his actions and George Mukora, chairman of the Kenya Olympics Association, first vice chairman of the Commonwealth Games and IOC member since 1990 later resigned. USOC official Alfredo La Mont, and further IOC members, Pirjo Häggmann and Bashir Mohamed Attarabulsi (Libya) resigned during the same period (Mallon, 2000).

Mackay (1999) reported an overhaul of the bidding process to award cities the Olympic Games that emerged in January 1999. This reform meant that most IOC members lost the right to vote in such elections with the duty being concentrated on 'an independent committee' made up of eight IOC members, athletes, and a representative of the Winter Sports Federation and the National Olympic Committee. The reform arguably served to strengthen the grip of the most senior IOC members on the organisation rather than deeply changing many of its practices. At the later event, the newly formed IOC 2000 Commission announced further changes which included banning all expense-paid visits to the cities bidding for the Olympic Games; lowering the age limits for new and future members of the IOC by 10 years to 70 years old and, the implementation of a new screening procedure for that board, where proposed candidates would be judged by seven IOC members (including at least one athlete). Above all else, Jennings (2011: 393) points out that Samaranch dealt with the public pressure to change how the IOC was run by setting up an ongoing 'reform commission' which headed. Havelange, former U.S. Secretary of State Henry Kissinger, and global public relations company, Hill & Knowlton, were called upon to assist in this group. On this, Jennings (2011: 392) said:

> President Samaranch's reform programme was organized by Hill & Knowlton and one of its figureheads was Henry Kissinger. These are not the kind of people you employ to help launch a new brand of mascara. Hill & Knowlton are *the* spin-doctors of choice for global capitalism in trouble. When big tobacco wanted us to believe that smoking wasn't a health issue, Hill & Knowlton did the spinning. They've spun for McDonalds, Coca Cola, Adidas. And now Hill & Knowlton were master-minding Samaranch's reform programme. Let's reflect on that for a moment. Feeling comfortable? And Henry Kissinger was there too. Henry Kissinger hasn't changed since he made his name carpet-bombing Cambodia, making the world safe for American capital. He hasn't retired. He's gone freelance! His international consulting firm, Kissinger Associates, has advised, among others, Coca Cola, American Express, Freeport-McMoRan Minerals and J.P. Morgan-Chase. Hill & Knowlton based one team in New York, another in Washington and a third in Lausanne to keep a grip on the IOC members and massage the media. 'Safe' reporters were selectively leaked 'good news' documents.

In their company sat former U.S. Democratic party Senator, George Mitchell who was on the board of the Olympic sponsor Xerox. The 'reform' of the IOC seemed to be ensconced with commercial interests and, particularly, those with internal connections to the organisation. A reform that promised the opportunity to 'clean up' the IOC arguably failed because the actions of those designing such changes are those who might be committing the actions that provoke the allegations (Jennings, 2000). Indeed, ahead of the 2020 Tokyo Summer Olympics, staged in 2021, reports of corruption and bribery allegations in this edition's bidding process emerged again (see Boykoff and Gaffney, 2020). The 'powerful' at the IOC, it seems, can therefore redesign the 'rules' to protect their own interests.

FIFA, Sponsorship and Cash for Votes Allegations

Jűrgen Lenz was trained by Horst Dassler (Tomlinson and Young, 2006) and later headed up TEAM, the organisation responsible for marketing the UEFA Champions League (see King, 2017 [2003]). However, for several years, he worked for ISL, acting on behalf of FIFA (and the IOC) on issues related to marketing, media and sponsorship. When interviewed by sociologist Alan Tomlinson, he frankly reflected that 'FIFA's now so corrupt that it no longer knows that it is being corrupt' (Jűrgen Lenz, interview with Tomlinson, 2009; quoted in Tomlinson, 2014: 3; 172). Pielke (2013) points out that as a non-governmental organisation, the sole domestic government that has any immediate formal authority or control over its practices is Switzerland, where it is registered. Indeed, Jennings (2011) argues that despite FIFA being a multi-billion-pound business, it operates under Swiss charitable association rules – guaranteeing minimal disclosure about how it spends its money. As such, its 'transparency' in operations is difficult to judge. However, Pielke (2013) also argues that FIFA has found itself subject to legal proceedings in several jurisdictions over many years. This includes the 2002 presidential elections when 'the supreme leader' (Tomlinson, 2014: 71), President Joseph 'Sepp' Blatter was accused of litany of transgressions by the FIFA general secretary, Michel Zen-Ruffinen which specifically included claims of making improper payments using FIFA funds. Pielke (2013) stated that this led 11 members of FIFA's 24-member executive committee to file a complaint against Blatter in Swiss courts, although the prosecutors dropped the case for a lack of evidence in support of the claims. In many respects, allegations such as these have sensitised some segments of the international media to issues of governance and 'fair play' and, as such, 'corruption' has become a word associated with its institutional culture – even though if this lacks precision in its use (see Brooks et al., 2013). Indeed, from 2015 the Swiss and United States authorities investigated FIFA with Blatter ultimately deposed as president, but as will be discussed, doubts remain about the extent to which the world governing body of football is free of 'corruption'.

Jennings (2009: 9) places the main root of this institutional culture in 1974, when João Havelange defeated Sir Stanley Rous to become FIFA president. In doing so, Havelange became the first non-European to hold the post. He served the role until 1998, when he was succeeded by Sepp Blatter, receiving the title of Honorary President. Havelange resigned in April 2013 following the publication of FIFA's internal ethics committee report which detailed that he and former Brazilian FA president Ricardo Teixeira (who is his former son-in-law) had taken a series of bribes worth $100m (USD) over an 8-year period from the now defunct sports marketing agency ISL (Gibson, 2013). Sutherland (1974) argued that white-collar criminal actions are learned through processes of personal communication and interaction with others. Jennings (2014) points out that Havelange was close to both Dassler, and the new world of sport that he was modelling through the network of people in the Club, and Castor Andrade who, according to Misse (2007), was the uncontested leader of the main organised crime rackets Rio de Janeiro in the 1980s and 1990s, who had more than 100 policemen, public servants, prominent politicians and judges working for him.

Havelange had previously been an elite sports player, representing Brazil in the 1936 summer Olympic Games in the 400m freestyle and 1500m freestyle swimming heats before returning in 1952 summer Olympics to compete for his country as a water polo player. He then began his career in sports administration, first in the 1956 Olympic Games where he served as Brazil's Chef de Mission, then 2 years later he had 'taken control' (Jennings, 2009: 12) of the Brazilian Sports Confederation (which included football) before, as earlier noted, joining the IOC in 1963. Jennings (2009) and Sugden and Tomlinson (1998a, 2003) point out how different Havelange and Rous, the man he replaced, were in character. Havelange was gregarious and spoke four different languages, whilst Rous preferred the company of those close to him and spoke only English. Havelange and Rous also had very different professional backgrounds, the former employed in the private sector – running businesses as different as bus, chemical and insurance industries – whereas the latter was a Physical Education teacher and referee before beginning sports administration with the F.A. in 1934 and then replacing fellow Englishman Arthur Drewry as FIFA president in 1961.

Havelange was elected to the FIFA presidency after lobbying across the world; Rous had been loath to partake in a similar campaign tactics (Jennings, 2009: 10). Sugden and Tomlinson (2003: 50) point out that on a rare FIFA presidency duty trip to the Central and North American confederation in 1971, Rous 'called for the member associations to clean up their act'. These 'acts' included making sure that 'financial resources were effectively and correctly used', improving 'administration' – in part to – 'make committees properly representative and to take more care in nominating referees' (Sugden and Tomlinson, 2003: 50). They further suggest that visiting such confederations to deliver a 'strong schoolmasterly ticking-off . . . evoked stereotypes that were to be played upon with brilliance by Havelange' (Sugden and Tomlinson, 2003: 50). Rous, Havelange suggested, was a schoolteacher and neo-colonial Englishman with dated values and not the person to 'modernise' football. Havelange made seven key promises to change global football. First, as earlier discussed with reference to the relationship between him, Dassler and Samaranch, he pledged to increase the number of countries competing in the tournament from 16 to 24 from the 1982 World Cup in the process hinting that many of these places would go to teams in the 'developing' world. Second, he would work to improve youth competitions, making junior World Championships in which players would be aged 20 or younger. Third, promises were made to improve FIFA's administrative infrastructure, focussing on the desire to acquire new – larger and more modern – premises. Fourth, FIFA would move away from its focus on Europe to particularly support underdeveloped football nation, particularly, fifth, in assisting them to construct and improve their stadiums and, sixth, in offering provision of new technical and medical expertise to those associations. Seventh, Havelange also suggested that under him, FIFA would introduce new inter-continental club championships. Sugden and Tomlinson (2003) suggest that most of these proposals were aimed at improving opportunities for national associations on the margins of Rous' FIFA, appealing to the global regions where Havelange was chasing votes and lobbying in the presence of Pele and the Club's Patrick Nally.

Rous acknowledged that it seemed likely that Havelange's campaign was gaining support and asked Dassler for help. His response was to send support from his 'political team' in the form of Christian Janette and British former 800m runner, John Boulter. However, whilst Rous thought Janette and Boulter were acting in his interests, they were spying on him for Dassler who was supporting Havelange (Jennings, 2009: 14). Indeed, Jennings (2009: 16) reports that in the run-up to 1974 FIFA Presidential Election, Dassler 'distributed a wad of cash among officials who were holding out or who could bring in other votes to encourage them back to Havelange'. Ultimately, Havelange beat Rous by 16 votes in a second-round ballot, and FIFA had its first non-European president.

However, Havelange's FIFA did not have sufficient finances to resource the proposals he made, so sought financial support from Dassler (Simson and Jennings, 1992). This was not directly offered by Dassler who instead the services of Nally were enlisted to capture Adidas and Coca-Cola as primary event sponsors – and later 'partners' – of FIFA tournaments. Indeed, the two companies additionally underwrote the expenses of FIFA tournaments, with Coca-Cola guaranteeing the 1978 FIFA World Cup in Argentina (Yallop, 2011). Once the world-leading soft drinks brand associated itself with the sport, other sponsors competed to become additional 'FIFA partners' (Jennings, 2009: 20–21). Additionally, television rights agreements grew alongside sponsorship revenues, being attributable to a combination of, first, larger numbers of homes across the world began to own television sets and later there was an increase in the number of channels bidding for those rights as that market grew; and second, the marketing and negotiating capacity of Patrick Nally, working for ISL who had been 'commissioned' to act of FIFA's behalf with the European rights to the 1990, 1994 and 1998 World Cups. These rights sold for $440 (USD) million, and the global rights (excluding the United States) for the three tournaments from 1998 sold for $2.2 (USD) billion (*The Economist*, 1998). This rise in value may have been partially attributable to the expansion of the tournament from 16 to 24 (in 1982) to 32 (in 1998) teams, which boosted both the number of matches and the number of broadcast markets that had 'vested' interests in the World Cup finals. Havelange was replaced by his former Technical Director (1975–1981) and General Secretary (1981–1998), Sepp Blatter in 1998.

Like Havelange, Sepp Blatter also had strong personal connections to Horst Dassler. Prior to joining FIFA, Blatter had led public relations for a Swiss tourist board before moving on to become Director of Sports Timing and Public Relations at the pedigree watch-makers Longines, where Tomlinson (2014: 72) records that 'he was noticed by Adidas boss Horst Dassler'. Tomlinson also points out that Blatter had experience in sport business and administration experience, helping to organise the 1972 and 1976 summer Olympic Games. In August 1975, Blatter began 4 months training in sport business and marketing practices at Adidas' Landersheim headquarters, immediately joining FIFA as technical director afterwards. Despite working for FIFA, Tomlinson (2014: 72) notes that 'Dassler and Adidas paid Blatter's salary in those early days, and provided [his] office space', as such the two worked closely together. One of Blatter's first roles was to work with Nally and Havelange to capture corporate interest in FIFA to be able to fund the new president's programme of change. From the beginning, the FIFA that Blatter engaged with was in the process of commercialising. Tomlinson (2014) states that Blatter rose quickly through FIFA's hierarchy and became general secretary in 1981, a role he held until he became president. Whilst doing this, Blatter married the daughter of Helmut Käser, the previous incumbent of the general secretary role who had been in role since before Havelange took up post but was not one of his close associates. When Blatter became FIFA President in 1998, UEFA President Lennart Johansson stood against him in the election.[2] By then, Jennings (2009: 32–38) points out that Blatter and Havelange's relationship had weakened after the former had unsuccessfully challenged the latter for presidency in 1994. However, Jennings (2009: 70) also states that Havelange supported Blatter because whilst he might publicly 'call for transparency, there was no danger he'd actually open the shutters and let some light in. So Havelange's secrets might stay safe in a FIFA ruled by President Blatter'.

That the World Cup changed in form, format and the sums of money involved under the guidance of Havelange and Blatter is not surprising; many sports across the world 'commercialised' in the same time period but the issues for concern are how the increasing sums of money were spent and invested. *CNBC* (2018) state that the 2014 World Cup generated more than $4.5bn [USD] for FIFA through broadcasting rights, sponsors, hospitality and licensing sources. Of this, it suggests that FIFA paid out $400m [USD] between the 32 nations that compete in the finals of the tournament, with the Deutscher Fußball-Bund (The German F.A.) – as the tournament winners – taking a $35m [USD] in prize money.[3] Those teams eliminated at the group stages received $8m [USD]. These sums of money can be used in whatever each F.A. that is awarded the money sees fit but often covers the costs of staffing, travel, accommodation and player bonuses for the tournament. FIFA also sets aside $70m [USD] to reimburse the clubs that employ the players, at a rate of £2,800 [USD] per player per day. This left an excess of $4bn [USD].

Owen (2014) argues that on the surface most other expenditure from FIFA's revenues is transparent, pointing out that the governing body's 2014 financial report sub-divides its expenditure into six core areas: development projects, the World Cup, other competitions, football governance, operational expenses and rights exploitation. Within this, the development budget for the projected period of 2015–2018 accounts for $900m. This sum is largely made up of the money that is invested in – for instance – developing football's infrastructure and facilities amongst the poorer associations within its membership of 209 countries through its 'Goal' programme. In 2009, the sum attached to 'development' for 2011–2014 period accounted for $800m. 2014 figures show a 12.5 per cent growth, but this lagged the 31.6 per cent growth in FIFA's revenues over the same period (Owen, 2014). Indeed, 'operational expenses and services' which Owen (2014) describes as 'the amount sucked in by the central FIFA organisation' was projected to be $990m [USD] for 2015–2018, representing a 69.2 per cent increase from the $585m [USD] that was budgeted for 2011–2014. These figures prompt questions about what 'operational expenses and services' and the miscellaneous 'other' category (which has grown from $97m [USD] budgeted for 2011–2014 to $228m [USD] for 2015–2018) specifically refer to. The answers remain unclear. The likelihood is that most of the sum was used in legitimate ways. However, Jennings (2009: 18) has argued that a culture of 'little brown envelopes being passed around with such fraternal sentiments as "if that's not enough, please tell me" had grown with FIFA since the run up to Havelange's election in 1974'. Jennings' (2009, 2014) and Tomlinson's (2014; Sugden and Tomlinson, 1998a, 1998b, 1999, 2003) shared concern is that some of the excess FIFA revenues could be sliced off and used in such illegitimate ways. This might happen in two areas: first, in the pursuit of FIFA presidency and second, in the competition to host World Cup finals. We first explore the issue of presidential elections.

In 1999, a story broke that 20 figureheads from national associations had allegedly each accepted $50,000 [USD] from the ruler of a Middle Eastern state in exchange for their vote for Sepp Blatter to be elected as FIFA president (see Campbell and Kuper, 1999). Rather than launch an internal enquiry, FIFA responded with an attempt – through the Dutch legal system – to have David Yallop's *How They Stole The Game* (1999; second edition 2011), the book that exposed this story, banned. However, the judge ruled that Yallop's allegations to be 'sufficiently concrete that Blatter and FIFA can defend themselves against it' and the book was published (Campbell and Kuper, 1999: 62). More recently, in December 2010, *The Sunday Times* ran an expose that stated that through sourcing 'hundreds of millions' of documents accessed 'electronically' and by gaining 'whistle-blowers' within FIFA and the Asian Football Confederation (AFC), it had evidence that AFC president, Mohammed Bin Hammam had covertly bought voting influence for Qatar bid to host the 2022 World Cup after it had just beaten the English bid to hold the sporting mega-event (Radnedge, 2014). It followed this story up with further exposés that strongly evidenced their claims shortly before the 2014 World Cup (see Blake and Calvert, 2015). In May 2011, *The Sunday Times'* allegations from 2010 were built upon when Lord David Triesman of the English FA said that four members of FIFA's executive committee – Jack Warner, Nicolas Leoz, Ricardo Teixeira and Worawi Makudi – had taken bribes in return for their support of Qatar's bid to host the World Cup (*BBC*, 2011). These accusations were based on information provided by a whistleblower involved with that bid (*BBC*, 2011). Mohammed Bin Hammam, who played a key role in securing the games for Qatar, launched himself as a candidate to replace Blatter as president in 2011 but withdrew from the election after being accused of bribing 25 FIFA officials. The suggestion was that he had been helped in handing out these bribes by fellow Executive Committee member, vice-President of FIFA and President of the Confederation of North, Central America and Caribbean Association Football (CONCACAF), Jack Warner. Conn (2014: 72) described the leak of these allegations as being 'uncannily close [in timing] to the presidential vote'. Warner subsequently released an email exchange in which FIFA general secretary Jerome Valcke wrote that Qatar had 'bought the World Cup' after it had won the election to host the 2022 amid allegations that it had bought votes (Conn, 2014: 72).

Blatter had initiated the establishment of an ethics committee in 2004, claiming it to be one of the successes of his tenure (Tomlinson, 2014: 37). Its composition and terms of reference have been changed several times since then. Until 2012, FIFA was largely internally regulated, when it changed to appoint external chairs to its committees after public pressure and sponsors' concerns. Scott (2011) points out that Blatter's original choice to assume one of these roles was his 'long-term associate' and former U.S. Secretary of State, Henry Kissinger who Jennings (2011) said had helped to 'reform' transparency in the IOC. FIFA judging its own practices lead to several potential problems, including those that emerged in relation to Bin Hammam and Warner when Blatter, in his capacity of President and Executive Committee chair, convened a panel to interrogate allegations that the heads of the two confederations were bribing members of smaller football associations to vote for Bin Hammam in the 2011 presidential election. Jennings (2014) suggests that the major issue that concerned Blatter was Bin Hammam's large reserves of cash meant he could bribe more people – with more attractive enticements – than the gifts he could provide. Indeed, Jennings (2014) further argues that Bin Hammam had been providing similar incentives to help Blatter remain in power in previous elections. With reference to such matters, Jennings (2011: 395) stated:

> Sepp Blatter runs a tight ship, he recruits loyalists and keep them loyal. Nothing buys loyalty like money. And, there's dirt; if you've got some on your subordinates, terrific. And here we go again. First-class air travel, long limousines, five-star hotels, the full VIP-treatment. As for the critics: ban them, intimidate them, get their phone records, identify their contacts, threaten their publishers and try to destroy them.

Bin Hammam's withdrawal left Blatter unopposed in the presidential election that took place days later; taking 186 out of 203 possible votes, with the remaining 17 ballot papers spoiled. Conn (2014) points out that 2 months after the election the court of arbitration for sport found it did not have indisputable evidence that Bin Hammam provided the $1m cash in bribes, but stated that the ruling was not 'any sort of affirmative finding of innocence . . . It is more likely than not that Mr Bin Hammam was the source of the monies' (Conn, 2014: 72). If Bin Hammam was guilty of bribery, he is almost certainly not the only sports administrator connected to world football to have carried out such acts; it seems likely that his deviant act – in the eyes of those in influence at FIFA – was to launch a democratic challenge Blatter's position.

Indeed, Tomlinson (2014: 145) states that in April 2013 an internal FIFA report on its dealings with ISL during Havelange's presidency criticised him from 'a moral and ethical standpoint' and said that ISL's practices were sometimes 'deliberately fraudulent'. The report further stated that

> it is certain that not inconsiderable amounts were channelled to FIFA President Havelange and to his son-in-law Ricardo Teixeira as well as to Dr. Nicolás Leoz, whereby there is no indication that any form of service was given in return for them. These payments were apparently made via front companies to cover up the true recipient and are to be qualified as 'commissions', known today as 'bribes'. Known payments in this regard were made between 1992 and May 2000.
>
> *(quoted in Tomlinson, 2014: 145–146)*

These allegations stood at 'moral' and 'ethical' levels and did not become criminal for two reasons: first, the report stated that 'the acceptance of bribe money by Havelange, Teixeira and Leoz was not punishable under Swiss criminal law at the time' (quoted in Tomlinson, 2014: 146) because legal proceedings on ISL were closed. The report drew no conclusions about Blatter's involvement in such activities but called his initial period leadership 'clumsy', questioning whether he may have been complicit in FIFA paying ISL 2.5m (CHF) as it was threatened with bankruptcy. Blatter distanced himself from allegations of white-collar criminality and deviance and – for Jennings (2009, 2014) and Tomlinson (2014; Sugden and Tomlinson, 2003) – presented himself as a bastion of reform. Indeed *BBC* (2014) reported that 'United Passions', a FIFA-financed film released in only selected countries at the time of the 2014 World Cup, reflected Blatter's narrative. The film cost FIFA £19m to produce which is equivalent to the sum of money it sets aside for its 'Goal' programme, which supports the development of football in poorer nations but might give prioritise funds for those federations that have remained loyal to its politics (Doidge, 2014). Jennings (2012) stated that this creates a culture of dependency from individual members and associations to FIFA but, as Doidge (2014) pointed out, in the work of the social anthropologist Marcel Mauss, gifts are not without value as they serve to create bonds between givers and receivers, meaning that FIFA 'gifts' place future obligations on the receiver. These 'obligations' might have shaped the act of 'staying loyal' to the president and/or voting for host countries and leadership elections in the way he expected, which was until 27 May 2015, at least.

The End of Blatter's FIFA Presidential Era

That morning the sporting world awoke in shock as, on the eve of FIFA's 65th congress in Zurich, the Swiss authorities acted on behalf of the United States' Federal Bureau of Investigation (FBI) to arrest seven officials on corruption charges explicitly related to the process of awarding the 2018 and 2022 men's World Cups (Gibson and Gayle, 2015). Separately, Swiss federal prosecutors opened criminal proceedings, also in connection with the award of the 2018 World Cup to Russia and the 2022 tournament to Qatar. These decisions have been shrouded in claims of bribery and corruption ever since the vote in December 2010 (as noted, earlier in this chapter and featured in Blake and Calvert, 2015; Conn, 2017; Mersiades, 2018). To do this, the Swiss authorities took 'electronic data and documents' (Gibson and Gayle, 2015) in their raid on FIFA headquarters. Subsequently, they questioned 10 members of those who at the time sat on FIFA's executive committee, who took part in the World Cup votes. This number included senior vice-president Issa Hayatou of Cameroon and Vitaly Mutko, Russia's sports minister who is head of the country's 2018 World Cup organising committee, Angel Maria Villar Llona (Spain), Michel D'Hooghe (Belgium), Senes Erzik (Turkey), Worawi Makudi (Thailand), Marios Lefkaritis (Cyprus), Jacques Anouma (Ivory Coast), Rafael Salguero (Guatemala) and Hany Abo Rida (Egypt).

The FBI and the Internal Revenue Service Criminal Investigation Division (IRS-CI) launched an inquiry into wire fraud, racketeering and money laundering that mostly revolved around officials of continental football bodies CONMEBOL (South America) and CONCACAF (Caribbean, Central and North America), and the sports marketing executives. The issue was collusion in the sale of media and marketing rights for high-profile international competitions, such as the Americas' FIFA World Cup qualifying tournaments and their major tournaments CONCACAF Gold Cup and Copa América. Fourteen people were indicted by the FBI and the IRS-CS, whilst The United States Attorney General simultaneously announced the unsealing of the indictments and the prior guilty pleas by four football executives and two corporations. CONCACAF President Jeffrey Webb, also serving president of the Cayman Islands Football Association, was arrested in connection with the investigation, as were two sitting FIFA Executive Committee members: Eduardo Li of the Costa Rican Football Federation and Eugenio Figueredo, formerly of the Uruguayan Football Association, and former CONMEBOL President Nicolás Leoz. The investigation lasted several years, with the first arrest, of former CONCACAF president Jack Warner's son Daryll, made in July 2013 (Papenfuss and Thompson, 2017). The charge was that they had collectively received £65m of bribes over a three-decade period (Gibson and Gayle, 2015).

The arrests came 2 days before Sepp Blatter had expected to be re-elected for a fifth term as FIFA president. Blatter has been closely entwined with many of those charged at that point during his 40 years at FIFA, including the Paraguayan Leoz and the Trinidadian Warner, whilst Webb and Figuero were then current FIFA vice-presidents. To repeat earlier stated material, Jennings (2011: 395) had previously written: 'Sepp Blatter runs a tight ship, he recruits loyalists and keep them loyal. Nothing buys loyalty like money. And, there's dirt; if you've got some on your subordinates, terrific'. At that point, Blatter was not under investigation but many of those that were appeared to be 'loyalists', destabilising his tenure and prompting the FIFA president to attempt to call for a delay to the election process that was due to take place 2 days later.

That delay did not occur, but Blatter was re-elected as FIFA president on 29 May 2015. Blatter had polled 133 votes to his challenger, Jordanian Prince, Ali Bin al-Hussein's 73 in the first round. Under FIFA's presidential election protocol, which would have been enough to take the contest to a potential second round, his 39-year-old challenger withdrew ahead of that process taking place (Gibson, 2015a). Upon his victory, Blatter offered that: 'For the next four years I will be in command of this boat called FIFA and we will bring it back ashore, we will bring it back to the beach' and when closing the conference stated: 'What football needs right now is a strong leader, an experienced leader, a leader who knows all the ins and outs of the situation' (Gibson, 2015a). He did not elaborate on the specifics of the 'situation', but it seemed clear that bringing FIFA 'back ashore' required a leader who knew 'all the ins and outs of the situation', or perhaps, paraphrasing Jennings (2014), a knowledge of where the 'bodies were buried'. However, his fifth term did not last 4 years and only got to the following Tuesday (2 June 2015) when he resigned from his role. This was just hours after evidence emerged showing that FIFA's secretary general, Jérôme Valcke, was aware of a $10m [USD] payment from South African officials to the former Concacaf president Jack Warner, which US investigators saw as a bribe (Gibson, 2015b). In his resignation speech, Blatter had noted that he expected to serve a period of grace in which he would oversee a process of appointing his successor. As Jennings (2011: 395) had noted, Blatter – like Dassler, Samaranch and Havelange – liked to run 'a tight ship', recruiting 'loyalists and keep[ing] them loyal'.

Blatter did not serve the period of grace, however. Rather on 25 September 2015, the Swiss authorities opened criminal proceedings against him as the corruption crisis engulfing FIFA further escalated (Gibson, 2015c). In the same process, UEFA president, Michel Platini – the former European footballer of the year and Blatter protégé – who was favourite to become next FIFA leader was also dragged into the web of allegations engulfing football's governing body. In particular, the investigations centre on a 'disloyalty payment' of two million Swiss francs (£1.35m) made to Platini by Blatter 4 years earlier. According to the attorney general's office, the payment was made 'at the expense of FIFA' for work allegedly performed between January 1999 and June 2002, when Blatter was in his first term as president. Platini helped him to win that election, as a paid consultant. However, the attorney general's office said FIFA did not execute this payment until February 2011. Of potential temporal significance, this was 3 months after Qatar had won the right to host the 2022 World Cup with the help of Platini and 3 months before Blatter was re-elected unopposed as president (Gibson, 2015c). This was a tough period for Blatter's 'tight ship' (Jennings, 2011: 395) which given that another of his 'loyalists' (Jennings, 2011: 395), Jérôme Valcke, had been suspended FIFA amid allegations that he had profited from the sale of black-market tickets on 17 September (Gibson, 2015d).

A 'disloyalty payment' to Platini was not the only allegation the Swiss attorney general levelled at Blatter at that point, neither. Indeed, it is said that it believed: 'on 12 September 2005 Mr Joseph Blatter has signed a contract with the Caribbean Football Union [with Jack Warner as the president at this time]; this contract was unfavourable for Fifa' (quoted in Gibson, 2015d).

Within a month, on 8 October, Sepp Blatter, Michel Platini and Jérôme Valcke had all been suspended for 90 days by FIFA. This period oversaw the period until the emergency presidential elections, effectively ending Blatter's presidency prematurely and curtailing Plantini's hopes of succeeding him. Interestingly, given discussions earlier in this chapter about corruption and white-collar crime at the IOC, its president, Thomas Bach, released a statement stating that: 'FIFA must realise that this is now about more than just a list of candidates. This is also a structural problem and will not be solved simply by the election of a new president' (quoted in Gibson, 2015d). As Jűrgen Lenz, like Blatter a fellow Horst Dassler trainee and former ISL employee who acted on behalf of FIFA and the IOC on issues related to marketing, media and sponsorship, told Tomlinson: 'FIFA's now so corrupt that it no longer knows that it is being corrupt' (quoted from Tomlinson, 2014: 3; 172).

On 21 December, both Sepp Blatter and Michel Platini were banned from football for 8 years by FIFA (although this length of time was reduced to 6 years on appeal in February 2016). At this point, the organisation cleared both of corruption charges but found them guilty of a series of other breaches including a conflict of interest and dereliction of duty over the 'disloyalty payment' Platini had received (Gibson, 2015e). A 6-year investigation by Swiss prosecutors into that payment ensued and on 2 November 2021, Blatter and Platini were charged with fraud and other offences, however by then the former president's successor, Giovanni (Gianni) Infantino, had been elected on 26 February 2016, re-elected until 2023 on 5 June 2019 and – mimicking Havelange and Blatter – had become a member of the IOC in January 2020.

Enter Gianni Infantino: A New FIFA?

Gianni Infantino was born in Brig, a Swiss-German-speaking Alpine town close to the border with Italy. He qualified in law from Fribourg University, before working as the secretary general of the International Centre for Sports Studies at the University of Neuchâtel. Infantino started collaborating with UEFA in August 2000 and was appointed to the confederation's role of Director of Legal Affairs and Club Licensing Division in January 2004. Under Michel Platini's tenure as UEFA President, Infantino became Deputy General Secretary of UEFA in 2007 and Secretary General of UEFA in October 2009, but nonetheless had a much lower profile than either the former UEFA or FIFA president. Conn (2016) reports that once Platini was effectively ruled out of the race to replace Blatter, 'Infantino was the substitute candidate to stand for the presidency of FIFA . . . but [is] shrewdly aware of football's political heart: self-interest'.

In the case that Infantino needed to define his growing public profile in opposition to both Blatter and Platini, his election manifesto was built upon the planks of transparency, good governance, and support for reforming FIFA whilst, in common with Havelange, also explicitly seeking to further maximising the governing body's revenue-generating activities. Indeed, just as Havelange grew the number of teams competing in men's World Cups, under Infantino FIFA is exploring ideas that would see the frequency of the tournament increase from one every 4 years to one every 2 years (Lahm, 2021). From 2026, meanwhile, the World Cup will include 48 (as opposed to 32) competing teams. The questions are therefore how different is Infantino to Samaranch, Havelange, Blatter and the school of other sports administrators that were spawned by Dassler's 'club' and has a 'new FIFA' emerged during his presidency.

Jens Sejer Andersen is International Director of 'Play the Game', an INGO which was been developed under the auspices of the Danish Institute for Sports Studies (in 1997) and aims to strengthen sport's ethical foundation and promote democracy, transparency and freedom of expression in sport. For him 'the jury is still out' in response to the previous questions (Andersen, 2020). He suggests that Infantino's reforms have brought about a series of 'internal checks and balances' that 'are stronger' in so far as 'less power than before is vested in one very small group of corrupt allies' (Andersen, 2020). These make the 'disloyalty payment' and other bonus scandals unlikely to reoccur at the present time.

However, Andersen (2020) also feels that 'we are very far from a new FIFA that has earned public confidence, such as Gianni Infantino promised when he was elected' and that 'Infantino's own behaviour is one of the reasons why FIFA still is surrounded by scepticism'. To elaborate he draws upon three examples.

First, Andersen (2020) notes that a key element in Infantino's reforms involved establishing independent committees of ethics and governance in a way that stood in contrast to Blatter. However, he argues that there have been instances when such committees make decisions that go against the interests of the Infantino, and when that has happened their chairpersons have been dismissed. He outlines the concrete example in 2017 when the Portuguese Miguel Maduro blocked the then Russian deputy prime minister and Russian FA President Vitaly Mutko from being re-elected to a seat in the FIFA Council, citing FIFA rules on political neutrality. Whilst the incident ended Mutko's FIFA career, it also spelt the end for Maduro in the governing body. This led Maduro et al. (2017) to state 'We have concluded that FIFA cannot reform from within'.

Second, Andersen (2020) argued that Infantino's FIFA's decision to put its Secretary General Fatma Samoura in charge of the African Football Confederation (CAF) violated confederations autonomy. He records that FIFA continues to conceal a report by the audit firm PriceWaterhouseCoopers documenting corruption for millions of dollars by CAF leaders, including CAF President Ahmad Ahmad, who is also investigated by French prosecutors but who the current FIFA president actively lobbied for his election to role in 2017.

Third, in August 2020, the Swiss special federal prosecutor, Stefan Keller, announced a criminal investigation into Infantino relating to three meetings the FIFA president had after his election with Switzerland's then-attorney general Michael Lauber, who was investigating many different allegations of corruption under the previous president of 17 years, Sepp Blatter (Conn, 2020). Despite FIFA's deputy general secretary, Alasdair Bell, stating that there was 'no factual basis whatsoever' in any allegations of criminality (Conn, 2020), Andersen (2020) points out that Lauber was sanctioned for not reporting the meetings and a procedure to remove him from his position was started by the Swiss parliament. For Andersen (202), this leaves open questions of i) why did Infantino try to hide these meetings? ii) Were they aimed at neutralising legal procedures against FIFA and himself? And, iii) are they the reason no court case has been raised in Switzerland after the 2015 raids on football's world governing body, despite Swiss police opening up investigations alongside the FBI? The answers are not clear.

Additionally, in October 2021, Infantino and his family moved to Doha, with his children being educated there. Whilst residing in Qatar does not mean for suspicion of wrongdoing, the initial reports by *SonntagsBlick* which revealed the story were denied by FIFA, it was eventually forced to confirm them following a probe in early 2022 (Morgan, 2022). This denial of demonstrable fact, allied to Andersen's (2020) presentation of concerns, leave the jury out as to the extent that FIFA has changed without external reform.

Summary: Corruption and Critical White-Collar Criminologies of Sport

ISL is at the core of Jennings and Tomlinson's analyses of FIFA and/or the IOC.[4] At the centre of such discussions is evidence that the Jennings uncovered from various whistle-blowers over several years which suggest ISL won the right to sell the broadcasting and marketing rights to World Cup finals and Olympic Games without a transparent and competitive tender. These suspicions are strengthened by the suggestion that before ISL was founded, its lead member, Horst Dassler, formed 'the Club' whose membership included future presidents of the IOC and FIFA in Juan Antonio Samaranch and João Havelange. A 'crooked practice' (Sutherland, 1940: 2) that may have emerged is the lack of external competition that stood against ISL in achieving these rights, given the cross-over of interests between ISL and the two governing bodies. The Club formalised and became ISL. However, the interlocking sporting and business interests are not the only practices involved with ISL and it acts on behalf of the IOC and FIFA that might be considered 'crooked'. Jennings and Tomlinson ask at least three questions about these relationships in their respective writing. First, given that ISL did not compete with other external agencies for the right to act on the IOC and FIFA's behalf, how were the prices and the commissions that were paid to the agency set? The answer is not clear but the heavy suggestion in Jennings' (2009, 2012, 2014; Simson and Jennings, 1992) work was that in the late 1980s and early 1990s the remuneration that ISL received may have been too high. Second, given that the broadcasting and marketing landscapes in the wider society were changing through, for instance, increased television ownership in Western Europe and North America, the global spread of television across the world, and the proliferation in the number of channels (which included subscription and pay-to-view outlets) that needed filling – the revenues that ISL assisted in the generation of continued to grow, making FIFA and the IOC increasingly wealthy. Despite ISL's collapse in 2001, leaving behind debts of £153m, it had also generated unquantifiable large sums of revenue. ISL was a private company and so it has no obligation to show how it invested its resources, but Jennings (2009) suggests that it paid out multiple large sums of money to FIFA members for over two decades. For what purposes and how the members spent this money is largely unknown. However, in 2008, following a 4-year investigation by prosecutors in the Swiss canton of Zug, six former ISL executives, including its former chairman Jean-Marie Weber, were accused of a series of charges including fraud, embezzlement and the falsification of documents, strengthening the case for greater transparency in elite sports organisations such as the IOC and FIFA. Third, given growing calls for transparency, Jennings and Tomlinson both point out that the IOC and FIFA have usually internally dealt with such problems through 'reforms' that may simply cover up the allegations rather than deal with their issues.

Edwin Sutherland (1939) introduced the concept of 'white-collar crime' by suggesting that criminal acts committed by those from wealthy and powerful positions, secure home lives and 'sound' minds. To do this, Sutherland offered a theory of differential association. We connect with eight touchstones in his theory. First, Sutherland argued that criminal behaviour is learned and second, he suggested that such learning accrued through processes of communication and interaction with others. We find that a root of the way in the IOC and FIFA self governs could be learned from the association of Horst Dassler's 'Club' which embraced and engineered sponsorship and free-market principles in sport. Third, Sutherland pointed out that personal communication is the most important form of interaction in this learning process. In relation to this, the influential position that Dassler held over Samaranch, Havelange and Blatter (amongst others) and their alleged connections to the KGB (Gulko et al., 2010: 48) and Jennings (2014) suggest that Castor Andrade, the uncontested leader of organised crime rackets, and Rio de Janeiro in the 1980s and 1990s are worth noting. 'Underhand' codes of behaving may have been learned through such socialisation. Fourth, Sutherland suggests that social learning processes may be complicated but usually include developing the techniques to commit the crime (which may range in complexity) and also a socialisation of the specific directions of motives and attitudes and, indeed, Dassler trained Blatter – who looked up to him as a mentor – at his Adidas offices immediately before he became FIFA General Secretary.

Jűrgen Lenz was also trained by Horst Dassler and worked for ISL, acting on behalf of FIFA and the IOC on issues related to marketing, media and sponsorship. In an interview with Tomlinson, he said that 'FIFA's now so corrupt that it no longer knows that it is being corrupt' (quoted from Tomlinson, 2014: 3; 172). This connects to Sutherland's fifth and sixth points which are that the specific direction of such motives and desires is learned through the group's cultural definitions of specific legal codes and individuals may engage in criminal behaviour through repeated exposure and individual internalisation of definitions that are favourable to violations of law. Given that FIFA 'no longer knows it is being corrupt', it reflects an internalisation of its members' views that the nature of their transgressions is menial and they rise above legal codes. The repeated exposure to this attitude only strengthens the institutional view further, and so its culture is internally self-produced.

However, seventh, for Sutherland, these views sit relative to the social bonds within the group and the value and contact with those in positions of subcultural influence meaning that people can exit the way in which it operates, as is the case of Patrick Nally who Simson and Jennings (1992: 23) quote as 'getting to the point where I was finding it difficult to know which side I was on' and left 'the Club' before it formalised into ISL. Eighth, the learning of criminal behaviours is such that rewards and anticipated rewards encourage the take up of such behaviour whereas the punishments and the anticipation of punishments dissuade the learning of behaviours; thus the institutional culture of acceptance at the selling of votes (or match tickets) amongst FIFA and the IOC members may produce rewards without fear of reprisal, as long as – as Jennings (2011: 342) argues 'the Club', the IOC and FIFA had to 'recruit loyalists and keep them loyal. Nothing buys loyalty like money. And, there's dirt; if you've got some on your subordinates, terrific' in order to re-orientate their institutional cultures towards a deeper commercialisation, thus producing both the incentive and fear to govern the way members behave.

In making these points, we wish to extend Sutherland's work to discuss white-collar crime more broadly through the illustrative examples of ISL, the IOC and FIFA. To do so, we make four key points. First, Gerber and Jensen (2007: xi) state that white-collar crime is a 'residual category' category into which many indiscretions can be gathered. Similarly, Brooks et al. (2013: 5–6) argue that 'white-collar criminality' and 'corruption' in sport describe a wide range of actions, including bribery, collusion, conflicts of interest, embezzlement, extortion, cronyism, fraud, lobbying and money laundering. The issues we recount in connection to ISL, the IOC and FIFA would clearly support these claims: 'white-collar criminality' is a useful way to gather up 'crooked practices' (Sutherland, 1940: 2) but the potential legality is better questioned through the labels for actions that Brooks et al. offer. As we unpacked literature in the field of 'white-collar criminality' and 'corruption' in sport, we argued that three broad areas to interrogate potential 'wrongdoing' emerged. These were a) white-collar criminal actions, defined by set of nationally or internationally prescribed judicial laws which are 'illegal' and could be referred to as 'white-collar crime'; b) 'white-collar rule-breaking' as those actions that are 'against the rules' of a governing body in a given sport but not 'against the law' and c) borrowing from Simon (2006), 'white-collar deviancy' as actions that runs against widely held ethical or moral positions in sport. White-collar deviancy is 'softer' and more malleable than white-collar crime and white-collar rule-breaking, being formed through cultural judgements of norms and values. Most of the analysis that Jennings offers is white-collar deviancy: it does not seem – from our cultural position – to be 'right', 'fair' or within the 'spirit' of the sport, but this is open to counter allegations of normative analyses of sport. Indeed, we should not forget that Sugden and Tomlinson (1998a, 1998b, 1999, 2003) point out that the argument offered against Rous' ideas for FIFA's future was that they were rooted within a neo-Colonial culture of spreading the British practices of 'fair play' to the rest of the World. Adding further nuance to this understanding, Goldstraw-White's (2012) interviews with offenders of white-collar crimes showed that in their afterthoughts many recount narratives about how such actions can contribute to a subjectively defined wider 'social good'. Undoubtedly, if a culture of bribe exists/existed within the IOC and/or FIFA it should not automatically be assumed that all 'beneficiaries' took gifts for personal gain but instead the 'illegitimately' gained resources may have investments into sporting facilities to improve elite and/or grassroots participation in sport. Allegations of about bribe being passed around turn into mediatised scandals, written and reported on to 'sell' news outlets. For instance, 2 weeks before the 2014 World Cup began, Hill and Longman (2014) suggested in *The New York Times* that match-fixing could be rife at the tournament, but Jennings reported that he did not believe this to be the case. Therefore, in measuring white-collar criminality/deviance through media channels, it is important to be alive to the possibility that such reports could be exaggerations of a reality, creating a 'moral panic' (Cohen, 2011 [1972]). Thus, whilst we call into question most actions that might be called 'white-collar deviance/criminality', it is important that in making such judgements we acknowledge that intellectual black holes exist in strictly normative frameworks about 'wrongdoing'.

Second, legality might be rooted within cultural judgements about what is 'right' and 'wrong' (Elias, 1983; Taylor et al., 1973) but it facilitates a (often questionable) position that goes beyond soft judgements. In making this point, clearly defined judicial systems also often take normative positions, reflecting the 'powerful' (however defined) in society. However, most legal judgements are nationally hemmed. The IOC and FIFA are positioned within Switzerland, and their tournaments have to abide by the national laws. Therefore, any legal cases levelled at the organisations must be questionable according to Swiss Law. However, the country's economy is strengthened by its position as the world's largest tax haven (Urry, 2014) and has secrecy laws, designed to protect this status (Crawford and Drucker, 2014). As post-2015 investigations into FIFA show, this makes acts of white-collar criminality at the IOC and FIFA difficult to police; a point especially pertinent given that white-collar crime is notoriously difficult to detect in most countries across the world (Tombs, 2007, 2018).

Our third point is attached to this. Namely, Slapper and Tombs (1999) point out that a key reason 'white-collar crime' is underreported is that it is the expression of those holding – and shaped by – powerful hegemonic positions. When their actions are questioned in the media, they mobilise actors within their 'powerful' (however defined) networks and a 'cover up' begins. In making this point with reference to the IOC and FIFA, Andrew Jennings' (2011) vignette that we open up this chapter with is worth returning to. He recounts that in trying to uncover the questionable activities of some leading figures in the IOC and/or FIFA, he was banned from accessing their grounds, had logs of his telephone calls secretly recorded by both organisations and was criminalised through the Swiss judicial system on account of 'deep contempt towards the International Olympic Committee [IOC], its president and its members, criticizing their personalities, their behaviour and their management' (Jennings, 2011: 388). Fourth, when allegations become too pervasive to attack individuals, both the IOC and FIFA have a propensity to internally govern – through the formation of ethics panels and reform procedures – often drawing upon the same individuals (for instance, Kissenger, Blatter and Havelange have all been connected to IOC and FIFA reform procedures). Even in the context of post-2015 FIFA, Maduro et al. (2017) have 'concluded that FIFA cannot reform from within'. This means that the shield of 'dealing' with white-collar criminality can be projected to the world but often such reforms reflect the interests of those leading the organisations, thus potentially deepening rather than addressing the issues that have spiked the interests of the public.

Notes

1. See Croall (2001: 29) for specific discussions of tax evasion and money laundering as white-collar crime.
2. Havelange retired shortly after agreeing that Nigeria could host the World Youth Soccer Championships in 1997. Shortly after this award, the activist Ken Saro-Wiwa was executed in Nigeria on the order of military dictator Sani Abacha. Jennings (2009: 62) points out that Havelange and Abacha had been 'sipping tea' together 2 days before this execution. Indeed on this Tomlinson records Havelange stating: 'I don't want to make any comparisons with the Pope, but he is also criticised from time to time, and his reply is silence. I too am sometimes criticised, so explanations about such matters are superfluous' (2014: 67).
3. This is less than Cardiff City earned in Premier League prize money when it finished bottom of the competition in 2013/2014 season.
4. ISL also acted on behalf of the International Athletics Association Federation.

References

Andersen, J.S. (2020) 'FBI vs. FIFA: How deep an impact?' *Play the Game*, 28 May, available from: www.playthegame.org/news/comments/2020/1003_fbi-vs-fifa-how-deep-an-impact/#:~:text=The%20coordinated%20raid%20of%20Swiss,raid%20was%20indeed%20a%20surprise [accessed 1/2022].

BBC. (2011) 'Triesman claims four Fifa members sought 2018 bribes', 10 May, available from: http://news.bbc.co.uk/sport1/hi/football/9481461.stm [accessed 11/2021].

BBC. (2012) 'The Olympic spirit', available from: www.bbc.co.uk/wales/raiseyourgame/sites/dedication/2012/pages/olympic_history.shtml [accessed 1/2022].

BBC. (2014) 'United passions: How Fifa spent £16m on a film where Sepp Blatter is a hero', 19 June, available from: www.bbc.co.uk/news/magazine-27868764 [accessed 11/2021].

Becker, H.S. (1967) 'Whose side are we on?' *Social Problems* 14(3): 239–247.

Blackshaw, T. and Crabbe, T. (2004) *New Perspectives on Sport and 'deviance': Consumption, Performativity and Social Control*, Abingdon: Routledge.

Blake, H. and Calvert, J. (2015) *The Ugly Game: The Qatari Plot to Buy the World Cup*, London: Simon & Schuster.

Bonger, W. (1916) *Criminality and Economic Conditions*, Boston: Little Brown.

Bond, D. (2008) 'The £66m bribe shadow hanging over FIFA', *The Telegraph*, 13 March, available from: www.telegraph.co.uk/sport/columnists/davidbond/2294323/The-66m-bribe-shadow-hanging-over-Fifa.html [accessed 11/2021].

Bose, M. (2012) *The Spirit of the Game: How Sport Made the Modern World*, London: Constable Press.

Boykoff, J. (2016) *Power Games: A Political History of the Olympics*, London: Verso.

Boykoff, J. and Gaffney, C. (2020) 'The Tokyo Olympics and the end of Olympic history', *Capitalism, Nature, Socialism*: 1–19.

Braithwaite, J. (1984) *Corporate Crime in the Pharmaceutical Industry*, London: Routledge.

Braithwaite, J. (1985) 'White collar crime', *Annual Review of Sociology* 11(1): 1–25.

Breuer, M. (2019) 'Multi-club ownerships', *The Palgrave Handbook on the Economics of Manipulation in Sport* (Eds. M. Breuer and D. Forrest), Basingstoke: Palgrave Macmillan.

Brooks, G., Aleem, A. and Button, M. (2013) *Fraud, Corruption and Sport*, Basingstoke: Palgrave MacMillan.

Campbell, D. and Kuper, S. (1999) '$1m "fixed" the FIFA poll, author claims', *The Guardian*, 21 March, available from: www.theguardian.com/uk/1999/mar/21/sport.sportfeatures [accessed 11/2021].

Canning, V. and Tombs, S. (2021) *From Social Harm to Zemiology: A Critical Introduction*, Abingdon: Routledge.

Carson, W.G. (1970a) 'White-collar crime and the enforcement of factory legislation', *The British Journal of Criminology* 10(4): 383–398.

Carson, W.G. (1970b) 'Some sociological aspects of strict liability and the enforcement of factory legislation', *Modern Law Review* 33(4): 396–412.

Carson, W.G. (1974) 'Symbolic and instrumental dimensions of early factory legislation: A case study in the social origins of criminal law', *Crime, Criminology and Public Policy: Essays in Honour of Sir Leon Radnowicz* (Eds. R. Hood), London: Heinemann.

Carson, W.G. (1979) 'The conventionalization of early factory crime', *Journal of the Sociology of Law* 7(1): 37–60.

Carson, W.G. (1980a) 'Early factory inspectors and the viable class society', *International Journal of the Sociology of Law* 8(2): 187–191.

Carson, W.G. (1980b) 'The institutionalization of ambiguity: Early British factory acts', *White Collar Crime: Theory and Research* (Eds. G. Geis and E. Stotland), London: Sage.

Carson, W.G. (1982) *The Other Price of Britain's Oil: Safety and Control in the North Sea*, New York: Rutgers University Press.

Carson, W.G. (1985a) 'Hostages to history: Some aspects of the occupational health and safety debate in historical perspective', *The Industrial Relations of Occupational Health and Safety* (Eds. B. Creighton and N. Gunningham), Sydney: Croomhelm.

Carson, W.G. (1985b) 'Technology, safety and law: The case of the offshore oil industry', *Social Responses to Technological Change* (Eds. A. Brannigan and S. Goldenberg), London: Greenwood Press.

Coleman, J.W. (1985) *The Criminal Elite: The Sociology of White Collar Crime*, New York: St. Martin's Press.

Conklin, J.E. (1977) *"Illegal but Not Criminal": Business Crime in America*, Englewood Cliffs, NJ: Prentice-Hall.

Conn, D. (2017) *The Fall of the House of FIFA*, London: New Jersey Press.

Clinard, M. and Yeager, P. (1980) *Corporate Crime*, London: Routledge.

CNBC. (2018) 'Here's who is getting rich off the world cup', 19 June, available from: www.cnbc.com/2018/06/14/the-business-of-the-world-cup – who-makes-money-and-how-much.html [accessed 11/2021].

Cohen, S. (2011 [1972]) *Folk Devils and Moral Panics*, Abingdon: Routledge.

Conn, D. (2014) 'Qatar world cup: Bin Hammam 'acted like head of crime organisation', *The Guardian*, 1 June, available from: www.theguardian.com/football/2014/jun/01/qatar-world-cup-bin-hammam-qatar-fifa [accessed 11/2021].

Conn, D. (2016) 'Everything you need to know about Gianni Infantino, the new Fifa president', *The Guardian*, 26 February, available from: www.theguardian.com/football/2016/feb/26/gianni-infantino-fifa-president [accessed 1/2022].

Conn, D. (2020) 'Fifa comes out fighting in defence of accused president Gianni Infantino', *The Guardian*, 3 August, available from: www.theguardian.com/football/2020/aug/03/fifa-comes-out-fighting-in-defence-of-accused-president-gianni-infantino [accessed 1/2022].

Crawford, D. and Drucker, J. (2014) 'Swiss to relax bank secrecy laws', *The Wall Street Journal*, 14 March, available from: http://online.wsj.com/news/articles/SB123694252262918343 [accessed 11/2021].

Croall, H. (2001) *Understanding White Collar Crime*, Maidenhead: McGraw-Hill Education (UK).

Doidge, M. (2014) 'FIFA: World cups, commercialism and corruption', *Discover Society*, 5 August, available from: https://archive.discoversociety.org/2014/08/05/fifa-world-cups-commercialism-and-corruption/ [accessed 11/2021].

Downes, D. and Rock, P. (2011) *Understanding Deviance: A Guide to the Sociology of Crime and Rule-Breaking*, Oxford: Oxford University Press.

The Economist. (1998) 'The paymasters: Money is the name of every game', 4 June, available from: www.economist.com/node/168569 [accessed 1/2022].

Elias, N. (1983) *The Court Society*, Blackwell: Oxford.

Friedrichs, D.O., Schoultz, I. and Jordanoska, A. (2017) *Edwin H. Sutherland*, Abingdon: Routledge.

Gerber, J. and Jensen, E.L. (2007) *Encyclopedia of White-Collar Crime*, Westport: Greenwood Press.

Gibson, O. (2013) 'João Havelange resigns as Fifa honorary president over "bribes"', *The Guardian*, 30 April, available from: www.theguardian.com/football/2013/apr/30/joao-havelange-resigns-fifa [accessed 11/2021].

Gibson, O. (2015a) 'Sepp Blatter re-elected as Fifa president for fifth term', *The Guardian*, 29 May, available from: www.theguardian.com/football/2015/may/29/sepp-blatter-reelected-fifa-president-fifth-term [accessed 1/2022].

Gibson, O. (2015b) 'Fifa's secretary general Jérôme Valcke under new pressure over $10m "bribe"', *The Guardian*, 2 June, available from: www.theguardian.com/football/2015/jun/02/fifa-jerome-valcke-under-pressure-10m-bribe [accessed 1/2022].

Gibson, O. (2015c) 'Sepp Blatter: Swiss attorney general opens criminal investigation', *The Guardian*, 25 September, available from: www.theguardian.com/football/2015/sep/25/sepp-blatter-criminal-investigation-swiss-attorney-general [accessed 1/2022].

Gibson, O. (2015d) 'Fifa's Jérôme Valcke released from duties over world cup ticket claims', *The Guardian*, 17 September, available from: www.theguardian.com/football/2015/sep/17/fifa-jerome-valcke-world-cup-tickets [accessed 1/2022].

Gibson, O. (2015e) 'Sepp Blatter and Michel Platini banned from football for eight years by Fifa', *The Guardian*, 21 December, available from: www.theguardian.com/football/2015/dec/21/sepp-blatter-michel-platini-banned-from-football-fifa [accessed 1/2022].

Gibson, O. and Gayle, D. (2015) 'Fifa officials arrested on corruption charges as world cup inquiry launched', *The Guardian*, 27 May, available from: www.theguardian.com/football/2015/may/27/several-top-fifa-officials-arrested [accessed 1/2022].

Goldstraw-White, J. (2012) *White-Collar Crime: Accounts of Offending Behaviour*, Basingstoke: Palgrave Macmillan.

Gulko, B., Popov, V., Felshtinsky, Y. and Kortschnoi, V. (2010) *The KGB Plays Chess*, Milford, CT: Russell Enterprises.

Haines, F. (2020) 'You're a criminologist? What can you offer us? Interrogating criminological expertise in the context of white collar crime', *Routledge Handbook of Public Criminologies* (Eds. K. Henne and R. Shah), Abingdon: Routledge.

Hagan, J.L. (1998) *Crime and Disrepute*, London: Pine Forge Press.

Hanstad, D.V., Smith, A. and Waddington, I. (2008) 'The establishment of the world anti-doping agency: A study of the management of organizational change and unplanned outcomes', *International Review for the Sociology of Sport* 43(2): 227–249.

Helmkamp, J., Ball, R. and Townsend, K. (eds.) (1996) *White Collar Crime: Definitional Dilemma: Can and Should There Be a Universal Definition of White Collar Crime?* Morgantown, WV: National White Collar Crime Center.

Hill, C. (1996) *Olympic Politics*, Manchester: Manchester University Press.

Hill, D. and Longman, J. (2014) 'Fixed soccer matches cast shadow over world cup', *The New York Times*, 31 May, available from: www.nytimes.com/2014/06/01/sports/soccer/fixed-matches-cast-shadow-over-world-cup.html?_r=0 [accessed 11/2021].

Hillyard, P., Pantazis, C., Tombs, S. and Gordon, D. (eds.) (2004) *Beyond Criminology: Taking Harm Seriously*, London: Pluto.

Homer, A. (2020) 'HMRC investigations into footballer tax affairs reaches record level', *BBC News*, 3 March, available from: www.bbc.co.uk/sport/football/51698150 [accessed 11/2021].

Jennings, A. (2000) *The Great Olympic Swindle: When the World Wanted Its Games Back*, London: Simon & Schuster.

Jennings, A. (2008) 'Blatter & Havelange named in Swiss bribes trial', *Transparency in Sport*, available from: www.transparencyinsport.org/swiss_trial.html [accessed 11/2021].

Jennings, A. (2009) *FOUL! The Secret World of FIFA: Bribes, Vote Rigging and Ticket Scandals*, London: Harper Collins.

Jennings, A. (2011) 'Investigating corruption in corporate sport: The IOC and FIFA', *International Review for the Sociology of Sport* 46(4): 387–398.

Jennings, A. (2012) 'The love that dare not speak its name: Corruption and the Olympics', *The Palgrave Handbook of Olympic Studies* (Eds. H.J. Lenskyj and S. Wagg), Basingstoke: Palgrave Macmillan.

Jennings, A. (2014) *Omertá: Sepp Blatter's FIFA Organized Crime Family*, London: Transparency.
Jennings, A. (2016) *The Dirty Game: Uncovering the Scandal at FIFA*, London: Random House.
Jennings, A. and Simson, V. (1992) *The Lords of The Rings*, London: Simon & Schuster.
King, A. (2017 [2003]) *The European Ritual: Football in the new Europe*, Abingdon: Routledge.
Lahm, P. (2021) 'A world cup every two years would finally kill football's golden goose', *The Guardian*, 19 October, available from: www.theguardian.com/football/blog/2021/oct/19/a-world-cup-every-two-years-would-finally-kill-footballs-golden-goose [accessed 1/2021].
Lilly, J.R., Cullen, F.T. and Ball, R.A. (2018) *Criminological Theory: Context and Consequences*, London: Sage.
Mackay, D. (1999) 'Olympic bribery scandal: The six IOC members recommended for expulsion', *The Guardian*, available from: www.theguardian.com/sport/1999/jan/25/olympic-bribery-scandal-key-figures [accessed 01/2022].
Maduro, M.P., Pillay, N. and Weiler, J. (2017) "Our sin? We appeared to take our task at Fifa too seriously', *The Guardian*, 21 December, available from: www.theguardian.com/football/2017/dec/21/our-sin-take-task-fifa-seriously [accessed 1/2022].
Mallon, B. (2000) 'The Olympic bribery scandal', *Journal of Olympic History* 8(2): 11–27.
McNamee, M.J. and Parry, S.J. (eds.) (2002) *Ethics and Sport*, London: Routledge.
Mersiades, B. (2018) *Whatever It Takes: The Inside Story of the FIFA Way*, Wyoming: Powderhouse Press.
Miller, D. (1992) *Olympic Revolution: The Biography of Juan Antonio Samaranch*, London: Pavilion Books Limited.
Millward, P. (2011) *The Global Football League: Transnational Networks, Social Movements and Sport in the New Media Age*, Basingstoke: Palgrave Macmillan.
Millward, P. (2013) 'New football directors in the twenty-first century: Profit and revenue in the English Premier League's transnational age', *Leisure Studies* 32(4): 399–414.
Misse, M. (2007) 'Illegal markets, protection rackets and organized crime in Rio de Janeiro', *Estudos Avançados* 21(61): 139–157.
Morgan, L. (2022) 'FIFA president Infantino moves to Qatar, Swiss newspaper reports', *Inside the Games*, 18 January, available from: www.insidethegames.biz/articles/1117954/infantino-moves-to-qatar-world-cup [accessed 1/2022].
Owen, D. (2014) 'FIFA's development spending conundrum', *Inside Football*, 26 March, available from: www.insideworldfootball.com/2014/03/26/david-owen-fifa-s-development-spending-conundrum/ [accessed 1/2022].
Papenfuss, M. and Thompson, T. (2017) *American Huckster*, London: HarperCollins.
Pearce, F. (1976) *Crimes of the Powerful*, London: Pluto.
Philippou, C. (2021) 'Anti-bribery and corruption in sport mega-events: Stakeholder perspectives', *Sport in Society* (Online First): 1–18.
Pielke Jr, R. (2013) 'How can FIFA be held accountable?' *Sport Management Review* 16(3): 255–267.
Radnedge, K. (2014) 'Qatar 2022 decision may appear dubious but re-vote unlikely', *World Soccer*, 2 June, available from: www.worldsoccer.com/columnists/keir-radnedge/qatar-corruption-re-vote-352307 [accessed 1/2022].
Rafter, N.H. (2009) 'Edward Alsworth Ross: The system of social control, 1901', *The Origins of Criminology: A Reader* (Eds. N.H. Rafter), London: Routledge.
Rios, R., Rivera, E., Roberts, K. and Rojas, S., et al. (2013) *Ethical Analysis of Salt Lake City, the Olympics, and Bribery*, 23 April, available from: https://nanopdf.com/download/view-evelyn-riveras-portfolio_pdf [accessed 1/2022].

Ross, E.A. (1909) 'The criminaloid', *White-Collar Criminal: The Offender in Business and the Professions* (Eds. G. Geis, 2017 [1968]), Abingdon: Routledge.
Scott, M. (2011) 'Henry Kissinger recommended for Fifa anti-corruption squad', *The Guardian*, 2 June, available from: www.theguardian.com/football/2011/jun/02/henry-kissinger-sepp-blatter-fifa [accessed 1/2022].
Shapiro, S.P. (1984) *Wayward Capitalists: Targets of Securities and Exchange Commission*, New Haven: Yale University Press.
Siddons, L. (1999) 'IOC expels six members in Salt Lake City scandal', *The Guardian*, 17 March, available from: www.theguardian.com/sport/1999/mar/17/ioc-expels-members-bribes-scandal [accessed 1/2022].
Simon, D.R. (2006) *Elite Deviance* (8th Edition), London: Pearson/Allyn & Bacon.
Simpson, S.S. (2019) 'Reimagining Sutherland 80 years after white-collar crime', *Criminology* 57(2): 189–207.
Simson, V. and Jennings, A. (1992) *Dishonored Games: Corruption, Money & Greed at the Olympics*, London: SP Books.
Slapper, G. and Tombs, S. (1999) *Corporate Crime*, Harlow: Longman.
Smit, B. (2007) *Pitch invasion: Adidas, Puma and the Making of Modern Sport*, London: Penguin.
Smit, B. (2008) *Sneaker Wars: The Enemy Brothers Who Founded Adidas and Puma and the Family Feud That Forever Changed the Business of Sports*, London: Harper Perennial.
Sugden, J. and Tomlinson, A. (1998a) *FIFA and the Contest for World Football: Who Rules the People's Game?* Cambridge: Polity Press.
Sugden, J. and Tomlinson, A. (1998b) 'Power and resistance in the governance of world football: Theorizing FIFA's transnational impact', *Journal of Sport and Social Issues* 22(3): 299–316.
Sugden, J. and Tomlinson, A. (1999) *Great Balls of Fire: How Big Money Is Hijacking World Football*, London: Mainstream.
Sugden, J. and Tomlinson, A. (2003) *Badfellas: FIFA Family at War*, London: Mainstream.
Sugden, J. and Tomlinson, A. (2017) *Football, Corruption and Lies: Revisiting 'Badfellas', the Book FIFA Tried to Ban*, Abingdon: Routledge.
Sutherland, E. (1939) 'The white-collar criminal', 52nd American Sociological Association Conference, 27 December.
Sutherland, E. (1940) 'The white collar criminal', *American Sociological Review* 5: 1–12.
Sutherland, E. (1949) *White-Collar Crime*, New York: Dryden.
Sutherland, E. (1974) *Principles of Criminology*, Chicago: Lippincott.
Sutherland, E. (1983 [1949]) *White-Collar Crime*, New Haven: Yale University Press.
Taylor, I., Walton, P. and Young, J. (1973) *The New Criminology: For a Social Theory of Deviance*, London: Routledge & Kegan Paul Books.
Taylor, I., Walton, P. and Young, J. (eds.) (1975) *Critical Criminology*, London: Routledge & Kegan Paul Books.
Tombs, S. (2007) '"Violence", safety crimes and criminology', *The British Journal of Criminology* 47(4): 531–550.
Tombs, S. (2018) 'Official statistics and hidden crime: Researching safety crimes', *Doing Criminological Research* (Eds. V. Jupp, P. Davies and P. Francis), London: Sage.
Tombs, S. and Whyte, D. (2003) 'Unmasking the crimes of the powerful', *Critical Criminology* 11(3): 217–236.
Tomlinson, A. (2014) *FIFA (Fédération Internationale de Football Association): The Men, the Myths and the Money*, Abingdon: Routledge.
Tomlinson, A. and Young, C. (eds.) (2006) *National Identity and Global Sports Events: Culture, Politics, and Spectacle in the Olympics and the Football World Cup*, Albany: Suny Press.
Urry, J. (2014) *Offshoring*, Cambridge: Polity Press.

Whyte, D. (2007) 'The crimes of neo-liberal rule in Occupied Iraq', *The British Journal of Criminology* 47(2): 177–195.
Whyte, D. (2009) 'Paradoxes of regulation', *Regulating the Illicit Market in Antiquities* (Eds. P. Green and S. MacKenzie), London: Hart, pp. 159–177.
Yallop, D. (1999) *How They Stole the Game*, London: Poetic Publishing.
Yallop, D. (2011) *How They Stole the Game* (2nd Edition), London: Constable & Robinson.

4
GOVERNING YOUNG PEOPLE AND COMMUNITIES THROUGH SPORT

Introduction

Sport is commonly considered to possess a transformative capacity for disadvantaged young people and communities (Kelly, 2011, 2012, 2013; Spaaij, 2009, 2012; Coakley, 2011; Ekholm and Dahlstedt, 2021). Indeed, such assumption has both impacted and informed policymaking related to issues of youth crime and 'anti-social' behaviour amongst young people. Youth programs that involve (to some degree) or revolve around sport now constitute local, regional and national crime reduction strategies (Kelly, 2011, 2012). Accurately demonstrating this, the UK Government (2019) recently announced that it would: 'work with sports organisations such as the [English] Premier League and basketball, boxing and cycling bodies to increase sports activity in youth crime hot spots'.

The widespread and influential assumption sustaining that sport remains an 'effective' tool in reducing or deterring 'crime' and/or 'anti-social behavior' is also commonly amplified by 'ad hominem stories' about how sport had a rescuing effect on an individual from a 'life of crime' (Coalter, 2007: 115). Thus, official rhetoric, public discourses and pre-existing policies surrounding sport and its potential for 'crime reduction' typically set the scene in the growing literature examining sport-based interventions (heron SBIs) (for example, Crabbe, 2000; Kelly, 2011; Spaaij, 2009).

Yet, targeted programmes disproportionately target disadvantaged and vulnerable young people (Kelly, 2012). This has raised a number of questions around the advantages of participating. Furthermore, the extent to which targeted youth projects like SBIs *actually* 'work' remains unclear. This, despite the fact that a corpus of research exists in the area that is evaluative of nature and aims to examine or determine sport's, SBI's and recreation programs' 'effectiveness' or 'success' in reducing youth crime (Witt and Crompton, 1996; Coalter, 2007; Nichols, 2007).

DOI: 10.4324/9781003276791-4

However, the evidence base – which not uncommonly has impacted relevant policies – suffers from being both occasionally anecdotal and underdeveloped. This makes it a difficult exercise to extract any generalisable conclusions from the several isolated cases to overarching questions surrounding SBIs 'effectiveness'. This is further complicated by the fact that terms such as 'effectiveness', 'impact' or 'success' can be defined in a multitude of loose and (in)tangible ways and with the deployment of or emphasis on different indicators of effectiveness.

This chapter will first provide a discussion and some examples of what SBIs involve in practice as a response to 'youth crime' and 'risks'. Then, it will present an overview of and map the contours of the existing, contemporary debates speaking to sport's and SBI's 'effectiveness' in improving young people's lives and reducing 'crime'. This chapter also places SBIs in the theoretical contexts of 'governance' (Kelly, 2011; Ekholm and Dahlstedt, 2021) and wider strategies of social control (Spaaij, 2009). By borrowing insights from the extant literature (e.g. Kelly, 2011; Hartman, 2001; Spaaij, 2009; Chamberlain, 2013), this chapter argues that ongoing criminological perspectives and debates about the community of governance of youth may be useful and applied to understand the current role of SBIs and its governance of young people within them. Moreover, we suggest that the Foucault-inspired concept of 'governing by fun' (for a longer discussion, see Lauss and Szigetvari, 2010) may be usefully applied to targeted sport interventions, as an analytical relation. Finally, an emerging research agenda and our conclusions are outlined. Importantly, we argue for a shift away from questions mainly preoccupied with whether SBIs 'work'. Instead, the argument we present maintains that our understanding of SBIs can be significantly enhanced by in-depth, inter-disciplinary examinations of the exact situations in which SBIs seem to have 'worked' and what the key factors in ensuring this was. It also remains crucial to examine whom exactly the relevant SBI has 'worked for' in light of some of the *dual* purposes that have been attributed to SBIs (see Spaaij, 2009; Kelly, 2011).

Unpacking SBIs and Assumptions Around Sport as a 'Hook'

With this chapter's overarching focus being on sport programs and SBIs, primarily in relation to young people, crime and communities, it remains both useful and necessary to unpack what SBIs entail in closer detail. This again should be seen in context of how 'youth', 'youth crime' and 'youth risk' and the 'appropriate' or punitive responses to the two latter have impacted policies since the early 1990s (for a longer discussion, see Kelly, 2012: 103–104). As mentioned, it can be observed that governments, international organisations, criminal justice agencies, and local and international sporting bodies, confronted with issues of youth crime and 'anti-social' behaviour, have set up, supported or emphasised the need for sporting programs that, in various ways (i.e. social or personal development exercises), tackle, pre-empt or address youth crime and delinquency (Kelly, 2011; Crabbe, 2000; Spaaij, 2009; UN, 2015).

This is hardly a new phenomenon, however. In fact, Crabbe (2000: 382) writes that, historically, in a UK context, 'organized modern sport owes its very existence to the Victorians' attempts to influence and shape attitudes within British public schools and to service the needs of the Empire through the concept of "Muscular Christianity"'. And, at least since the nineteenth century, SBIs have been employed throughout the UK as a response to 'troublesome youth' (Kelly, 2011). Notwithstanding, in the current era, SBIs are linked much tighter to broader policy agendas and even attached to some political parties' major policies. Ultimately, sport has come to play a central role in crime reduction strategies on local, regional and national levels.

A number of targeted youth projects are offered or available for young offenders. These include programs based around athletics, track and field, basketball, boxing, football (soccer) and table tennis. The programs are most commonly organised by criminal justice agencies, sporting professionals, coaches, charities and community-based volunteers, and they share a common and overarching aim that is closely knitted to the idea of providing young people with a diversionary avenue away from an adult life impacted by 'crime' and, more generally, 'criminal behaviour' (Chamberlain, 2013; Smith and Waddington, 2004). Exemplifying this multi-agency approach and the coalescence of different stakeholders that are involved in the diverse sporting programs, Kelly (2012: 105) points out that 'Positive Futures', which she examines, was 'funded primarily by the Home Office and nationally managed by the charity "Catch 22"' and then 'locally delivered by statutory and voluntary agencies'.

It can be argued that sport has been regularly offered as a 'catch-all' intervention and response for loosely defined ideas and conceptualisations of 'youth crime'. SBIs, therefore, are primarily sporting (based) initiatives wherein a mix of public and private stakeholders in the prevention of crime collaborate in order to reduce, pre-empt or deter 'youth crime', whilst concurrently making a path-breaking change for the relevant young individuals impacted by these interventions (Crabbe, 2000; Hartmann and Depro, 2006; Meek, 2014).

On a global level, several examples of SBIs can be identified that offer programs for individuals excluded from school, known to social services or who may have been involved with criminal justice services (Chamberlain, 2013). That includes, inter alia, Midnight Basketball in the US (Hartmann and Depro, 2006), Midnight Football in Sweden (Ekholm and Dahlstedt, 2021), the Sport Steward Program in the Netherlands (Spaaij, 2009), the Vencer Program in Brazil (Spaaij, 2012), the Leyton Orient Community Sports Programme (Crabbe, 2000), the Tottenham Boxing Academy (Chamberlain, 2013) and the Positive Futures in the UK (Crabbe, 2007; Kelly, 2011, 2012).

Questions may then be asked about *why* and under which conditions this pronounced turn *towards* sport has occurred. Not uncommonly, SBIs have been appraised and endorsed by government departments and sporting bodies for their alleged capacity and sheer potential in contributing to 'youth crime reduction' and 'social inclusion' (see Kelly, 2013). And indeed, such assumptions and discourses suggest not only that SBIs are constructive tools in the reduction of crime – since they repeatedly are deployed – but the continued reliance on such programs, to an extent, implies that there is a degree of 'effectiveness' or 'success' attached to SBIs with regard to fulfilling their stated aims or rationales related to crime reduction. It is also interesting to observe that governmental agencies now have resorted to sport interventions to tackle the political and religious radicalisation of young people (see Giulianotti et al., 2019).

As the next sections explain in closer detail, the actual potential or ability of sport to address social issues has been critically questioned (Coakley, 2011; Ekholm, 2013). Yet it is also important to point out that these programs are not solely confined to sport, athletic training and exercises. The programs also deploy sport as a tool to 'help young people realize their potential, obtain training and recognize the importance of the shared community bonds' (Chamberlain, 2013: 1282). Typically, programs also involve educational components that young people must partake in besides sporting activities.

For example, Chamberlain (2013) writes that the students at the Tottenham Boxing Academy also were required to attend lessons that helped them obtain GCSE qualifications in Maths and English. Aspects of education, as well as personal and social development and employability skills are thus some of the key reasons that SBIs are commonly regarded as a 'way out' for 'at-risk' individuals (Coakley, 2011) and considered to have the capacity of providing 'social' and 'cultural capital' and social mobility (Spaaij, 2009, 2012). Fundamentally, sport is often viewed as a 'hook' that attracts young people and steers them away from the streets during late-night hours (Hartman, 2001), the peak hours of crime or other contexts in which 'youth crime' may occur or develop within.

However, according to Coakley (2011), it remains problematic that this exact notion, maintaining that sport is unequivocally 'positive' for development (including Sport for Development and Peace and SBIs), becomes an established assumption. Especially when this assumption is:

> woven into popular narratives, reproduced in uncritical forms, and used by well-meaning people and organizations from wealthy nations to justify the creation of sport programs for populations that lack participation opportunities and face challenges caused by poverty, war, natural disasters, or oppression.
>
> *(ibid.: 307)*

Coakley (2011) goes deeper into the widespread assumptions and beliefs, often held by what he calls the 'sports evangelists', which assist such 'popular narratives'. As he argues, 'sports evangelists' forward a number of evangelistic claims about youth sports. Yet he divides the claims into three main categories. First, that sport assists personal character development and a 'positive development'. This assumption is attached to the belief that sport has *'fertilizer effect'* which can develop young characters and growth. The second assumption is that sport can reform 'at risk' populations'. This view attributes a *'car wash effect'* to sport. Sports become something that 'cleanses character and washes away personal defects so that young people become acceptable to those in mainstream society' (ibid.: 308). Third, Coakley notes that 'sports evangelists' typically proclaim that sport can foster 'social capital', which again can contribute to occupational success and/or civic engagement. Accordingly, this is sport's alleged *'guardian angel effect'*. The practical implications of these claims, when promoted individually and collectively, become evident when they proceed to inform or justify policies and funding decisions, despite being given limited critical evaluation (ibid.).

Against the backdrop of the appraising claims surrounding sport's alleged benefits as a policy tool for young people and their communities, it is highly important that 'sport' is not seen or approached as some idyllic safe-haven for young people: free from any 'undesirable' behaviours, substances or actions (see Chapters 3 and 6). Whereas the mentioned, targeted programs can provide a constructive educational route, facilities and support staff, sport can simultaneously – from a recreational to a professional level – be associated with crime, drugs (Crabbe, 2000; see Chapter 5) and violence (Armstrong, 1998). Concerning the notion of sports as a useful tool for reducing youth drug use, Crabbe (2000) notes that young people in sporting context may instead use or be exposed to 'performance-enhancing drugs' rather than 'recreational drugs' that are more prevalent in non-sporting contexts (see Silverstone, 2006). Following this, sport may in fact serve as an entry route into youth crime or deviance.

As such, sport's potential advantages for young people and communities should not just be passively accepted by academics, commentators, think-tanks or policy-makers. Rather, as this chapter argues, they should be critically explored, interrogated and questioned. The next section provides a scholarly base for such an argument to rest more firmly upon, as we present the lack of empirical and longitudinal evidence for subscribing to such positions. Thus, this section has outlined what SBIs are, and what they generally encompass and offer young people at a basic program level. Furthermore, the basic, but seemingly deeply anchored assumption holding tight to the idea of sport fundamentally changing young individuals' lives – and as a means to reduce or steer away from crime – has been outlined and critically challenged.

Questioning the Effectiveness of SBIs: Young People, Crime and Communities

Against the background of some of the mentioned official discourses and existing arguments, like those holding that SBIs are 'effective in early intervention' and in 'preventing youth crime' (Sport for Change, 2011 cited in Chamberlain, 2013: 1282), Chamberlain (2013: 1282) also warns us about uncritically accepting such claims at face value because of the evidence base which, as he highlights, is 'not as extensive as might be presumed'. Drawing from this, this section seeks to revisit and review this evidence base and go deeper into the discussions or claims that exist surrounding the 'success', 'impact' or 'effectiveness' of SBIs.

A substantial part of the SBI and sports programs research is evaluative in its nature (Witt and Crompton, 1996; Coalter, 2007; Nichols, 2007; Spaaij, 2009, 2012; Meek and Lewis, 2014; Jugl et al., 2021). And moreover, to paint a portrait of the '(in)effectiveness' of SBIs, we review not only existing research – not as confined to SBIs and crime reduction – but also SBIs and their relationship to 'at risk' youth (Witt and Crompton, 1996), 'social inclusion' and 'exclusion' (Kelly, 2013), social mobility and types of 'capital' (Spaaij, 2009, 2012). It is also crucial to highlight that the existing literature is both contemporary and transnational in nature. Despite this, our main argument will resemble that of Crabbe (2000) from the start of the new millennium. He argued that 'little definitive evidence [exists] to support the notion that sports programmes *are effective* in reducing crime and deviance' (p. 382, emphasis added). Almost two decades later, Crabbe's argument can be largely echoed.

The early literature on SBIs and socially vulnerable or disadvantaged youth was predominantly positivist and employed agency developmental approaches (Haudenhuyse et al., 2012). Some early assessments were also positive of sport programs' effectiveness (see West and Crompton, 2001; MacMahon, 1990), which of course is one potential explanation for why policymakers have turned towards and relied on sport as a solution for social ills (Williams et al., 2015). However, the academic research on SBIs has advanced over the last decades. It has become more complex and pluralistic methodologically. Still, it is merely a few years ago that Chamberlain (2013), who examined SBIs effect on 'at risk' individuals and 'youth crime', could reach a conclusion maintaining the following:

> Indeed it was noted that research evidence exists which reinforces the positive role that sport can play in changing the lives of some young people for the better. *But the limitations of the available literature to conclusively support SBIs claims to success were also noted. There is a lack of methodologically robust evidence to support the argument that participation in sporting activity can directly lead to a reduction in antisocial and offending behaviour.* In addition, it was noted how SBI's can act as a social control mechanism and in doing so may serve to mask the broader structural inequalities, which often shape a young person's lived experience of growing up in marginalized and stigmatized communities.
> *(Chamberlain, 2013: 1288, emphasis added)*

Thus, there is some evidence that SBIs can be 'effective': both in reducing crime and in developing young individuals. So, it remains crucial to highlight that we do not contest the immediate, but often individual or isolated success stories. For instance, Nichols (1997) argued that sport can play a role in reducing youth crime by diverting youths and assisting a pro-social development as well as enhancing self-esteem. Whilst being alive to the issues of providing tangible evidence, Nichols argues that sport has the capacity for creating a sense of control over one's life and that sport can act as a 'hook' and reduce young individuals' opportunities or abilities to commit crimes. For example, Nichols writes that '[a] simple explanation of programmes' effectiveness in reducing crime is that whilst participating on a programme the participant is not able to take part in crime at the same time' (ibid.: 183). However, this does not automatically or necessarily mean 'sport' is *the* component that renders a program 'effective'. Rather, it could be the basic availability of a space or location to be present at, or a program to attend. As Chamberlain (2013) writes, the evidence of 'effectiveness' typically lack robustness and is commonly anecdotal. Further, the indicators of 'effectiveness' deployed by researchers differ, and must be contextualised.

One obvious way of measuring SBIs programs 'effectiveness' in this context could be by exploring before-and-after crime rates. Nichols (1997), for instance, claimed that a program in Huddersfield (taking place from schools finished and until 6 pm) resulted in 'substantial reduction in vandalism on the school premises' (p. 183). However, there are problems with this type of evidence because there are inherent difficulties involved in separating the effect of an SBI program from the effect of other utilised crime reduction strategies in the same region, city, neighbourhood or even schoolyard.

Moreover, rather than offending rates *per se*, SBI's 'impacts' and 'effectiveness' on youth lives must also be seen as related to their contribution to participants' socio-economic conditions, forms of capital (see Spaaij, 2009, 2012), inclusion (Kelly, 2013), employability opportunities, as well as decrease or increase in anti-social behaviour and recorded crimes. Especially SBIs are not merely aiming to achieve 'crime prevention' but, as mentioned, have certain educational and social components (and thus related aims) attached to them, too.

Whilst there is anecdotal evidence that SBIs can be 'effective', Coalter (2007) questions why these assumptions are maintained, and yet writes that participating in a sport-based program can have certain impacts on participating individuals. Indeed, certain findings add to Coalter's sceptical stance. Such warnings are also issued by Kelly (2012), who writes that over-stating SBIs' abilities to prevent crime can be problematic. In a UK context, Kelly's (2011, 2012, 2013) findings make it possible to critically question the 'success' or 'effectiveness' of SBIs when it comes to 'social inclusion' and 'crime reduction'. Kelly (2011, 2013) qualitatively examines four Positive Futures projects in the UK. Here, in some isolated incidents, SBIs have been impactful or successful.

Kelly (2013) evaluates 'success' according to four delineated themes. First, that is 'sports for all' – which is how sport facilitates access to otherwise unaffordable or inaccessible leisure provisions and/or provides sport activities for groups likely to be excluded from mainstream sporting services. The second theme is 'social cohesion' or 'community development' related to the outcome of bringing (divided) communities together. Third is a 'pathway to work' – which is the ways in which an SBI can encourage labour market participation and/or (re)engagement with education or training. Fourth, some programs maintained that they were 'giving a voice' to young people by enabling active participation via consultation. Indeed, Kelly finds that the research sites achieved 'varying degrees of "success" as a method of social inclusion in relation to these themes' (p. 131).

Thus, whilst finding some evidence of 'effectiveness' or 'success', Kelly notes that this was, and could only be inherently restricted because SBIs still failed to transform the root causes for the same young people's initial social exclusion. Therefore, whilst providing access to free sporting activities indeed suggests a level of 'social inclusion' – that sporting programs can provide – Kelly also emphasises that access does not 'address the socio-structural foundations of young people's initial exclusion' (ibid.: 144), whereas access and activities are highly dependent on available funding streams. Therefore, 'social inclusion' is highly funding-dependent and, overall, SBIs are 'inevitably restricted' (ibid.: 145). This does, of course, connect with the argument that sport, fully and wholly by itself, is no straightforward recipe for 'positive' impacts (Coakley, 2011) and that sport must not be viewed in 'isolation from other social spheres, such as the family, education, labour market and government' (Spaaij, 2009: 262). Essentially, there is nothing ingrained in the nature of sport that means it, by default, is an effective crime prevention tool or emancipatory activity.

Kelly (2011) also examines SBIs in relation to wider strategies for governing youth crime and anti-social behaviour. Crucially, Kelly argues that SBIs 'govern at distance' and serve a purpose of being 'agents of social control' (Kelly, 2011: 276). As argued, SBI staff, managers, partners and participants suggest that SBIs contribute to 'crime reduction' by providing alternative environments, supporting social relationships and changes to how transgressive behaviour is being dealt with, through a range of community partners. By drawing upon criminological perspectives speaking to community's governance of youth, Kelly writes that SBIs thus become tools for regulating 'at risk' youngsters under broader 'responsibilisation' strategies whilst failing to address structural inequalities. Significantly, this feeds into our discussion in the next section on how sport can conceal social problems that are often seen as generating crime (i.e. poverty, unemployment). Therefore, SBIs and targeted youth projects more broadly can be interpreted as neoliberal governance mechanisms, although they – for obvious reasons – are not signposted as such.

Arguments carrying some resemblance to those of Kelly are provided by Spaaij (2009) in the Dutch context. In Rotterdam, Spaaij examines the 'Sport Steward Program'. Indeed, Spaaij also finds several immediate positive impacts and success stories on young individuals' lives, employment prospects, attitudes and friendships. Nonetheless, the Steward Program, he argues, 'contributed to objective and subjective social mobility of some participants, in most cases it is more suitable to highlight participants' relatively modest increases in cultural, social and/or economic capital' (ibid.: 261). In the wider context, Spaaij also views the program as fulfilling neoliberal agendas, though these are camouflaged as a progressive sporting initiative that ultimately seeks to have a civilising effect on 'at risk' individuals, prevent large-scale urban unrest, segregation and a culture of unemployment. He argues that:

> Ultimately, they [sport-based programs like SSP] are a means through which governmental organizations and their partners seek to civilize and regulate

these 'at risk' minority ethnic youth to normalize their behaviour (i.e. not 'dropping out', contingent work, refrain from criminal behaviour), to make them meet their 'societal responsibilities' and to 'integrate' them into Dutch society. Rather than simply being a sign of 'individual freedom and opportunity', sport-based intervention programs of this kind also serve as a form of social control and regulation. Sport is increasingly becoming a substantial aspect of the neoliberal policy repertoire of cities like Rotterdam aimed at generating social order in disadvantaged inner-city neighbourhoods.

(ibid.: 263)

Whilst we set out to discuss the implications of such arguments in the next section, the findings again point towards a modest impact on these young people's socio-economic situations and social mobility. Ultimately, the program did not effectively prevent systems of social reproduction. Therefore, this connects with Coakley (1998: 2), who powerfully argued for the need to see 'sports as *sites* for socialisation experiences, not *causes* of socialisation outcomes' and that we need to 'de-mythologise' sport to understand better when sport work, for what subjects and under what conditions.

The mentioned literature to this point has mostly examined SBIs in what can be considered the 'Global North'. Spaaij (2012), however, provides insight into an SBI in the 'Global South', in Brazil. Drawing upon Bourdieu's forms of capital, Spaaij examines how SBIs here may – or may not – contribute to 'social' and 'cultural' capital. The program that is being examined aims to provide employment prospects for young people in Rio de Janeiro's *favelas* that are characterised by high unemployment levels and poverty (Spaaij, 2012: 80). Again, it is found that the program had some immediate positive impacts on the enhancement of 'social capital' and 'cultural capital' amongst disadvantaged youngsters, whereas it is argued that the program's contribution was related to its ability of developing links with institutional agents. The 'major success marker' for the program was its 'multi-agency approach', Spaaij writes (p. 92). Therefore, the single case study suggests that SBIs indeed have transformative potential – and holds that if there is significant focus on the matters of 'ownership, participation and partnership' (ibid.: 94), *then* SBIs may have long-term impact on participating young people's lives. The study thus provides some answers on *how* an SBI situated within the Brazilian context works.

To summarise, one key issue with the existing research and available data on SBIs is its anecdotal nature, small samples and relatively short time span of existing studies (Chamberlain, 2013). Simply put, there is limited available evidence to conclude that participation in an SBI directly reduces crime. Of course, this is somewhat paradoxical because the conventional presumption and official rhetoric typically endorse sport as a tool for crime reduction and positive youth development. Clearly, there a discrepancy between these discourses, the social realities and the available empirical evidence. Furthermore, it is noted that it is inherently difficult to attribute any potential crime reduction to young people playing or engaging in sport – or if it simply is related to other crime prevention strategies at a national, local or even neighbourhood level. The problem of separating the effect or effectiveness of the different programs employed in the same city or area is, however, not unique to SBIs which is important to underline.

The argument that emerges from this section is one that we share with Chamberlain (2013: 1289), namely that 'Clearly, many people do benefit in one way or another from participating in sport'. Denying this would be cynical (see Van Hout and Phelan, 2014) as there is existing evidence suggesting that SBIs sometimes do benefit participants in individual cases (Kelly, 2012; Spaaij, 2009). Though, as seen, existing studies committed to the social study of SBIs show that this, *in itself* is no panacea. The studied SBIs provide limited scope for social mobility (Spaaij, 2009), and do little – if anything – to challenge, eradicate or impact structural inequalities (Kelly, 2013). This momentously impedes SBI's transformative potential. Moreover, since sport does not operate in isolation from its socio-political contexts, an SBI's 'success' must not be based completely upon its sports-related goals. 'Success' must relate to improvements in young individual's wider, socio-economic contexts. Albeit evidence suggests that SBIs generate some desired and intermediate impacts for their participants, this does not necessarily provide any solutions to wider social problems (Coalter, 2007), inequality, social class or mobility. Therefore, it remains especially problematic that SBIs may come to work as wider strategies or mechanisms for social control (see Spaaij, 2009; Kelly, 2011; Chamberlain, 2013).

Sport-Based Social Control? Governing by Fun and Governing from a Distance

This chapter argues that ongoing criminological debates about community governance of disadvantaged and 'troublesome' youth can be usefully applied to explore and develop our understanding of the role that SBI play within the frameworks for governing young people and the professionals working with them. In that sense, we build largely upon Kelly (2011) when we situate SBIs in the wider context of crime prevention, crime control and risk management in contemporary capitalist societies.

Similarly, Chamberlain (2013) attributed the increased reliance on SBIs over the past decades to a broader shift 'towards a more surveillance heavy "risk aware" punitive system of criminal justice in the UK' (p. 1286). This wide shift happens structurally in crime control contexts (see Mythen and Walklate, 2010) and involves inter alia community-based surveillance and profiling of young people (Chamberlain, 2013). Arguably, such shift also connects with why sport now has become increasingly used as a tool for countering different forms of radicalisation (Giulianotti et al., 2019). SBIs, on a policy level, must hence be seen as moulded by wider pre-emptive strategies of crime prevention, regulation and social control which may enable or reproduce social categorisations or inequalities.

Furthermore, the previous section points out the extant arguments holding that sport can be used as a neoliberal 'policy repertoire' in disadvantaged urban neighborhoods (Spaaij, 2009). SBIs and sporting programs can indeed be analyzed as governmental attempts to regulate, control or monitor individuals that are seen to be or labelled 'at risk', 'criminal', 'violent' or 'deviant'. As such, it may be prudent to also talk about 'sport for social control' (see Chamberlain, 2013). In this view, SBIs work as control mechanisms through which 'troublesome' or underprivileged youngsters are identified, monitored, choreographed and controlled – by public/private institutions – whilst thought to not be 'disturbing' their communities.

It is here we seek to extend the already discussed ideas related to SBIs and 'social control' (Kelly, 2011; Spaaij, 2009; Chamberlain, 2013). We argue that this is where Foucault's concept of 'governmentality' can be usefully applied: particularly to the strategic employment of sport – symbolising something 'fun' – to bring 'at risk' individuals into a controlled, regulated and monitored environment. Foucault (1979) advanced the concept of governmentality as one understanding of 'power'. For Foucault, governmentality referred to 'the organizing of practices (e.g., mentalities, institutions and techniques) through which regulatory power is achieved' (Anderson and Brown, 2010: 546). These practices of control, according to Foucault (1979), encompassed both organisational governance and self-governance. As Anderson and Brown (2010: 547) write, '[n]ew forms of knowledge, rationality, and technology are [consequently] invoked to manage this governance, including strategies such as risk screening, case management insurance, and situational crime prevention'. Yet, such regulatory strategies may also be enacted through neoliberal leisure and sporting contexts or initiatives.

Building further upon the governmentality framework, Lauss and Szigetvari (2010) use Foucault's ideas of 'governing by fun' to hyper-surveilled fan zones at sport mega-events. They argue that fan zones essentially serve to govern and regulate fans, whilst the fans are occupied and having 'fun' due to the range of sporting and commercial activities which the fan zones have to offer. Thus, the fan zones' regulating components are normalised and the fan zones' appealing power serves to organise large crowds, acting as a social control strategy. To be sure, the fan zone differs fundamentally from SBIs. However, we can draw inspiration from this idea and argue that this conceptual relation can benefit an analysis of SBIs.

Arguably, SBIs provide individuals different types of 'fun'. 'Fun' could be in the form of playing different sports, making new friends, increasing self-esteem or feeling a sense of achievement. But simultaneously, some SBIs are found to serve dual purposes as it controls and regulates participants' behavior and essentially normalises and reproduces social categorises and socially excluded youth. As such, the structural inequalities, often seen to be at the roots of 'criminal' or 'anti-social' behaviors (which SBIs seek to challenge), are only paid insufficient attention. Instead, they are 'masked' (Chamberlain, 2013) behind a façade of sporting fun. Processes of 'governance by fun' therefore occur since SBIs – at a distance – can contribute towards the governance of 'disorderly' youth (Kelly, 2011). This occurs superficially without any 'real' commitment to addressing the 'structural inequalities associated with increased "risk" of crime or criminalization' (ibid.). Therefore, it can be argued – as Kelly (2011) notes – that SBIs reflect how the state 'governs at distance'. Adding to this, it may also be appropriate to view SBIs as reflections of attempts to 'govern by fun'. Ideas of 'fun' are thus firmly embedded into the disciplinary and precautionary structures of SBIs and work as a regulator, which can harmonise the interests of stakeholders in 'crime reduction'.

According to Kelly (2011: 236), 'SBI practice is shaped by broader control strategies [and] SBI practitioners contribute to the local interpretation and implementation of youth crime and antisocial behavior reduction policies'. Sport may thereby serve as an entrée for the state and other institutions for the governance of young people and their communities. Significantly then, these mechanisms of social control again call into question the alleged and discussed 'successes' which the political and public narratives not uncommonly claim or use as justifications for SBIs. So, despite existing anecdotal evidence and isolated cases of 'effectiveness', it is argued here that SBIs seemingly are limited in terms of their ability to deal with root causes of structural inequalities. Essentially, this becomes increasingly problematic when sport, in fact, may serve as a site for processes of 'social control', where socially constructed categories of 'at risk' individuals are reinforced or (covertly) normalised.

Shifting the Focus: Towards a Better Understanding of 'How' SBIs Work

This section outlines a number of pathways for future research into the fields of young people, sport programs and crime reduction. Indeed, Giulianotti et al. (2019) recently provided an emerging research agenda for Sport for Development and Peace (SDP) research. Here, they noted that sports-related interventions and activities now had grown into a 'heavily researched subject' (ibid.: 411). This chapter shares their view. Indeed, a body of literature exists that empirically examines SBIs, SDP and other sporting programs. However, as their articulated research agenda suggests, and as our chapter mutually reinforces, there is still a pressing need for critically informed research within the global field of SDP and sporting programs such as the ones we have discussed, mostly related to crime reduction objectives. Such research does not need to be confined to criminology and would benefit from insights from scholars of sociology, social policy, education and youth studies, to name a few.

As initially noted in this chapter, a volume of the pre-existing literature on SBIs has been evaluative (Witt and Crompton, 1996; Coalter, 2007; Nichols, 2007; Spaaij, 2009, 2012). However, as our key contentions maintain: despite this pronounced focus on and drive to evaluating SBIs, this has not taken us much closer to an established understanding of sport's impacts on young people and communities. In fact, against the backdrop of such a pronounced focus on evaluating sport-based programs, the evidence base remains limited, and it cannot empirically support claims surrounding sport's 'good' or 'positive' impacts on young people and local communities. Moreover, the existing literature suggesting that sport does not work is also commonly based upon single case studies and occasionally anecdotal evidence.

Therefore, concerning future inter-disciplinary research seeking to understand SBIs and sport-related programs, we argue that the oft-pursued question about whether sport or (more specifically) SBIs '*do work?*' may be somewhat misplaced. That is because we simply are left with little fixed idea of what 'working' means or looks like in the relevant context. For this reason, a more appropriate question to be guided by may be to ask in what situations and under which conditions SBIs looked to have 'worked', and what the key factors were. Moreover, as our discussion about 'social control' and monitoring implies, it may also be necessary to ask whom sport programs and SBIs ultimately are beneficial for. Fundamentally, this links up with the call made by Chamberlain (2013: 1289) for 'SBI advocates to pursue a "bottom-up" rather than "top down" view of how SBIs can and should operate'.

Upon proceeding, it is therefore crucial to gather the individual, lived experiences and perceptions of participants in SBIs. Following Kelly (2012), it remains important that both intended and unintended consequences are better understood in targeted programmes, through both interviews and more field immersed approaches such as ethnographies (see Chapter 6). This could provide in-depth answers in relation to some of the previous questions, whilst allowing for the adaption of a 'bottom-up' stance. Importantly, this would facilitate the continuation of transnational case studies that are both empirically and theoretically informed (see Spaaij, 2009; Kelly, 2011) by critical theories. However, it remains extra pertinent to examine SBIs in a 'Global South' context (i.e. Spaaij, 2012) given the clear dominance of studies focussed on sport programs situated within the 'Global North'.

Finally, this chapter proposes that future SBI-related work should consider the official narratives and rhetoric that commonly are constructed or employed when SBIs are justified and then become established notions and presumptions impacting policy and funding decisions (Crabbe, 2000; Kelly, 2011; Spaaij, 2009). By deployment of critical discourse analysis techniques, the narratives surrounding and portrayals of sport – as an unequivocal 'good' that *will* benefit young people – could be further examined and unpacked. Such discourses must be seen as particularly important, accounting for their capacity to impact policy and decision-making, funding, and ultimately, impact in some way or another, young people's futures and lives. Therefore, paying closer detail to the justifications, rationales, reasoning and promises that are made in official policy documents, announcements and media releases remains important in the future study of SBIs. The evidence that is derived from such examination could then, of course, be juxtaposed with the social realities of sporting programmes, which underscores how the points on our research agenda are inter-linked.

Summary: Young People, Communities and Governing through Sport

The United Nations (UN) (2015: 10) has maintained that sport 'is an important enabler of sustainable development' and that it contributes to the 'empowerment of women and of young people, individuals and communities as well as to health, education and social inclusion objectives'. In the present day, sport is commonly believed to represent a positive and empowering tool, and, against this backdrop, this chapter has critically explored current issues related to the governance of young people and communities through the lens of sport. It is evident that sport is often assumed to have transformative capacities for disadvantaged or 'troublesome' youth (Coakley, 2011). Such assumption, which has often rested upon limited empirical evidence, has impacted and directed policymaking: sport currently plays a role in crime reduction and social inclusion strategies (Kelly, 2011) and simultaneously as mechanisms for social control (Spaaij, 2009).

To be sure, this chapter does not contest that sport or SBIs in isolated cases have had positive effects on individuals in both the immediate and longer terms. However, this chapter critically interrogates the previous perspective concerning sport and then the employment of SBIs as programs which aim to have a transformative effect on young people's lives and to reduce crime. As our chapter has demonstrated, sport undeniably creates different attitudes, in different young people, in different places, at different times. This renders the ideas of employing sport as a 'catch-all' intervention extremely complicated. This remains one of the reasons why Chamberlain (2013: 1292, emphasis added) holds that:

> Sport Based Initiative advocates must seek to promote a *less homogenous idea of what an SBI is*, as well as be more sensitive to the diverse needs of young people, particularly if they are to tackle the underlying structural inequalities that arguably create the social problem, that is youth crime in the first place.

In this chapter, we have also restated the potential for governmentality theories to be applied to SBIs, and how SBIs may proceed to normalise and reproduce social categorisations that facilitate conditions for inequalities to preserve or even grow. As suggested, the state's and other agencies' 'governance at distance' (Kelly, 2011) can be embedded in sport through SBIs. And as we propose, SBIs may, by following Foucault's (1979) lead, be interpreted as efforts to 'govern by fun' (cf. Lauss and Szigetvari, 2010). This is closely linked to the idea of sport being utilised for its social 'goods', 'positives' and elements of joy and pleasure (Coakley, 2011). Yet, the risk is that this concurrently distracts us from, conceals or mutes SBI's neoliberal agendas as well as the wider power relations and structural issues impacting young people and their communities (see Spaaij, 2009).

So, overall, we argue that if sport programs are to play a sustainable role in crime prevention or in challenging social and structural inequalities, then the aims of the relevant program must also exceed 'merely' the provision of access to sport. Considering the paradoxical lack of robust evidence (Chamberlain, 2013), we also maintain that academic and practitioner-oriented evaluations of SBIs must move away from the common question of whether SBIs *work* and progressively towards critical examinations of in which situations SBIs seem to have worked; and what the key conditions for these outcomes were. And, finally, whom SBIs actually work for, given the range of organisations, communities and individuals that impact or are impacted by SBIs. Considering this, it may be useful to adopt a program theory approach (see Coalter, 2007) which identifies 'the critical success factors of an intervention [and] the mechanisms via which it works' (Giulianotti et al., 2019: 426). Finally, we have argued for a bottom-up approach that gathers lived experiences of SBI participants and marginalised youth. Overall, such bottom-up approaches would assist our current understanding of the different types of programs and what is required to fulfill their potential and could help unpack the potential of SBIs as effective crime reduction and policy tools.

References

Anderson, L. and Brown, M. (2010) 'Expanding horizons of risk in criminology', *Sociology Compass* 4(8): 544–554.
Armstrong, G. (1998) *Football Hooligans: Knowing the Score*, Oxford: Berg.
Chamberlain, J.M. (2013) 'Sports-based intervention and the problem of youth offending: A diverse enough tool for a diverse society?' *Sport in Society* 16(10): 1279–1292.
Coakley, J. (1998) *Sport in Society: Issues and Controversies*, Boston, MA: McGraw-Hill.
Coakley, J. (2011) 'Youth sports: What counts as "positive development?"' *Journal of Sport and Social Issues* 35: 306–324.
Coalter, F. (2007) *A Wider Social Role for Sport: Who's Keeping the Score?* London: Routledge.
Crabbe, T. (2000) 'A sporting chance? Using sport to tackle drug use and crime', *Drugs: Education, Prevention, and Policy* 7(4): 381–391.
Crabbe, T. (2007) *Positive Futures: Putting the Pieces Together? The 2007 Annual Positive Futures Monitoring and Evaluation Report*, London: Home Office.
Ekholm, D. (2013) 'Sport and crime prevention: Individuality and transferability in research', *Journal of Sport for Development* 1(2): 26–38.
Ekholm, D. and Dahlstedt, M. (2021) 'Pedagogies of (de)liberation: Salvation and social inclusion by means of Midnight Football', *Sport, Education and Society* 26(1): 58–71.
Foucault, M. (1979) 'Governmentality', *Ideology and Consciousness* 6: 5–21.
Giulianotti, R., Coalter, F., Collison, H. and Darnell, S.C. (2019) 'Rethinking Sportland: A new research agenda for the sport for development and peace sector', *Journal of Sport and Social Issues* 43(6): 411–437.
Hartman, D. (2001) 'Notes on midnight basketball and the cultural politics of recreation, race, and at-risk urban youth', *Journal of Sport and Social Issues* 25(4): 339–371.
Hartmann, D. and Depro, B. (2006) 'Rethinking sports-based community crime prevention: A preliminary analysis of the relationship between midnight basketball and urban crime rates', *Journal of Sport and Social Issues* 30(2): 180–196.
Haudenhuyse, R.P., Theebom, M. and Coalter, F. (2012) 'The potential of sports-based social interventions for vulnerable youth: Implications for sport coaches and youth workers', *Journal of Youth Studies* 15(4): 437–454.
Jugl, I., Bender, D. and Lösel, F. (2021) 'Do sports programs prevent crime and reduce reoffending? A systematic review and meta-analysis on the effectiveness of sports programs', *Journal of Quantitative Criminology*: 1–52.
Kelly, L. (2011) '"Social inclusion" through sports-based interventions?' *Critical Social Policy* 31(1): 126–150.
Kelly, L. (2012) 'Representing and preventing youth crime and disorder: Intended and unintended consequences of targeted youth programmes in England', *Youth Justice* 12(2): 101–117.

Kelly, L. (2013) 'Sports-based interventions and the local governance of youth crime and antisocial behavior', *Journal of Sport & Social Issues* 37(3): 261–283.

Lauss, G. and Szigetvari, A. (2010) 'Governing by fun: EURO 2008 and the appealing power of fan zones', *Soccer & Society* 11(6): 737–747.

MacMahon, J.R. (1990) 'The psychological benefits of exercise and the treatment of delinquent adolescents', *Sports Medicine* 9: 344–351.

Meek, R. (2014) *Sport in Prison: Exploring the Role of Physical Activity in Correctional Settings*, London: Routledge.

Meek, R. and Lewis, G. (2014) 'The impact of a sports initiative for young men in prison: Staff and participant perspectives', *Journal of Sport & Social Issues* 38: 95–123.

Mythen, G. and Walklate, S. (2010) 'Pre-crime, regulation, and counter-terrorism: Interrogating anticipatory risk: Gabe Mythen and Sandra Walklate explore the extent to which risk is being utilised more intensively in the development of crime control policies', *Criminal Justice Matters* 81(1): 34–36.

Nichols, G. (1997) 'A consideration of why active participation in sport and leisure might reduce criminal behaviour', *Sport, Education and Society* 2(2): 181–190.

Nichols, G. (2007) *Sport and Crime Reduction: The role of Sports in Tackling Youth Crime*, London: Routledge.

Smith, A. and Waddington, I. (2004) 'Using "sport in the community schemes" to tackle crime and drug use among young people: Some policy issues and problems', *European Physical Education Review* 10(3): 279–298.

Silverstone, D. (2006) 'Pub space, rave space and urban space: Three different night-time economies', *Drugs, Clubs and Young People* (Eds. B. Saunders), Aldershot: Ashgate, pp. 141–151.

Spaaij, R. (2009) 'Sport as a vehicle for social mobility and regulation of disadvantaged urban youth: Lessons from Rotterdam', *International Review for the Sociology of Sport* 44(2–3): 247–264.

Spaaij, R. (2012) 'Building social and cultural capital among young people in disadvantaged communities: Lessons from a Brazilian sport-based intervention program', *Sport, Education and Society* 17(1): 77–95.

UK Government. (2019) 'Press release: Government to harness power of sport to help tackle youth violence', available from: www.gov.uk/government/news/government-to-harness-power-of-sport-to-help-tackle-youth-violence [accessed 01/2020].

UN. (2015) 'Resolution adopted by the general assembly on 25 September 2015', A/RES/701, available from: www.un.org/ga/search/view_doc.asp?symbol=A/RES/70/1&Lang=E [accessed 01/2022].

Van Hout, M.C. and Phelan, D. (2014) 'A grounded theory of fitness training and sports participation in young adult male offenders', *Journal of Sport & Social Issues* 38: 124–147.

West, S.T. and Crompton, J.L. (2001) 'A review of the impact of adventure programs on at risk youth', *Journal of Park and Recreation Administration* 19: 113–140.

Williams, D., Collingwood, L., Coles, J. and Schmeer, S. (2015) 'Evaluating a rugby sport intervention programme for young offenders', *Journal of Criminal Psychology* 5(1): 51–64.

Witt, P.A. and Crompton, J.L. (eds.) (1996) *Recreation Programs That Work for at-Risk Youth: The Challenge of Shaping the Future*, State College, PA: Venture Publishing.

5
MODES OF SECURITY, GOVERNANCE AND SURVEILLANCE IN SPORT

Introduction

Sport can be a significant site for social control and specific modes of governance and monitoring. Indeed, wider social, economic and political developments in the fields of security and surveillance have impacted sport. So, in the context of sport mega-event security and the surveillance of athletic bodies and performances, this chapter will probe further into current debates surrounding security, surveillance and governance in sport. Research into 'security risks', 'terrorism' and 'surveillance' at sport mega-events or in sport has grown apace following the 9/11 attacks on the United States in 2001 (Falcous and Silk, 2005; Silk and Falcous, 2005; Taylor and Toohey, 2007; Lee Ludvigsen and Millward, 2020; Lee Ludvigsen, 2022; Cleland, 2019; Armstrong et al., 2017). The term 'mega-events' is commonly used to describe 'large-scale cultural (including commercial and sporting) events which have a dramatic character, mass popular appeal and international significance' (Roche, 2000: 1). This chapter will draw upon currents in critical criminological research into 'security' and 'terrorism' to explore issues associated with attempts to secure safety at sport mega-events. In particular, this chapter will draw upon the concept of a 'security legacy'. The concept of 'legacy' has become the standard way in which the civic benefits believed to follow from hosting a sports mega-event are presented in bids for events (e.g. job creation, increased tourism, infrastructure investment, urban regeneration, etc.). The concept of a security legacy refers to the similarly lasting impacts of security strategies and technologies after the games have taken place (Eick, 2011; Giulianotti, 2013; Giulianotti and Klauser, 2010; Toohey and Taylor, 2012). Importantly, however, this chapter is not solely concerned with surveillance and security as applied to the rather exceptional moments like sport mega-events. We also seek to explore

DOI: 10.4324/9781003276791-5

typologies of surveillance that, more broadly, are identifiable in sport and also serve as broader mechanisms of governance for the monitoring of behaviours, athletic bodies, performances and doping. Thus, this chapter situates these modes of governance – which again may be understood as forms of power (cf. Coleman and Sim, 2000) – in sport, and as apparent in both exceptional and far more 'mundane' settings. This illuminates the time and space diffuse nature of security and surveillance in sport.

Maurice Roche (2000) led the way in critically investigating the history, politics and sociology of structure, organisation, planning and delivering of 'mega-events'. His book *Mega Events and Modernity* (2000) provided an investigation of two wide-scale mega-events, World Fairs/Expos and the Olympic Games. Specifically he examined the Crystal Palace Expo (1851), the Olympic Games that were held in Berlin (1936) and Barcelona (1992) to argue that sport (in both local and international senses) offers the potential to provide significant cultural resources for people in late-modernity to use in order to adapt to the economic and political opportunities for life and that mega-events provide citizens with enduring motivations and special opportunities to participate in collective projects which have the characteristics of structuring social space and time. Host cities use the opportunities afforded by global coverage of sport mega-events as ways of demonstrating the cultural distinctiveness of their regional and aim to capitalise upon this with wider economic impacts, such as attracting increased numbers of tourists or new industry to the area (Roche, 2000). Mega-events are therefore culturally, economically and politically important in national and international domains. Roche's book proved to be influential and spawned a growth of social scientific interest in the field. When Roche (2006) returned to these debates, the study of mega-events – and in particular sports mega-events – had grown (see Horne and Manzenreiter, 2004; Jones, 2001).

Taking into account the diversity in which sports mega-events are conceptualised, this chapter will use ideas borrowed from critical security studies to reconsider social science of sport literature discussing the themes of 'safety' and 'security', interrogate the idea of sports mega-events 'security legacies', before moving on to examining 'surveillance' in the wider fields of sport. By doing the latter, we combine and provide an extension to the two existing sets of literature on 'surveillance' in sport. These are focussed on anti-doping (Park, 2005; Waddington, 2010; Hanstad and Loland, 2009; Møller, 2011) and mega-event surveillance (Sugden, 2012; Klauser, 2017). Crucially, this chapter advances three relevant typologies of 'surveillance' in sport. Corresponding with this chapter's first half, one typology involves 'surveillance' for 'safety' and 'security' purposes. However, we also explore 'lateral surveillance', and finally, 'surveillance' of the athletic performance and body. Whilst we acknowledge that other types of surveillance still exist across sport, the types we discuss collectively demonstrate how modes of security and surveillance governance in sport should not be conflated with technological hardware whilst translating into a blurredness around 'who is watching who' in diverse settings.

Critical Security Studies, Critical Terrorism Studies and Sport

Critical security studies share an epistemological position with much in the critical criminological canon, by viewing state and the economy as shaping social relations and articulating 'security measures' as the concretisation of 'power' (see Loader and Walker, 2007). However, like critical criminology, critical security studies are not a uniform and uncontested terrain. Indeed, Wyn Jones (1999) argued that there are at least two different ways in which it is understood. A first broad approach to understanding critical security studies (lower case) has been to include all approaches that are critical of the realist orthodoxy within security studies, in much the same way that critical criminology can be discussed as including a multitude of critical responses to dominant official discourses of criminality. Second, there is the tighter defined 'Critical Security Studies' (CSS) school of thought (which is sometimes referred to as the 'Welsh School' of security studies), from which members argue that the application of Frankfurt School-inspired 'Critical Theory' (upper case) to the field of security studies generates a range of theoretical, methodological, and normative issues that seek to promote emancipatory rather than restrictive politics, which Wyn Jones (1999: 166) – a key figure in the CSS – argued 'focus', 'deepen', 'broaden' and 'extend' security studies. Thus, for Wyn Jones (1999), CSS should be *focussed* on its theory and practice by promoting emancipatory politics; *deeper* by understanding 'security' to be a derivative concept given that differing understandings in world politics see it to mean different things, with different referents; *broader* in viewing the threat and possible usage of military force as proving the sole threat or means of providing 'security' (in other words, a security that extends beyond the military) and, *extended* through a growth in the security studies agenda to recognise both a multiplicity of issues and actors beyond the state as sites of insecurity – thus, taking into account the actions of individuals. In short, the CSS approach fits inside the first broad definition but not all broad approaches fit within the Welsh School's understanding of CSS. Tying the two approaches together, Bellamy (2005) argues that both broadly share a view that security is a process as much as a condition and throughout history this process has focussed on determining the most appropriate relationship between individuals and political communities.

In both variants of the approach, critical understandings of 'security' emanate from established accounts of 'whom' or 'what' is to be secured. It follows, then, that there can be no real threats or 'security' without any referents to what might be 'secured'. However, what is truly 'secured' might be an open question. When it is nation-states that are secured, there is an open debate as to whether that country is the true referent or its citizens (as typically argued in the realist traditions).[1] Bellamy (2005: 141) argues that CSS scholars maintain that human beings should be ultimate referents of security because it is only with reference to real people that the concept of security can have any meaning. A CSS critique would therefore be levelled when the referent for security is something that is not an individual, group or community but – for instance – a political or economic structure. Thus, in the

CSS tradition, critical questions have to be asked about who – if anyone – that is ultimately made safer by security measures (see also Loader and Walker, 2007; Lee Ludvigsen, 2022).

In the post-9/11 period, 'security' has become a sizable part of the budgets planning and delivery of sport mega-events (Sugden, 2012; Armstrong et al., 2017; Lee Ludvigsen, 2022). For instance, Giulianotti (2013: 96) points out that the security expenditure for the 2000 Sydney Olympics was $180m, whilst at London in 2012 it reached an estimated $1.9bn. Further, in light of the announcement that the 2022 FIFA World Cup would be held in Qatar, *The International Centre for Sport Security (ICSS)* was launched in Doha in March 2011. ICSS is a non-profit-making international organisation aimed at becoming a global hub of expertise in the field of major event security. The need to 'secure' Qatar, football fans and other visitors to the country during the event is understood, what/who they are being 'secured' from remains questionable? To answer, an examination of the key premises within 'critical security studies' is needed.

An obvious answer might be 'terrorists'. However, Castells (2011 [1997]) suggests we should ask 'what is a "terrorist"?'. To begin to answer this question, we turn to critical terrorism studies which is a subfield within the study of terrorism in the light of 9/11 by adopting some of the theories and ideas prevalent in critical security studies to change the epistemological grounds upon which 'terrorism' is understood. To be sure, Simons (2018: 324) pointed out that 'there are some 200 different definitions of terrorism in existence' and this led Jackson et al. (2009) to question 'the treatment of "terrorism" as an objective, ontologically stable phenomenon that can be studied unproblematically'. As such, Jackson et al. (2020) claim that the surrounding discourse of the Western state-centrism on research into terrorism has led to a complete reluctance to consider the motivations of terrorists. They argue that the hegemonic discourse that emerges from this casts 'terrorists' as evil 'individuals' neglecting a focus on their actions because of the risk of appearing to justify or condone the outcome of their acts.[2]

Through surveying the academic literature on 'security' in sport, two labels emerge to describe what are often thought of as 'wrong doers' (although these labels are sometimes problematised): the 'hooligan' and the 'terrorist'. This is interesting given that 'hooligan' and 'terrorist' have: first, both been described as emotive signifiers that usually stir negative feelings amongst the public (see Braun and Vliegenthart, 2008; Rahmani Khalili and Safavian, 2019 on hooliganism and Clément, 2021; Macagno and Walton, 2019; Palmer, 2012; Taylor, 2007 on terrorism) and whilst second, there has been great dispute within both the sociology of sport and critical security studies about what a 'hooligan' or a 'terrorist' might definitely be (see Free and Hughson, 2003).[3] For instance, Primoratz (1990: 129) points out that the word 'terrorism' is used in 'so many incompatible ways' to describe many different actions but points out that its usages cause 'most of us to view it with moral repugnance'. Making these points does not mean that we deny that either 'terrorist' actions or 'hooligan' violence can exist, but it does mean that – following from CSS scholars – critical thought must go into unpacking what such labels mean in a socio-political context, along with whom or what is secured in challenges to the labelled individuals.[4]

Unpacking 'Safety' and 'Security': The Absence of 'Hooligans' and 'Terrorists'?

In *The Transparency of Evil* (1993), Jean Baudrillard likens 'hooliganism' to 'terrorism':

> Behind the tragedy at the Heysel Stadium, in fact, lies a kind of state terrorism. . . . Mrs Thatcher successfully destroyed the miners by means of just such a calculated bloody-mindedness: the strikers ended up discrediting themselves in the eyes of society. She has a similar strategy towards unemployed hooligans: it is as though she turns them into commandos herself, then sends them abroad; she condemns them, of course, but their brutality remains the very same brutality that she demonstrates in the exercise of her power. Liquidation policies of this kind, more or less drastic in their application, are the stock in trade, justified by the appeal to crisis, of all modern states. They inevitably entail extreme measures of the sort mentioned, which are merely the diverted effects of a terrorism to which the State is in no way opposed.
>
> Baudrillard (1993: 77–78)

Baudrillard talks with specific reference to 1985's Heysel Stadium football disaster in which 39 Juventus F.C. fans died before the club's European Cup final against Liverpool on 29 May. In the immediate aftermath, the British Prime Minister, Margaret Thatcher and many media sources blamed Liverpool F.C. supporters for the disaster – castigating all of the club's fans for the involvement of just a few and calling for all English clubs to be banned from European club competition for 5 years (Scraton, 2016; Young, 1986). This request was granted by UEFA.[5] Incidents such as Heysel colored a populist image that conflated football fans with 'hooliganism' in the 1980s (Goldblatt, 2006). The subsequent Belgian Parliamentary Commission of Inquiry told how the disaster unfolded by pointing out that the Heysel stadium was 'dilapidated' with structurally weak 'columns, crush barriers and steps' and terracing inside the stadium that was 60 years old and poorly maintained (Scraton, 2016: 25). This did not remove all 'blame' from the shoulders of some fans but clearly attributed it to a complex set of circumstances.

Baudrillard (1993) draws upon the disaster to critique banal and more extreme ideas associated to 'evil' within 'The Mirror of Terrorism'. In this chapter, Baudrillard connects 'hooligan' fan behaviour to 'state terrorism' that used governmental structures that crush, rather than help, poorer segments of society. As such, Baudrillard inverts the meaning of 'terrorism' from its conventional usage in so far as the state provides the terror over individuals not the other way around; indeed, individual or smaller groups of 'terrorists' are, for Baudrillard, 'hyper real' occurring in a vacuum, with no witnesses, but broadcast as 'news' on massive screens, often to an international audience.

Atkinson and Young (2012) utilise Baudrillard's idea of 'hyper reality' to compare the mass mediation and discursive framing of 'terrorism' at the Salt Lake City 2002 Winter Games – the first post-9/11 Olympic event – in the British and North American press. Their analysis found concerns about security at the Olympics plugged into an 'everyday xenophobia' (see Gotsbachner, 2001) by paralleling American fears about terrorism with the extent to which systems of civil protection could be breached by 'foreigners'. In the subsequent Olympic Games, they found that the British and North American press talked about many global events as acts of 'terrorism', especially in the lead into the 2004 Athens Summer Olympics, as readers were 'reminded' of the sport mega-events were potential 'war zones'. This is not to imply that all security 'risks' to spectators and athletes and sport mega-events are 'hyper real' but that these 'risks' should be critically explored and the labelling of 'perpetrators' as 'terrorists' (or indeed 'hooligans') could be questioned.

Indeed, the post-9/11 media coverage of 'terrorist threats' at sports mega-events is more than matched by their rising financial costs (Lee Ludvigsen, 2022). For instance, Bernhard and Martin (2011: 28) point out that '$300m [USD] was deemed obscenely large at Salt Lake City [2002 Winter Olympics], Vancouver [2010 Winter Olympics] spent approximately $1bn [USD] on security'. Continuing this trend, Samatas (2011) estimated that Athens' 2004 Summer Olympics security bill was $1.5bn [USD]. Bernhard and Martin (2011: 28) argue that racketing up is partially because 'the Olympic demonstration is as much about opulence as it is anything else. No stadium is too magnificent, and no security measure is too expensive for the Games'. Ultimately, security budgets rise in step with sensationalist mega coverage around 'terrorist' threats.

Giulianotti and Klauser (2012) have read 'terrorism' and 'security issues' through broad critical theoretical lenses to provide a potted history of events and issues related to the broad umbrella of 'sport' and 'terrorism'. They point to a clear example of a subversive political action that killed and harmed security personnel and athletes, as well as assailants, developed at the 1972 Summer Olympics in Munich when 11 members of the Israeli squad and one German police officer were taken hostage and eventually killed by the 'Black September' Palestinian group, who had demanded the release of 234 prisoners from Israeli prisons (see also Radomyski, 2021; Silke and Filippidou, 2020). This type of 'terrorist' action is different in severity to the 'three bomb blasts outside a suburban police station threatened civil security in Athens' that Atkinson and Young (2012: 298) detail.

The work of Bairner (1999) and Tsoukala (2008, 2009) further underlines the confluence of research on 'terrorism' and 'hooliganism'. Bairner (1999) argues that the paramilitary ceasefires in Northern Ireland in 1994 meant that many working-class men wanted to find other ways of engaging with violence against rival groups. The results were that this form of aggression against 'the other' has been channeled into vociferous support for football teams (which are often founded on religious and political grounds) and may manifest violence against rival supporter groups or the police. Thus, for Bairner (1999), 'terrorism' and football 'hooliganism' in Northern Ireland might become intertwined for two reasons. First, they are the same action – violence against 'others' – that is more explicitly political when branded the former but contains these strains in the latter. The similar groups undertaking the actions may have simply taken on an alternative noun ('hooligan' replacing 'terrorist'). Second, where this is not the case, Bairner (1999: 299) suggests that a mutual support system operates between the two named groups in that supporters' chants sanction the actions of 'terrorists', providing those fan groups with a 'prized commodity' within the masculine hegemonic environment of 'male hardness'.

Tsoukala (2008, 2009) finds another overlap between 'terrorism' and hooliganism'. Bearing some similarities to Atkinson and Young (2012), her research sought to analyze a 'social construction of threat' through the British media and in doing so, found that the timed coverage of terrorists and football hooligans reveals rational processes of drawing boundaries around what constitutes the groups on the basis of the position of the target group in the political field rather than an 'objective' seriousness of the threat. In doing so, the press selectively reports actions undertaken by the labelled groups and gives only minimal discussions of the social context of their actions. As such, they become feared rather than understood. She argues that the media are powerful cultural communicators and so the threats that they identify and therefore their labelling of groups of people as 'terrorists' or 'football hooligans' means that they cease to be engaged with, both on 'everyday' and – potentially – on policymaking levels, further enforcing the view that they are 'deviant'. In addition, Breen Smyth et al. (2008: 1) point out that 'notwithstanding the exceptional and anomalous events of 2001, acts of clandestine non-state terrorism are committed by a tiny number of individuals and result in between a few hundred and few thousand casualties *per year over the entire world*' [original emphasis], whilst a range of studies into football hooliganism have argued that the problems associated with football hooliganism have been similarly overstated across a number of decades (Marsh et al., 1978; Pearson, 2012).

This literature, when read through critical theoretical lenses (for example, Loader and Walker, 2007), allows us to make three inter-connected points about 'safety' and 'security' at sports mega-events. First, following Bain (2006), it is important to point out that the two adjectives may be related but are not always the same.[6] On one level, 'security' might evoke formal measures of protection taken to ensure public safety, whereas 'safety' is taken to refer more vaguely to the state of being safe from harm. Thus, 'secured' might have a very restricted meaning – police or other personnel might be guarding something from someone.[7] Threats can be real but are also constructed and imagined and so it is important to critically think through what the 'threat' might be and 'who' is being secured from 'what' or 'whom'. Hence, it is important to question what sports mega-events (or the people within them) are being secured from (Lee Ludvigsen, 2022). In short, whilst we recognise the need for 'safety' and some measures of 'security', it is important that the two terms are not be automatically conflated – a situation can be made 'safer' by reducing the risk of a person hurting themselves but 'security' might address a safety from 'others' (such as political activists, other spectators, police/security staff) hurting the individual. Second, through providing 'security', spectators' experiences of sport mega-events should not be unduly 'sanitised'. Sport fans often stress the need to 'authentically' experience events (Millward, 2011) and 'security' measures to improve safety should not unduly impinge on this, even if the measure is to secure supporters from the harm they can carry out on themselves. Many sports spectators are likely to want to feel 'secure' in the sense that they want to be safe from the perils of structurally weak stadiums, 'terrorist' and 'hooligan' threats but not always if that comes at the price of the removal of freedoms such as various forms of carnival-esque behaviours through restrictive policing (see King, 2002 [1998]; Taylor and Toohey, 2011). By cautiously making this point, we clearly acknowledge that although the time in which the absence of freedom becomes described as too much security is individually subjective. In the event of *too much* 'security' enforcement, many spectators will stop attending sports events or find 'unsanitised' ways of behaving that will protect their experiences and this may present problems for security staff and supporter safety. Third, if 'security' is not to become a synonym for 'safety' or 'sanitisation', it also should not be reduced to a word that means the exercising of influence by the 'powerful' in sport (i.e. authorities, clubs, governing bodies, police or other security organisations) on the 'less powerful', who might be the spectators. Incidents surrounding the Hillsborough disaster (in 1989) in which 97 Liverpool Football Club (Liverpool F.C.) supporters died are pertinent here (see Scraton, 2016). From the immediate aftermath of the incident, Liverpool F.C. supporters were largely blamed for the disaster, despite many witness accounts suggesting that policing strategies and management practices were largely responsible. Despite some fan pressure contesting these official narratives, the accounts stood for 23 years until 2012 when an Independent Panel, ordered by the House of Commons, reopened the inquiry and removed liability from the supporters and argued that there were 'operational failings' (*Hillsborough: The Report of the Independent Panel*, 2012). Thus, in this case, it seems that senior members of the principal security staff for the event, South Yorkshire Police, management of the event caused the incident. As such, security was not safety and yet traces of 'blame' were initially disguised by the 'powerful' (senior members of South Yorkshire Police) and placed upon supporters, who represented less powerful groups in society. This process is not replicated in all instances of crowd management and whilst it is important to recognise that a critical analysis of security cannot simply become a simple alternative labelling exercise of rendering the 'real' villains to be the powerful, it is worth pointing out that close and rigorous examination of safety failings might reveal alternative stories to initial official accounts. Therefore, we argue that 'security' at sport mega-events 'security' cannot become a way in which the 'powerful' control the 'powerless'.[8]

Security Legacies: Definitions, Types and Challenges

Sport mega-events have become imbued with promises to deliver a 'legacy', usually to the host city, region or nation in which it is based on the point that 'the

IOC amended the Olympic Charter to include a particular reference to the creation of positive legacies from the Games' (Misener, 2013: 345; see also Bloyce and Lovett, 2012). Whilst representing a slippery concept (indeed, Boykoff (2020: 24) characterises 'legacies' as 'promises and follow through'), mega-event legacies have been claimed to be with respect to tourism (Dansero and Puttilli, 2010), urban renewal/change (Carlsen and Taylor, 2003; Essex and Chalkley, 1998; Hall, 2006; Armstrong et al., 2017), sport participation (Widdop et al., 2018), national economies (Horne and Manzenreiter, 2004; Pillay and Bass, 2008; Whitson and Horne, 2006) and even the healing domestic political wounds (Cornelissen and Swart, 2006). Measuring the impacts and legacies of sport mega-events is clearly important in deciding the extent to which they have 'succeeded' in meeting their aims away from the sports pitch, track or field. However, these 'legacies' are notoriously difficult to measure – a society is not a laboratory-based experiment on which a mega-event would not be held, with all future events observed and then run again, this time with the mega-event held but with all 'impacts' observed and measured (Garcia, 2010; Thornley, 2012). On this point, Giulianotti (2013: 95), when writing in the *ICSS* journal, argued:

> [H]ost cities and nations need to extend this range of legacies in order to consider the security impact of sport events. Security legacies include the full range of security-related strategies, practices and effects that continue to have significance beyond the life of the sporting event. These legacies may include top-down aspects, such as risk-management policies; bottom-up aspects, for example new policing techniques; and more generalised effects, such as in regard to employment or technological innovations.

Continuing to define the idea, Giulianotti and Klauser (2010: 53) describe a security legacy as 'a range of security-related strategies and impacts which continue to have significance beyond the life of the sport event'. The task of measuring a 'security legacy' is as difficult as gauging the impact of a sport mega-event as in other economic, social, cultural and political spheres but as Giulianotti points out, it has become another promise that sports mega-events deliberately pledge to deliver as they compete for the right to host an event. Here, Clavel (2013) and Lee Ludvigsen (2022) extend this discussion by arguing that sports mega-events are often viewed by governments or security actors to be laboratories for security management techniques. This point may be contentious if, given Roche's (2000) arguments about the events being an international platform of opportunity to showcase local cultures, they would be unlikely to unduly 'experiment' with security measures.

Nonetheless, Clavel (2013) states that sport mega-events leave long-lasting security legacies on their host locations and he points out that the Olympic Games often provide the moments where surveillance technologies – such as CCTV – are introduced or increased in number in city spaces (as discussed further later). Indeed, such position was recently reinforced by Hutchins and Andrejevcic (2021) in relation to potential COVID-19 related surveillance technologies ahead of Tokyo's

2020 Summer Olympics. Thus, once technologies have been introduced for a sport mega-event, they tend to stay. Clavel (2013) argues that Olympics are important moments in such developments and dispersals, given that in anticipation of the Games many citizens are more tolerant of intrusive security measures, like CCTV. However, some critical criminologists such as Coleman (2012 [2004]) strongly argue that the normalisation of these technologies of surveillance on the streets of the UK is a key to understanding strategies for material and ideological re-mapping of urban space in neoliberal cities. In short, he states that surveillance cameras are part of a social control strategy that hides the unequal consequences of neoliberalisation by implicitly making public spaces increasingly exclusionary (see also Coleman and Sim, 2000). Thus, Coleman (2012 [2004]) would regret any legacy of sport mega-events being the introduction of more surveillance technologies.

Giulianotti and Klauser (2010: 54) extend the argument about what security legacy from sports mega-events might constitute by suggesting that they might come in six distinct forms. These are i) 'security technologies'; ii) 'new security practices', which are utilised at the sports mega-event but then extended into other areas of society after the event; iii) 'governmental policies and new legislation' such as new laws 'that restrict public association or the movement of specific individuals' and stay in place after the event; iv) 'externally imposed social transformations' that might directly or indirectly relate to 'security issues' such as 'the clearing of specific [subjectively] "undesirable" or "unloved" populations' from the urban spaces in which the sport mega-event takes over; v) 'generalized changes in social and transsocietal relationships' such as long-lasting different relationships between people in local communities and police officials. These changes may improve or worsen these relationships; and vi) 'urban redevelopment' which may impact upon future 'security' issues. This may include physical landscape changes such as 'slum clearance' and 'rebuilding programs' that are intended in part to repopulate and commodify specific inner-city localities.

This may also have subjectively negative, as well as positive, impacts. For instance, Allen (2008) argues that working-class households in cities where housing market renewal strategies have been imposed have generally benefitted very little from such programmes but have instead experienced losses of community or, worse still, the homes in which they live. Similarly, Lewis (2015) looked at the longer-term legacy of the 2002 Commonwealth Games in the East Manchester area in which the City of Manchester Stadium is located 10 years after the sport mega-event and found that many local residents were less than happy about the spatial changes to the district, arguing that the legacy had mostly negative consequences for them.

Giulianotti and Klauser (2010) map out specific details of 'security legacies' along with how they have been operationalised. As such, they give meaning to the term 'security legacy' in the academic press. Moreover, Giulianotti (2013: 96–101) returned to further explore the issues 3 years later and further elaborated upon its meaning. As such, he argued that sports mega-events might have six potential security legacies: 'new technologies' (pp. 96–97), 'strategic partnerships' (pp. 97–98), 'knowledge and expertise' (p. 98), 'economic aspects' (pp. 98–99), 'legislation and policing' (pp. 99–101) and 'public effects' (p. 101). First, Giulianotti (2013) fleshes out the possibility of new surveillance technologies, such as CCTV, being a key security legacy. He points out that CCTV may be commonplace in the global North but elsewhere they are 'less evident in public places, hence sports events may lead host cities to install these cameras' (p. 96). In making this point, he demonstrates that it was reported that the 2010 Commonwealth Games in Delhi saw 2,000 CCTV cameras installed in the city. In the global North, he argues that further advances in surveillance technologies may be developed for sports mega-events, for instance, at the 2006 FIFA World Cup, held in Germany, CCTV cameras that has facial recognition software installed on them – so that individuals who were stored on national 'hooligan databases' – could be monitored.[9] Second, Giulianotti suggests that 'strategic partnerships' between security providers at local, national and international levels might be a legacy. This means that intelligence on outlined 'security issues' may be drawn together and networked across the various agencies. In principle, this would mean that 'good practice' could be replicated at either a) the next sport mega-event held anywhere in the world or b) subsequent events that are held in that host city or region. Third, 'knowledge and expertise' might be a security legacy (see also Lee Ludvigsen, 2022). By this, Giulianotti (2013) is referring to the ways that they might be advanced by their testing during a sport mega-event. For instance, he argues that a 'broad legacy' might be 'to demonstrate the security resilience of the host city or nation', if this task is successfully completed it seems likely that 'a robust security track record . . . places the host city or nation in a stronger position when bidding to stage future events' (Giulianotti, 2013: 98). Fourth, security legacies might have 'economic aspects', particularly given that the budgets for security at sports mega-events have continued to grow in an era dominated by a global recession – and the number of people employed in the security-related industry may be partially sustained after the event (Giulianotti, 2013). He also points out that a further economic aspect of sports mega-events is that they firmly connect the hosts to the transnational security industry, and that this development occurs in both the global South and the global North. Fifth, Giulianotti states that sport mega-events mean that the hosts develop new security legislation and policing strategies that remain in the country as a long-term legacy. For instance, he suggested that at the 2006 FIFA World Cup:

> more than 1,000 Dutch fans entering one stadium were told to remove their trousers, as their clothing bore the insignia of a beer company (Bavaria) that was not sponsoring the event. . . . [While] One family at the 2003 [cricket] World Cup in South Africa was ejected from a stadium after opening a soft drink produced by the main market rival of a tournament sponsor.
>
> *(2013: 101)*

Many people would not see this as necessarily improving the safety of spectators or participants; it could reasonably be viewed as a new dimension in the 'hyper-commodification' of sport (Walsh and Giulianotti, 2001). Sixth, Giulianotti (2013) contends that public understandings of security issues, provisions and practices are heightened by their experiences of sports mega-events, and he argues that this offers some potential to reduce 'urban crime' (however defined) and make the host city 'safer' after the event has passed. Resultantly, as Mastrogiannakis and Dorville (2013) argue, security practices do change as a result of sport mega-events, and this constitutes clear legacies. However, their impact on human behavior is less easy to measure, and the point remains with respect to asking what security legacies genuinely mean for the 'safety' of spectators, athletes and ordinary citizens as opposed to the sanitising interference in the quest for 'authentic' fan experiences or the exercising of influence of the politically or economically 'powerful' over the relatively 'powerless' at sports events. Some of these issues will also be returned to and highlighted in the following discussion, which turn more specifically towards diverse 'surveillance' forms in modern-day sport.

Sharpening the Blurry Contours of Sport 'Surveillance'

As another contested concept that must be approached with some caution, 'surveillance' can be defined as *'the systematic monitoring of people or groups in order to regulate or govern their behavior'* (Monahan, 2011: 498, original emphasis). The prominence of 'surveillance' in present-day societies must be seen in context of wider socio-political developments speaking to security governance and risk management, as well as technological progression (Bauman and Lyon, 2013). Moreover, 9/11 resulted in the 'increase in the routine surveillance of citizens' (Lyon, 2007: 161). As Haggerty et al. (2011: 231) observe, this has 'inspired [a] growing criminological interest' in the study of 'surveillance'. Now, the evolving criminological literature on surveillance 'demonstrates how various forms of exclusion or banning are commonly linked to problematic surveillance, identity authentication and pre-emptive law enforcement methods' (Warren et al., 2014: 441). Notwithstanding, as Bennett and Haggerty (2011) assert, contemporary 'surveillance' can no longer be accurately explained by merely borrowing Orwell's 'Big Brother' or Foucault's 'panopticon', which help explain how the state surveils its citizens. As observed, 'surveillance' is now considerably more globalised, 'fragmented and dispersed throughout different computer networks within government, outside government, and within grey areas in between' (ibid.: 3).

This is also the case in sport. Indeed, it may even be prudent to talk of 'surveillance studies of sport', although such field would be both recent and tightly interconnected with the growing area of research concerned with sport's anti-doping policies (Warren et al., 2014; Park, 2005) and SME securitisation (Bennett and Haggerty, 2011; Giulianotti and Klauser, 2011). Furthermore, it is important that the practice of 'surveilling' someone (or something) in sport is not conflated with what occurs in exceptional contexts like mega-events or, moreover, something that is being done solely for crime prevention purposes *with* technological hardware.

Rather, in the criminological and sociological studies of sport, 'surveillance' should be approached as a pluralised practice occurring on different levels (i.e. by the state, private companies, individuals), which seek to govern and/or control distinctive types of behaviors (whether that is doping, corruption, violence or a player's 'diving') or individuals ('deviant' or 'anti-social' individuals, 'hooligans', athletes, fans). Notwithstanding, behind surveillance is always the 'domination and power of those in authority and privilege' (Bale, 2003: 174). Further, as Klauser (2017) shows, surveillance techniques commonly serve as practices of control and power which enable disciplined spaces or populations. Thus, placed within this chapter's overarching focus on modes of governance, security and surveillance in sport, such points are essential because they invite and allow for an understanding of the nexuses between sport, crime and social control and power relations in sport. This will be elaborated on now, as we advance three types of surveillance in sport that demonstrate this argument.

Surveillance for Safety and Security

The first and perhaps most obvious type of surveillance in sport is the hinted monitoring strategies that are utilised at separate events and mega-events in order to achieve the normative yet basic aim of public safety and security (Roche, 2017) and to prevent 'crime' (Garland and Rowe, 1999). When critically approaching 'surveillance' in sport, the application of surveillance to sport mega-events and single-day events like the Super Bowl or UEFA Champions League finals and professional sports leagues must be revisited briefly.

In his examination of Olympic surveillance, Sugden (2012: 426) asks rhetorically whether: 'Perhaps it is time we got used to the fact that rather than us watching the Games, for the foreseeable future, it is more a case of the Games watching us'. Sugden's study, rooted in ideas of 'surveillance' and 'social control', investigates the rise of 'surveillance' complexes at post-9/11 mega-events under threat from 'terrorism' and how this has profound implications for citizens' civil liberties throughout events and if the tools of 'surveillance', as discussed earlier, translate into 'security legacies'.

Mega-events are crucial for any understanding of 'surveillance' in sport because the attempt to establish 'control' under the climates of uncertainty is one reason why surveillance techniques are increasingly incorporated into sport settings (Boyle and Haggerty, 2009). For instance, in the North American context of the National Football League (NFL), Schimmel (2011) investigates Super Bowl's security complexes. He observes that for almost every annual Super Bowl, 'a "new technology", often "used for the first time at a Super Bowl", is discussed by reporters' (p. 3283). Schimmel also provides a description of the exceptional realities of 'Super Bowl security':

> 'Super Bowl security' has included the installation of (permanent) surveillance cameras that extend from stadia into downtown communities, the (unannounced) use of biometric face-matching technology on fans attending the game, (covert) federal immigration dragnets arresting undocumented

workers and game-day volunteers, and expanded powers for urban police forces. Planning for security now begins at least two years prior to game day.

(ibid.: 3279)

Such trends have continued and before the 2019 Super Bowl final, taking place over one night in Atlanta, it was reported that 'a network of about 10,000 cameras' would assist the 65 law enforcement agencies involved in the associated security operation (Reuters, 2019). In a way, 'surveillance' is a highly normalised feature in the contemporary sport world that is bundled together into and formulates a 'surveillant assemblage' (Haggerty and Ericson, 2000) which remains under continual finessing, revision and development, following Schimmel's (2011) ideas.

Such an argument is supported by another recent event. Before the 2016/17 UEFA Champions League final hosted in Cardiff (Wales) in May 2017, between Juventus and Real Madrid, it was reported that the South Wales Police would employ facial recognition which then could be matched against '500,000 "custody images" stored by local police forces' (BBC, 2017). In a public statement from the South Wales Police, it was announced that the Champions League final which involved thousands of fans travelling to Cardiff, served as a testing ground for surveillance technology:

> The UEFA Champions League finals in Cardiff give us a unique opportunity to test and prove the concept of this technology in a live operational environment, which will hopefully prove the benefits and the application of such technology across policing.
>
> *(quoted in BBC, 2017)*

As Fussey et al. (2021: 340) observe, '[d]uring South Wales' initial deployments for the Champions League Final when the system was still being configured, it was slow and often produced "lag"'. Collectively, this underlines how sport, as mentioned, may act as a 'testing ground' for the piloting or configuration of new 'surveillance' technologies (Clavel, 2013; Samatas, 2007; Hodges, 2019; Lee Ludvigsen, 2019a, 2022). However, in English football this can be traced back to the 1980s when CCTV cameras were introduced into the stadium in the crackdown on supporter violence 'ahead of other areas in society' (Garland and Rowe, 1999: 39). Though, such practices are not unique to the UK, as Hodges (2019) finds in his study of Croatian 'ultras'.

Notwithstanding, the developments in the aftermath of the Champions League final were remarkable and invite critical inquiry. Reports emerged, holding that in relation to the 2016/17 Champions League final, more than 2000 individuals had been 'wrongly identified as potential criminals' (The Guardian, 2018) although none were wrongly arrested (BBC, 2018). *The Guardian* reported that '2,470 potential matches were identified. However, according to data on the force's website, 92% (2,297) of those were found to be "false positives"'. A few years later, the surveillance of fans in Cardiff was again criticised: this time Cardiff fans expressed discontent with being subject to facial recognition technology following a game against Swansea. As a way of marking their resistance at the game played in late October 2019, some Cardiff City fans went to the game wearing Halloween masks in a protest against the 'surveillance' technology (FSA, 2019). The intrusive surveillance techniques in sport hence prove problematic and have caused public debate.

For example, in Scottish football, fans perceived some surveillance measures to be provocative and offensive by fans who were targeted (Hamilton-Smith et al., 2021). Moreover, this is paradoxical since the technologies employed with the intention of creating 'security' and 'safety' may ultimately categorise 'innocents' who become at risk (Bauman and Lyon, 2013). It is also particularly problematic when monitoring and data gathering technologies which prove inaccurate (The Guardian, 2018) or are contested (FSA, 2019) are installed elsewhere in sporting settings or public life. In the UK, it has been found that CCTV is a 'socially invisible' crime control technology that fade into the background of urban life and seldom is noticed (Goold et al., 2013). Meanwhile, surveillance measures sometimes are implemented in a 'low key' manner in sport (Toohey and Taylor, 2012). Such combination, a 'socially invisible' tool introduced 'low key', may have critical implications and add substantial weight to this chapter's main argument. It also raises a series of important questions about what happens to the collected data, captured video images, and technologies when the relevant event's days are over (Lee Ludvigsen, 2019a). As such, this section demonstrates how one type of sports surveillance is commonly justified in the banner of 'security' and 'safety' against 'threats' such as 'terrorists', 'hooligans' or 'criminals'. Yet, occasionally, such technologies' workings are highly contested.

Lateral Surveillance

The second type of 'surveillance' this chapter advances and builds upon is what Dixon (2014) and Rees et al. (2014), in a sport context, refer to 'lateral surveillance'. 'Lateral surveillance' can also be referred to as 'peer monitoring' (Andrejevic, 2005) and must be deemed highly relevant in the study of sport and surveillance. Particularly so, if we read 'surveillance' as the establishment or reinforcement of power relationships (Monahan, 2011) across sport. However, as argued, even though 'lateral surveillance' is based upon individuals 'surveilling' their peers, it is occasionally encouraged and promoted by authorities and organisations. In essence, 'lateral surveillance' as a concept can help us comprehend:

> the use of surveillance tools by individuals' (rather than institutions) as they attempt to monitor the behaviour of family and peers and consequently replicate or reject forms of observed practice as 'authentic' or 'inauthentic'.
> *(Dixon, 2014: 424)*

As touched upon, this type of 'surveillance', when occurring in practice or in situ differs in some fundamental ways from the orthodox state (or even corporate) 'surveillance' discussed previously. Significantly, peers monitor each other. But 'lateral surveillance' might still be state driven, which is illustrated by how citizens occasionally are encouraged to perform 'vigilance' and report 'suspicious behavior' (Reeves, 2012). Indeed, this has happened in line with the broader trend where everyday citizens increasingly are becoming encouraged to act as active stakeholders in their own and national 'security' (Vaughan-Williams and Stevens, 2016) and in 'crime prevention'. Further, there are some certain conceptual and practical resemblances with that of 'self-policing'.

In sport contexts too, 'lateral surveillance' is sometimes encouraged. For example, fans that attend a game will be made aware of and encouraged via match-day programmes in English stadiums to contact the club if they want to inform other match-goers that engage in anti-social behavior (Giulianotti, 2011). Moreover, counterterrorism policing campaigns, including 'Know the Game Plan – Act', encourage vigilant action in the crowded places around stadiums and were promoted in numerous YouTube clips by former England football players Alan Shearer, Paul Parker and David Seaman ahead of the 2018 World Cup in Russia.[10] 'Kick It Out', an organisation battling 'racism' in English football, also encourages match-goers to report instances of discrimination at all levels including social media abuse via their smartphone app (Kick it Out, n.d.). Occasionally, police forces will also appeal for fans to provide mobile phone footage of public disorder and violent clashes in the context of football.[11] Hence, 'lateral surveillance' or peer monitoring is encouraged by relevant organisations and authorities in the governance of football or sport through specific campaigns. Yet, this depends on peer monitoring first, and second, on action to be taken. Thus, 'lateral surveillance' must be viewed as referring to the process in which fans – in this context – *monitor* each other, rather than the ways they report or act upon what they have monitored. This is one way in which 'lateral surveillance' can occur in sport, yet we have primarily focussed on monitoring potential 'anti-social' or 'suspicious' behavior. Nonetheless, the concept can also be used for other forms of 'surveillance' in sports.

Rees et al. (2014) employ it to understand how racing cyclists creates notions of 'team' and 'community' in a subcultural and competitive amateur training environment. Meanwhile, Dixon (2014) uses the 'lateral surveillance' to understand how football fans distinguish between each other and label each other according to 'authentic' and 'inauthentic' ideals. Such judgements are made against the background that, in football, 'authentic' fans are historically seen to be 'better', more 'loyal' and passionate and possess longstanding relationships with their clubs, compared to their 'inauthentic counterparts' – who, in fact, support the same team and should be considered 'fellows'. Dixon finds that fans create a distinctive 'otherness' through 'lateral surveillance'. This is based upon their observations of so-called 'inauthentic' of 'fake' fans and how these behave, dress or speak. Through such observations, idyllic perceptions around what it means to be an 'authentic' fan are created (Dixon, 2014). Thus, the element of 'surveillance' here relates to fans monitoring each other. Based on what they see, they either reject or replicate the observed behavior. The monitoring therefore has a regulating or governing effect on fans' behavior. Behaviors that were being monitored and subsequently seen as 'inauthentic' fandom would include lack of loyalty to the team, consumption activities or allowing the mass media to decide one's opinion on football or club matters (ibid.). Dixon also highlight that 'surveillance of otherness and perceptions of dirt also exist beyond conceptions of fake, inadequate or inauthentic fandom' (p. 434) such as the 'chav fan'.

The ways in which supporters monitor each other and make informal comparisons are found in other studies too, although not framed in terms of 'surveillance'. It occurs in and around the stadium and in online settings, such as message boards (Petersen-Wagner, 2015; Millward, 2011; Lee Ludvigsen, 2019b). In Petersen-Wagner's (2015) ethnographic study of Swiss and Brazilian Liverpool FC fans, he found that 'transnational fans', who commonly are considered to lack loyalty and commitment to their clubs, also made distinctions between fans according to what they saw, heard or experienced whilst present in the stands. For example, one transnational fan blamed other 'tourists fans' for contributing to bad atmospheres inside the stadium, when paradoxically, this fan was also technically a tourist visiting Liverpool for a short period. This is interesting as we can observe the applicability of 'lateral surveillance' to both offline and online settings in sport. Overall, 'lateral surveillance' can be applied to elite sport (Dixon, 2014), and it occurs both in relation to the desired prevention of 'anti-social' or 'deviant' behaviors, whilst it possesses more socio-cultural function in 'including' and 'excluding', or, determining who is an 'authentic' fan and who (supposedly) is not.

Surveilling Athletic Performances and Bodies

In line with the increased professionalisation of sport, so has the demand and need for being able to physically perform at the 'highest' or 'maximum' levels become increasingly important for professional athletes in an industry where revenue generation is fundamental. Moreover, the athletic body, representing or symbolising the 'state' can function as a sign of state power (Hargreaves, 1987). So, optimal performance represents an underlying aim in elite-level sport and has altered the ways in which athletes train, recover and eat in the sport industry's lucrative climate. However, it has also led some athletes to turn towards illicit performance-enhancing drugs. This section outlines the monitoring and surveillance of athletic bodies and performance levels as another broad type of sport-based 'surveillance'. Although this type of surveillance is not *always* linked to monitoring criminal or illicit activities, monitoring techniques like drug testing may still be felt as a disproportionate tool by athletes.

Giulianotti (2019: 7) locates elite sport's increased scientific focus on continually enhancing performances under the banner of 'rationalisation'. He writes that:

> Modern, analogue scientific rationalisation centred on producing a growing array of positional responsibilities, and early performance measures, directed at players by team managers and coaches. Big data points to the next,

postmodernised stage where vast volumes and varieties of digital information are gathered, compressed, and analysed, for example through the use of GPS and other monitoring devices attached to players, as well as the video-based classification and analysis of every conceivable incident during games.

(ibid.)

Hence, in both game and training situations, monitoring the individual athlete's daily training load comprises an essential component of the training regime. Although we cannot provide a full list here of the techniques, methods and tools that are used to ensure this, one device of particular interest in a chapter discussing 'surveillance' is the 'GPSports' tracking devices, including the activity-tracking vest that athletes typically wear, which allow for monitoring players' physical performances in sport such as rugby and football. Commonly, players are seen such 'bra-resembling' devices in photos from the training grounds,[12] and some of the benefits of the device are that it allegedly minimises injuries and maximises performance (STATSports, n.d.).

However, to ensure results and performances in an increasingly lucrative industry, Park (2005: 117) writes that some athletes, managers and coaches became attracted to 'pharmaceutical products and methods (i.e., blood doping) that could boost athletic performance' in the second half of the twentieth century. This has been accurately illustrated by numerous high-profile cases, such as former cyclist Lance Armstrong (Sefiha and Reichman, 2016). A key response to this has been the emergence of another key actor in the 'surveillance' of sport: the World Anti-Doping Agency (WADA) (Warren et al., 2014).

As such, parts of the surveillance/sport literature are anchored in sport's anti-doping policies and politics (see Sefiha and Reichman, 2016). WADA is centered on combatting and monitoring doping and drugs in sports and assist private sport organisations (Warren et al., 2014). Before proceeding, however, it remains important to underline that this section does not seek to answer or engage with the moral or philosophical questions around drug testing or whether to 'justify' it. Rather, we solely seek to outline this as another taxonomy of governance and surveillance in sport and touch upon key issues surrounding specific or notable cases.

WADA was established in 1999, and its headquarters are currently in Montreal, Canada. The year before, the 1998 *Tour de France* – the biggest cycling race in the world – had been a 'critical event' that assisted the 'collaborative fight' against doping in professional sport on a worldwide scale (Park, 2005). Throughout this edition of *Tour de France*, rumors emerged around illicit drug use amongst the riders, which meant the doping inspections were severe. This caused half of the participating riders to withdraw from *Tour de France*. It was only after the race that the IOC sought to address the ongoing 'drug crisis'. A 'World Conference on Doping in Sport' was held in Lausanne in February 1999, before IOC established WADA (ibid.). In her study of the rise, policies and structures of WADA, Park (2005: 185) concludes that 'WADA fundamentally works to police athletic bodies and how those ongoing projects in developing new drug-testing methods for currently undetectable drugs are implicated in the surveillance mechanism'. However, not all countries have the same resources and some currently have better infrastructures to set up effective surveillance systems than others (Dimeo and Møller, 2018).

In terms of drug testing, one contentious form of 'surveillance' in elite sport is the 'whereabouts' system that has received some scholarly attention (see Waddington, 2010; Møller, 2011; Hanstad and Loland, 2009). Since 2003, WADA introduced a system which meant that all elite-level athletes were obliged to provide anti-doping organisations with key information (including home address, telephone numbers, training, competition and travel plans) in order to enable no-notice and out-of-competition testing (Waddington, 2010). Then, in 2008 an updated system meant athletes had to provide increasingly detailed information about 'their precise whereabouts for each day in the following three months, with athletes being required to make themselves available for testing on every day of the year' (ibid.: 256).

As Waddington argues, this system faced much criticism from athletes with claims of WADA operating as 'a "Big Brother" system of surveillance and control' that was incompatible with athletes' rights to both privacy and civil liberties (ibid.). Whilst the question of whether this rule can be 'justified' – as stated – remain beyond the remit of this chapter, what remains central is the argument of Waddington holding that this system – although it may successfully deter or catch athletes using drugs – translates into an 'extraordinary system of surveillance and control of people who have committed no offence' (ibid.).

The whereabouts system can also lead to anxieties or grievances amongst athletes who may fail to turn up at their reported location due to unforeseen circumstances such as flight delays or cancels. As the Spanish tennis player, Rafael Nadal, commented, these procedures made him 'feel like a criminal'. Nadal's tennis rival, Andy Murray, meanwhile, described the 'whereabouts' procedures as 'draconian' (BBC, 2009). As Møller (2011) suggests, the 'whereabouts' system's implementation is both potentially 'counter-productive' and 'dehumanising' since it reduces the moral responsibility of the athletes and facilitates conditions of mistrust towards the athletes. As such, he argues it is one step too far, as opposed to Hanstad and Loland (2009), who defend the requirements as 'efficient'. Hence, whilst the 'whereabouts' system aims to enable a more transparent sporting arena, the modes of governance enabled by the whereabouts requirements may be synonymous with intrusive surveillance on athlete's bodies and privacy.

Also in the context of sport's professionalisation, and on another level, athletes' personal use of social media may be controlled, policed or acted upon by teams, leagues or football authorities. As known, sport, in itself, has distinctive on- and off-field justice systems that deal with the actions of athletes (Colluci and Jones, 2013). Reportedly, England players were banned from tweeting throughout the 2010 World Cup in South Africa, whilst the 'Spanish and Dutch squads certainly were' (Price et al., 2013: 449). Moreover, a high-profile incident was the £10.000 fine, then-Liverpool player, Ryan Babel, received from the FA after he had tweeted an edited picture of a referee, Howard Webb, wearing a Manchester United shirt, following a game between Liverpool and Manchester United (ibid.). This is not unique to association football. In a North American context, Los Angeles Rams linebacker, Clay Matthews, was fined £12.500 for criticising NFL referees via Twitter, referring to the NFL referees as unable to make accurate calls (Bleacher Report, 2019).

It is therefore reason to argue that the rise of digital technologies has added dimensions to the ways professional athletes are subject to constant scrutiny, monitoring and attempts to control or mold their behavior and discipline: First, by being 'caught' on (smartphone) cameras for this, subsequently, to be uploaded to social media and covered by newspapers; and second, by attempts to control, dictate and punish athletes' personal social media use and habits so that it conforms to normative ideals of 'professional' behavior. Therefore, as this section has explored, the surveillance of athletic bodies, performances and behaviors remains one important component situated within the surveillance of sport, especially so, in a hyper-professional, lucrative and physically demanding sport industry. However, mechanisms such as the 'whereabouts' policy could also have a series of unintended consequences and be perceived as intrusive or disproportionate.

Sport, Governance and Social Control: Emerging Research Priorities

Although the connections between 'sport', 'security' and 'surveillance' have been given increased attention over the past decades, there are still elements of these relationships that warrant further academic attention, both at future mega-events and more generally in sport. This chapter argues that there are still gaps in the literature speaking to how individuals that attend or live in the securitised spheres of a mega-event perceive 'security', 'safety' and 'threats'. As the discussion unpacking 'security legacies' implies, this also relates to their perceptions beyond the short-term duration of any mega-event. This is necessary to enhance the criminological and sociological understanding of what 'security' means for sport fans and what they perceive to be 'threatening' a 'security issue' or 'criminal behavior' in sport contexts.

Some studies reveal how sport fans talk about 'security', both in the early 2000s (Toohey et al., 2003; Toohey and Taylor, 2006) and more recently (Cleland and Cashmore, 2018; Cleland, 2019; Lee Ludvigsen and Millward, 2020). The research demonstrates that fans and attendees expect and accept the need for 'security' and that they appreciate that 'safety' is prioritised by event managers, law enforcements and wider stakeholders. Supporters also reflect on 'threats' or attacks elsewhere and its likely impact on their sport attendance (Lee Ludvigsen and Millward, 2020). Against the existing literature and this chapter's argument, it is undeniably necessary to – at a higher frequency – provide a voice to fans and residents of the event cities. Concerning to the latter, the residents, it may be of particular relevance to examine their perception of potential 'security legacies', as discussed. Particularly in the global South, which have recently hosted a number of SMEs, including South Africa (World Cup in 2010) and Brazil (World Cup in 2014; Olympics in 2016; Copa America in 2019) where 'security legacies' may have remained post-event in order to police local populations and spaces (Azzi, 2017).

Examining spectators' and residents' perceptions of 'crime', 'terrorism' and 'security' would not merely produce original ways of empirically and theoretically understanding 'security' in sport context but also have the potential to impact how stadiums, fan zones and mega-event spaces are managed or operated in the future. Further, there is a clear theoretical purchase in such studies in consulting literature from the broadly defined critical security studies. This again could enrich the dialogue between Criminology and International Relations, which Bigo (2016) has argued convincingly for. This includes CSS – which this chapter has worked within the premises of – but there are also other critical schools (for example, the 'Paris School' and the 'Copenhagen School') that still, as Lee Ludvigsen (2022) maintains, have not been made the most of in the academic study of sport-related security or surveillance.

The second aspect of 'security' and 'surveillance' in sport that warrants further enquiry is how citizens, increasingly, have become active stakeholders in their own 'security' and in preventing crime (Vaughan-Williams and Stevens, 2016). An examination of this would connect both to the previous point we made and to the discussion around 'lateral surveillance'. Essentially, it relates to exploring how citizens, when attending mega-events or another sporting context, perceive their own role as a security stakeholder, and then, how they feel they are reminded by or appealed to by authorities or agencies about reporting or looking out for 'suspicious' behaviors or items. Research into this could examine how such roles are adapted to, fulfilled or possibly resisted and how it takes place between the 'everyday' and the relevant sporting context.

Finally, the three advanced typologies of 'surveillance' invite further examination and extension. In particular, the type of social media-related 'surveillance' and other surveillance types that athletes and the 'athletic body' are subjected to. That includes the ways through which professional leagues (or teams) police, surveil and control players behavior and appearances. In North America, Lorenz and Murray (2014) argue that the dress code (including business attire) imposed by National Basketball League's (NBA) in 2005 on its players was one way to police and control young black athletes, disguised as an attempt to increase the league's professional aesthetic. Relevant sporting authorities and professional leagues thus do police and control their players (see also Kennedy and Silva, 2020). As highlighted, the rise of social media throughout the 2000s and 2010s has added another layer to the ways in through players now are controlled by their leagues, franchises or employers. Hence, it is argued here that critical criminological research could commit to examinations of this and explore how athletes' behaviors, public statements and appearances are controlled or responded to by sporting bodies, and naturally, how the intersections of gender, race and ethnicity play into this too.

Summary: Security, Governance and Surveillance in Sport

This chapter began with a statement maintaining that sport has been greatly influenced heavily by broader 'securitisation' and 'surveillance' processes. Since 9/11, a number of moral panics have emerged about the threat of (a catch-all term) of 'terrorists' threatening societies in the Global North. In the context of sport mega-events, these fears have been exceeded by reassurance from governments and other state apparatus and have become especially manifest in rising sports mega-event security budgets. The word 'security' is common in the everyday vernacular. Yet a critical analysis of this suggests that when it is talked about, for most people exactly what it means is unclear.

In the context of sport, we wish to underline three points with respect to this. First, we follow Bain (2006) in offering that 'security' and 'safety' may be related but are not uniformly the same. Thus, 'security' might include the formal measures of protection taken that give rise to public safety, but 'safety' more vaguely refers to the state of being safe from harm (see Chapter 7). 'Secured' might therefore have a restricted meaning such as police or other personnel might be guarding something from real or constructed threats. Second 'security' provisions should not unduly 'sanitise' spectators' experiences. To elaborate, sports fans will often emphasise their desires for 'authentic' experiences at events (accepting that 'authenticity' is a slippery concept). 'Security' measures to improve safety should not unduly remove this, even if the measure is to secure supporters from self-inflicted 'harm'.

In the event of too much 'security' enforcement, many spectators will stop attending sports events or find 'unsanitised' ways of behaving that will protect their experiences and this may present problems for security staff and supporter safety. Third, 'security' should not be reduced to a word that means the exercising of influence by the 'powerful' in sport (i.e. authorities, clubs, governing bodies, police, other security organisations) on the 'less powerful', who might be the spectators, as might have happened in the 1989 Hillsborough disaster during the F.A. Cup semi-final played between Liverpool and Nottingham Forest.

With reference to 'legacies' as soon as, or even sometimes before, a mega-event has ended calls for its direct impact on the urbanities and countries in which it held are made. Politicians, sports administrators and other stakeholders have often made wild claims as to what such 'legacies' might be and how far-reaching their impacts are. Indeed, the more impressive the legacy claims, the higher the bar for non-sporting achievement for the next. Such claims to 'legacy' from sports mega-events have included regeneration of an economy, improved health for local populations and even, the healing of political wounds. On these points, Giulianotti and Klauser (2010: 53) define sports mega-event security legacy as 'a range of security-related strategies and impacts which continue to have significance beyond the life of the sport event', whilst Giulianotti (2013) outlines six potential security legacies – 'new technologies', 'strategic partnerships', 'knowledge and expertise', 'economic aspects', 'legislation and policing' and 'public effects' – might emerge from sport mega-events. Addressing issues of 'what' is being secured, critical understandings of 'security' – such as those from critical security studies (in both upper- and lower-case variations) – suggest that there can be no real threats or 'security' without any referents to what might be 'secured'. Indeed, Bellamy (2005) states that those in the (upper case) CSS tradition hold that only humans should be ultimate referents of security for the term to hold meaning. Thus, the referent for security cannot be a political or economic structure. Who, then, was being secured by sport mega-events legacies? These answers are not clear, which Giulianotti and Klauser (2010) hint at. A common 'security legacy' is the spread of CCTV technologies which remain in place after the event.

However, Coleman (2012 [2004]) argues that CCTV is less effective in providing security than those from CSS would envisage to be 'meaningful', instead of targeting those who are judged on their appearance to be more likely social villains, observing them until they commit 'trivial' criminal acts and then criminalising them. There is a case to be made that in the global North, CCTV technologies are omnipresent in urban spaces (see Goold et al., 2013) and the biggest 'security' legacy of this form is in their spread to the global South after a sports mega-event has been held in one of its cities. The imposition of such technologies in other areas of the world could be read as neo-imperial in the spread of practices from the Global North to the Global South in the name of an unquestioned 'progress' and without specific reference to exactly *who* would be secured by their presence.

Towards this chapter's end, key typologies of 'surveillance' in sport were discussed under the aegis of 'social control' and with reference to the 'multiple modes of governance that impact on sports fans, athletes, coaches and administrative staff' (Warren et al., 2014: 451). By synthesizing the existing literature on 'surveillance' in sport, it can be argued that 'surveillance' in sport relates to a broader set of processes, policies, individuals and behaviors. However, 'surveillance' processes do not merely take place under the banner of 'security' or 'crime prevention', and it must not be solely read as a question of surveilling stadium spaces (Giulianotti and Klauser, 2011; Schimmel, 2011) or anti-doping policies such as unexpected doping tests (Park, 2005; Sefiha and Reichman, 2016). 'Surveillance', when situated in sport, refers to a set of diffuse practices, since these practices occur dispersedly over and in-between 'competition' days and 'non-competition days' and in-between athletes' private and athletic or professional lives. And so, in mapping the contours of this wide stretch between the 'everyday' and 'exceptional', and the blurred lines concerning 'who is watching who?', this chapter has combined and built upon existing literature and advanced three types of 'surveillance' and 'social control' *in, through* or *around* sport. Reasonably, it can be concluded that 'security' and 'surveillance' issues and strategies in sport are highly complex and invite further critical criminological inquiry, due to the potential counter-productive, discriminatory and exclusionary consequences they may have for social groups or individuals involved in (or sometimes banned from) sport.

Notes

1 This debate is further complicated by the lack of agreement about whether it can be assumed that the state protects its citizens (see, for instance, Cohen and Dawson, 1993; Takkac and Akdemir, 2012).
2 For an argument against critical terrorism studies that engages with – rather than merely rejects – its ideas, please see Horgan and Boyle (2008).
3 Crawford (2004) argues that the study of sports supporters has been dominated by extreme forms of fandom, such as 'hooliganism'. He is largely correct, although exactly what 'hooliganism' might mean is often not unpacked. There have also been multiple theorisations in the explanation and description of 'hooligan' incidents. We are not attempting to give readers an overview of these multiple theorisations but would suggest that these can be found in Bairner (2006), Best (2010), Carroll (1980), Frosdick and Marsh (2005), Redhead (1991), Rookwood (2009: 43–62) and Spaaij (2006: 9–53).
4 For instance, Crabbe (2003) points out that the national press sensationalising troubles which occur at football games and label a variety of actions – many that would not be considered to deviant in some 'everyday' circumstances – as 'hooligan'.
5 In Liverpool F.C.'s case, the ban was elongated to 7 years.
6 'Safe' can also be used as a verb but 'secure' is not. So, for instance, 'secure that weight' means making sure that the weight does not move, however, 'secure that neighbourhood, soldier' might mean rooting out any enemies in the area in question in order to call an area 'secure'.
7 Similarly, 'the safety of the event' might refer to the unlikelihood of an accident occurring, but 'the security of the event' would be in reference to protection from a form of 'threat'.
8 With this in mind, it must be acknowledged that Hough and Mayhew (1983) criticism of many branches of critical criminology as typically underdeveloping what is meant by 'power' might hold some value. In this case, it was a territorial police force (or senior members from it), but in other accounts 'power' might be the state or the economy.
9 Armstrong and Giulianotti (1998) argue that most local police constabularies responded to the threat of hooliganism by introducing CCTV at football matches, while a second surveillance technology that nearly came into operation in the 1980s was the introduction of identity cards for football fans. The implementation of this scheme would have meant that it would have been an offence to enter a football ground without a card, which would have further diminished match attendances that had – from the end of the Second World War until the end of the 1980s – been failing as it would have made it more difficult for casual fans to gain access to the football ground (King, 1998).
10 See: www.gov.uk/government/news/act-summer-security-know-the-game-plan [accessed 10/2019].
11 See: www.liverpoolecho.co.uk/news/liverpool-news/dozens-fans-pulled-police-arrested-16908331 [accessed 11/2019].
12 See for example: www.youtube.com/watch?v=Ttx8QuFMjZ8 [accessed 10/2019].

References

Allen, C. (2008) *Housing Market Renewal and Social Class*, Abingdon: Routledge.
Andrejevic, M. (2005) 'The work of watching one another: Lateral surveillance, risk, and governance', *Surveillance & Society* 2: 479–497.
Armstrong, G. and Giulianotti, R. (1998) 'From another angle. Police surveillance and football supporters', *Surveillance: Closed Circuit Television and Social Control* (Eds. C. Norris, J. Moran and G. Armstrong), Aldershot: Ashgate.
Armstrong, G., Giulianotti, R. and Hobbs, D. (2017) *Policing the 2012 London Olympics: Legacy and Social Exclusion*, London: Routledge.

Atkinson, M. and Young, K. (2012) 'Shadowed by the corpse of war: Sport spectacles and the spirit of terrorism', *International Review for the Sociology of Sport* 47(3): 286–306.

Azzi, V. (2017) 'Security for show? The militarisation of public space in light of the 2016 Rio Olympic games', *Contexto Internacional* 39(3): 589–607.

Bain, W. (eds.) (2006) *The Empire of Security and the Safety of the People*, Oxon: Routledge.

Bairner, A. (1999) 'Soccer, masculinity, and violence in Northern Ireland: Between hooliganism and terrorism', *Men and Masculinities* 1(3): 284–301.

Bairner, A. (2006) 'The Leicester school and the study of football hooliganism', *Sport in Society* 9(4): 583–598.

Bale, J. (2003) *Sports Geography: Second Edition*, London/New York: Routledge.

Baudrillard, J. (1993) *The Transparency of Evil*, London: Verso.

Bauman, Z. and Lyon, D. (2013) *Liquid Surveillance*, Cambridge: Polity Press.

BBC. (2009) 'Nadal attacks drug-testing rules', available from: http://news.bbc.co.uk/sport1/hi/tennis/7885314.stm [accessed 1/2022].

BBC. (2017) 'Police to use facial recognition at Champions League final', available from: www.bbc.co.uk/news/technology-39735637[accessed 1/2022].

BBC. (2018) '2,000 wrongly matched with possible criminals at Champions League', available from: https://www.bbc.co.uk/news/uk-wales-south-west-wales-44007872.

Bellamy, A.J. (2005) *Security Communities and Their Neighbours*, New York: Palgrave Macmillan.

Bennett, C.J. and Haggerty, K.D. (eds.) (2011) *Security Games: Surveillance and Control at Mega-Events*, Oxon: Routledge.

Bernhard, D. and Martin, A.K. (2011) 'Rethinking security at the Olympics', *Security Games: Surveillance and Control at Mega-Events* (Eds. C.J. Bennett and K.D. Haggerty), London: Routledge, pp. 20–35.

Best, S. (2010) 'The Leicester school of football hooliganism: An evaluation', *Soccer & Society* 11(5): 573–587.

Bigo, D. (2016) 'Rethinking security at the crossroad of international relations and criminology', *British Journal of Criminology* 56(6): 1068–1086.

Bleacher Report. (2019) ' "Rams" Clay Matthews fined for tweet criticizing NFL refs' controversial calls', available from: https://bleacherreport.com/articles/2858876-rams-clay-matthews-fined-for-tweet-criticizing-nfl-refs-controversial-calls [accessed 1/2022].

Bloyce, D. and Lovett, E. (2012) 'Planning for the London 2012 Olympic and paralympic legacy: A figurational analysis', *International Journal of Sport Policy and Politics* 4(3): 361–377.

Boykoff, J. (2020) *Nolympians: Inside the Fight Against Capitalist Mega-Sports in Los Angeles, Tokyo and Beyond*, Nova Scotia: Fernwood.

Boyle, P. and Haggerty, K.D. (2009) Spectacular security: Mega-events and the security complex, *International Political Sociology* 3(3): 257–274.

Braun, R. and Vliegenthart, R. (2008) 'The contentious fans: The impact of repression, media coverage, grievances and aggressive play on supporters' violence', *International Sociology* 23(6): 796–818.

Breen Smyth, M., Gunning, J., Jackson, R., Kassimeris, G. and Robinson, P. (2008) 'Critical terrorism studies–An introduction', *Critical Studies on Terrorism* 1(1): 1–4.

Carlsen, J. and Taylor, A. (2003) 'Mega-events and urban renewal: The case of the Manchester 2002 commonwealth games', *Event Management* 8(1): 15–22.

Carroll, R. (1980) 'Football hooliganism in England', *International Review of Sport Sociology* 15(2): 77–92.

Castells, M. (2011 [1997]) *The Power of Identity*, Oxford: Blackwell.

Clavel, A. (2013) 'Armed forces and sports mega events: An accepted involvement in a globalized world', *Sport in Society* 16(2): 205–222.

Cleland, J. (2019) 'Sports fandom in the risk society: Analyzing perceptions and experiences of risk, security and terrorism at elite sports events', *Sociology of Sport Journal* 36(2): 144–151.

Cleland, J. and Cashmore, E. (2018) 'Nothing will be the same again after the Stade de France attack: Reflections of association football fans on terrorism, security and surveillance', *Journal of Sport and Social Issues* 42(6): 454–469.

Clément, M. (2021) 'Emotions and affect in terrorism research: Epistemological shift and ways ahead', *Critical Studies on Terrorism* 14(2): 247–270.

Cohen, C.J. and Dawson, M.C. (1993) 'Neighborhood poverty and African American politics', *American Political Science Review* 87(2): 286–302.

Coleman, R. (2012 [2004]) *Reclaiming the Streets*, Abingdon: Routledge.

Coleman, R. and Sim, J. (2000) '"You'll never walk alone": CCTV surveillance, order and neo-liberal rule in Liverpool city centre', *British Journal of Sociology* 51(4): 623–639.

Colluci, M. and Jones, K.L. (eds.) (2013) *International and Comparative Sports Justice*, Rome: Sports Law and Policy Centre.

Cornelissen, S. and Swart, K. (2006) 'The 2010 football world cup as a political construct: The challenge of making good on an African promise', *The Sociological Review* 54(2): 108–123.

Crabbe, T. (2003) '"The public gets what the public wants" England football fans, "truth" claims and mediated realities', *International Review for the Sociology of Sport* 38(4): 413–425.

Crawford, G. (2004) *Consuming Sport: Fans, Sport and Culture*, London: Routledge.

Dansero, E. and Puttilli, M. (2010) 'Mega-events tourism legacies: The case of the Torino 2006 Winter Olympic Games – a territorialisation approach', *Leisure Studies* 29(3): 321–341.

Dimeo, P. and Møller, V. (2018) *The Anti-Doping Crisis in Sport: Causes, Consequences, Solutions*, Abingdon: Routledge.

Dixon, K. (2014) 'The role of surveillance in the construction of authentic football fandom practice', *Surveillance & Society* 11(4): 424–438.

Eick, V. (2011) '"Secure our profits!" The FIFA™ in Germany 2006', *Security Games: Surveillance and Control at Mega-Events* (Eds. C.J. Bennett and K.D. Haggerty), London: Routledge, pp. 87–102.

Essex, S.J. and Chalkley, B.S. (1998) 'The Olympics as a catalyst of urban renewal: A review', *Leisure Studies* 17(3): 187–206.

Falcous, M. and Silk, M. (2005) 'Manufacturing consent: Mediated sporting spectacle and the cultural politics of the "war on terror"', *International Journal of Media & Cultural Politics* 1(1): 59–65.

Free, M. and Hughson, J. (2003) 'Settling accounts with hooligans: Gender blindness in football supporter subculture research', *Men and Masculinities* 6(2): 136–155.

Frosdick, S. and Marsh, P. (2005) *Football Hooliganism*, Devon: Willian.

FSA. (2019) "Guinea pigs" – Cardiff City fans criticise facial recognition, available from: https://thefsa.org.uk/news/using-football-fans-as-guinea-pigs-cardiff-city-fans-criticise-facial-recognition-tech/ [accessed 11/2021].

Fussey, P., Davies, B. and Innes, M. (2021) '"Assisted" facial recognition and the reinvention of suspicion and discretion in digital policing', *The British Journal of Criminology* 61(2): 325–344.

Garcia, B. (2010) 'A cultural mega event's impact on innovative capabilities in art production: The results of Stavanger being the European capital of culture in 2008', *International Journal of Innovation and Regional Development* 2(4): 353–371.

Garland, J. and Rowe, M. (1999) 'The "English disease" – cured or in remission? An analysis of police responses to football hooliganism in the 1990s', *Crime Prevention and Community Safety* 1(4): 35–47.

Giulianotti, R. (2011) 'Sport mega events, urban football carnivals and securitised commodification: The case of the English premier league', *Urban Studies* 48(15): 3293–3310.
Giulianotti, R. (2013) 'Six security legacies of major sporting events', *ICSS Journal* 1(1): 95–101.
Giulianotti, R. (2019) 'Football events, memories and globalization', *Soccer & Society* 20(7–8): 903–911.
Giulianotti, R. and Klauser, F. (2010) 'Security governance and sport mega-events: Toward an interdisciplinary research agenda', *Journal of Sport and Social Issues* 34(1): 48–60.
Giulianotti, R. and Klauser, F. (2011) 'Introduction: Security and surveillance at sport mega events', *Urban Studies* 48(15): 3157–3168.
Giulianotti, R. and Klauser, F. (2012) 'Sport mega-events and "terrorism": A critical analysis', *International Review for the Sociology of Sport* 47(3): 307–323.
Goldblatt, D. (2006) *The Ball Is Round: A Global History of Football*, London: Penguin.
Goold, B., Loader, I. and Thumala, A. (2013) ' "The banality of security": The curious case of surveillance cameras', *British Journal of Criminology* 53: 977–996.
Gotsbachner, E. (2001) 'Xenophobic normality: The discriminatory impact of habitualized discourse dynamics', *Discourse & Society* 12(6): 729–759.
The Guardian. (2018) 'Welsh police wrongly identify thousands as potential criminals', available from: www.theguardian.com/uk-news/2018/may/05/welsh-police-wrongly-identify-thousands-as-potential-criminals [accessed 1/2022].
Haggerty, K.D. and Ericson, R.V. (2000) 'The surveillant assemblage', *British Journal of Sociology* 51(4): 605–622.
Haggerty, K.D., Wilson, D. and Smith, G.J. (2011) 'Theorizing surveillance in crime control', *Theoretical Criminology* 15(3): 231–237.
Hall, C.M. (2006) 'Urban entrepreneurship, corporate interests and sports mega-events: The thin policies of competitiveness within the hard outcomes of neoliberalism', *The Sociological Review* 54(2): 59–70.
Hamilton-Smith, N., McBride, M. and Atkinson, C. (2021) 'Lights, camera, provocation? Exploring experiences of surveillance in the policing of Scottish football', *Policing and Society* 31(2): 179–194.
Hanstad, D.V. and Loland, S. (2009) 'Elite athletes' duty to provide information on their whereabouts: Justifiable anti-doping work or an indefensible surveillance regime?' *European Journal of Sport Science* 9(1): 3–10.
Hargreaves, J. (1987) 'The body, sport and power relations', *Sport, Leisure and Social Relations* (Eds. D. Jay and A. Tomlinson), London: Routledge, pp. 139–159.
Hodges, A. (2019) *Fan Activism, Protest and Politics: Ultras in Post-Socialist Croatia*, Oxon: Routledge.
Horgan, J. and Boyle, M.J. (2008) 'A case against "critical terrorism studies"', *Critical Studies on Terrorism* 1(1): 51–64.
Horne, J.D. and Manzenreiter, W. (2004) 'Accounting for mega-events: Forecast and actual impacts of the 2002 football world cup finals on the host countries Japan/Korea', *International Review for the Sociology of Sport* 39(2): 187–203.
Hutchins, B. and Andrejevcic, M. (2021) 'Olympian surveillance: Sports stadiums and the normalization of biometric monitoring', *International Journal of Communication* 15: 363–382.
Jackson, R., Smyth, M.B. and Gunning, J. (eds.) (2009) *Critical Terrorism Studies: A New Research Agenda*, London: Routledge.
Jackson, R., Toros, H., Jarvis, L. and Heath-Kelly, C. (eds.) (2020) *Critical Terrorism Studies at Ten: Contributions, Cases and Future Challenges*, Abingdon: Routledge.
Jones, C. (2001) 'Mega-events and host-region impacts: Determining the true worth of the 1999 Rugby World Cup', *International Journal of Tourism Research* 3(3): 241–251.

Kennedy, L. and Silva, D. (2020) '"Discipline that hurts": Punitive logics and governance in sport', *Punishment & Society* 22(5): 658–680.

King, A. (2002 [1998]) *The End of the Terraces: The Transformation of English Football in the 1990s*, London: Leicester University Press.

Klauser, F. (2017) *Surveillance & Space*, London: Sage.

Lee Ludvigsen, J.A. (2019a) '"Safety first": Towards a security legacy and fan-oriented research agenda in the English premier league', *Sport in Society* 25(3): 880–900.

Lee Ludvigsen, J.A. (2019b) 'Transnational fan reactions to transnational trends: Norwegian Liverpool supporters, "authenticity" and "filthy-rich" club owners', *Soccer & Society* 20(6): 872–900.

Lee Ludvigsen, J.A. (2022) *Sport Mega-Events, Security and Covid-19: Securing the Football World*, London/New York: Routledge.

Lee Ludvigsen, J.A. and Millward, P. (2020) 'A security theater of dreams: Supporters' responses to "safety" and "security" following the Old Trafford "fake bomb" evacuation', *Journal of Sport and Social Issues* 44(1): 3–21.

Lewis, C. (2015) 'Dislocation and uncertainty in East Manchester: The legacy of the commonwealth games', *Sociological Research Online* 20(2): 185–191.

Loader, I. and Walker, N. (2007) *Civilizing Security*, Cambridge: Cambridge University Press.

Lorenz, S.L. and Murray, R. (2014) '"Goodbye to the Gangstas" The NBA dress code, ray emery, and the policing of blackness in basketball and hockey', *Journal of Sport and Social Issues* 38(1): 23–50.

Lyon, D. (2007) 'Surveillance, security and social sorting: Emerging research priorities', *International Criminal Justice Review* 17(3): 161–170.

Macagno, F. and Walton, D. (2019) 'Emotive meaning in political argumentation', *Informal Logic* 39(3): 229–261.

Marsh, P., Rosser, E. and Harré, R. (1978) *The Rules of Disorder*, London: Routledge and Kegan Paul Books.

Mastrogiannakis, D. and Dorville, C. (2013) 'Security and sport mega-events: A complex relation', *Sport in Society* 16(2): 133–139.

Mayhew, P. and Hough, M. (1983) 'The British Crime Survey', *British Journal of Criminology* 23: 394–395.

Millward, P. (2011) *The Global Football League: Transnational Networks, Social Movements and Sport in the New Media Age*, Basingstoke: Palgrave Macmillan.

Misener, L. (2013) 'A media frames analysis of the legacy discourse for the 2010 winter paralympic games', *Communication & Sport* 1(4): 342–364.

Møller, V. (2011) 'One step too far – about WADA's whereabouts rule', *International Journal of Sport Policy and Politics* 3(2): 177–190.

Monahan, T. (2011) 'Surveillance as cultural practice', *The Sociological Quarterly* 52(4): 495–508.

Palmer, C. (2012) *Global Sports Policy*, London: Sage.

Park, J.K. (2005) 'Governing doped bodies: The world anti-doping agency and the global culture of surveillance', *Cultural Studies? Critical Methodologies* 5(2): 174–188.

Pearson, G. (2012) *An Ethnography of English Football Fans: Cans, Cops and Carnivals*, Manchester/New York: Manchester University Press.

Petersen-Wagner, R. (2015) 'Cosmopolitan fandom: A critical postcolonial analysis of Liverpool FC's supporters discourses in Brazil and Switzerland', PhD thesis: Durham University.

Pillay, U. and Bass, O. (2008) 'Mega-events as a response to poverty reduction: The 2010 FIFA world cup and its urban development implications', *Urban Forum* 19: 329–346.

Price, J., Farrington, N. and Hall, L. (2013) 'Changing the game? The impact of Twitter on relationships between football clubs, supporters and the sports media', *Soccer & Society* 14(4): 446–461.
Primoratz, I. (1990) 'What is terrorism?' *Journal of Applied Philosophy* 7(2): 129–138.
Radomyski, A. (2021) 'Security of the 2014 Winter Olympics in Sochi', *Safety & Defense* 7(1): 93–106.
Rahmani Khalili, E. and Safavian, S.M. (2019) 'A sociological explanation of the phenomenon of soccer hooliganism case study: Soccer spectators of Tehran', *Social Sciences* 26(86): 123–156.
Redhead, S. (1991) 'Some reflections on discourses on football hooliganism', *The Sociological Review* 39(3): 479–486.
Rees, A., Gibbons, T. and Dixon, K. (2014) 'The surveillance of racing cyclists in training: A Bourdieusian perspective', *Surveillance & Society* 11(4): 466–480.
Reeves, J. (2012) 'If you see something, say something: Lateral surveillance and the uses of responsibility', *Surveillance & Society* 10(3/4): 235–248.
Reuters. (2019) 'With helicopters and dogs, massive Super Bowl security in Atlanta', available from: www.reuters.com/article/us-football-nfl-superbowl-security/with-helicopters-and-dogs-massive-super-bowl-security-in-atlanta-idUSKCN1PO35Z [accessed 1/2022].
Roche, M. (2000) *Mega-Events and Modernity: Olympics and Expos in the Growth of Global Culture*, London: Routledge.
Roche, M. (2006) 'Mega-events and modernity revisited: Globalization and the case of the Olympics', *The Sociological Review* 54(2): 27–40.
Roche, M. (2017) *Mega-Events and Social Change: Spectacle, Legacy and Public Culture*, Manchester: Manchester University Press.
Rookwood, J. (2009) *Fan Perspectives of Football Hooliganism: Defining, Analysing and Responding to the British Phenomenon*, Saarbrucken: VDM Verlag.
Samatas, M. (2007) 'Security and surveillance in the Athens 2004 Olympics: Some lessons from a troubled story', *International Criminal Justice Review* 17(3): 220–238.
Samatas, M. (2011) 'Surveillance in Athens 2004 and Beijing 2008: A comparison of the Olympic surveillance modalities and legacies in two different Olympic host regimes', *Urban Studies* 48(15): 3347–3366.
Schimmel, K.S. (2011) 'From "violence-complacent" to "terrorist-ready": Post-9/11 framing of the US super bowl', *Urban Studies* 48(15): 3277–3291.
Scraton, P. (2016) *Hillsborough: The Truth*, London: Mainstream Publishing.
Sefiha, O. and Reichman, N. (2016) 'When every test is a winner: Clean cycling, surveillance, and the new preemptive governance', *Journal of Sport and Social Issues* 40(3): 197–217.
Silk, M. and Falcous, M. (2005) 'One day in September and a week in February: Mobilizing American (sporting) nationalisms', *Sociology of Sport Journal* 22(4): 447–471.
Silke, A. and Filippidou, A. (2020) 'What drives terrorist innovation? Lessons from Black September and Munich 1972', *Security Journal* 33(2): 210–227.
Simons, G. (2018) 'Brand ISIS: Interactions of the tangible and intangible environments', *Journal of Political Marketing* 17(4): 322–353.
Spaaij, R. (2006) *Understanding Football Hooliganism: A Comparison of Six Western European Football Clubs*, Amsterdam: Amsterdam University Press.
STATSports. (n.d.) 'About us', available from: https://statsports.com/ [accessed 01/2022].
Sugden, J. (2012) 'Watched by the Olympics: Surveillance and security at the Olympics', *International Review for the Sociology of Sport* 47(3): 414–429.

Takkac, M. and Akdemir, A.S. (2012) 'Training future members of the world with an understanding of global citizenship', *Procedia-Social and Behavioral Sciences* 47: 881–885.

Taylor, T. and Toohey, K. (2007) 'Perceptions of terrorism threats at the 2004 Olympic games: Implications for sport events', *Journal of Sport & Tourism* 12(2): 99–114.

Taylor, T. and Toohey, K. (2011) 'Ensuring safety at Australian sport event precincts: Creating Securitised, Sanitised and stifling spaces?' *Urban Studies* 48(15): 3259–3275.

Thornley, A. (2012) 'The 2012 London Olympics. What legacy?' *Journal of Policy Research in Tourism, Leisure and Events* 4(2): 206–210.

Toohey, K. and Taylor, T. (2006) '"Here be dragons, here be savages, here be bad plumbing": Australian media representations of sport and terrorism', *Sport in Society* 9(1): 71–93.

Toohey, K. and Taylor, T. (2012) 'Surveillance and securitization: A forgotten Sydney Olympic legacy', *International Review for the Sociology of Sport* 47(3): 324–337.

Toohey, K., Taylor, T. and Lee, C.K. (2003) 'The FIFA World Cup 2002: The effects of terrorism on sport tourists', *Journal of Sport Tourism* 8(3): 186–196.

Tsoukala, A. (2008) 'Boundary-creating processes and the social construction of threat', *Alternatives* 33: 137–152.

Tsoukala, A. (2009) *Football Hooliganism in Europe: Security and Civil Liberties in the Balance*, Basingstoke: Palgrave.

Vaughan-Williams, N. and Stevens, D. (2016) 'Vernacular theories of everyday (in)security: The disruptive potential of non-elite knowledge', *Security Dialogue* 47(1): 40–58.

Waddington, I. (2010) 'Surveillance and control in sport: A sociologist looks at the WADA whereabouts system', *International Journal of Sport Policy and Politics* 2(3): 255–274.

Walsh, A.J. and Giulianotti, R. (2001) 'This sporting mammon: A normative critique of the commodification of sport', *Journal of the Philosophy of Sport* 28(1): 53–77.

Warren, I., Palmer, D. and Whelan, C. (2014) 'Surveillance, governance and professional sport', *Surveillance & Society* 11(4): 439–453.

Whitson, D. and Horne, J. (2006) 'Underestimated costs and overestimated benefits? Comparing the outcomes of sports mega-events in Canada and Japan', *The Sociological Review* 54(2): 73–89.

Widdop, P., King, N., Parnell, D., Cutts, D. and Millward, P. (2018) 'Austerity, policy and sport participation in England', *International Journal of Sport Policy and Politics* 10(1): 7–24.

Wyn Jones, R. (1999) *Security, Strategy, and Critical Theory*, London: Lynne Rienner.

Young, K. (1986) '"The killing field": Themes in mass media responses to the Heysel Stadium riot', *International Review for the Sociology of Sport* 21(2–3): 253–266.

6
CULTURAL CRIMINOLOGY, SPORT AND TRANSGRESSION

Introduction

Cultural criminology is underpinned by a theoretical, methodological and interventionist approach to the study of crime, deviance, transgression and criminal justice. Broadly, cultural criminologists place crime, crime control and criminality in the context of culture and cultural processes. Moreover, central to this 'new sort of criminology' that will be the focus of this chapter is the notion that 'cultural dynamics carry within them the "meaning of crime"' (Ferrell et al., 2008: 2). Considered a vibrant strand of criminology since the 1990s, cultural criminological approaches subscribe to a fundamental idea that crime and the cultural domain in which illicit activities and behaviours take place should not be separated.

Ferrell et al. (2008) discuss the multiple, sometimes similar but often diverging and occasionally paradoxical, 'cultural' meanings inherent within the differing forms of acts of violence that permeate complex disordered urban environments in the twenty-first century. Setting the scene for this, they analyse a police investigation into an alleged assault in Arlington, Texas (US), in 2006. The investigation made the local news media and is picked up on by Ferrell et al. as what was initially assumed by police to be a crime of assault was later uncovered to be part of a series of amateur 'fight videos' uploaded online. This represented a quasi-sporting spectacle, very real and perhaps not so new in its sensationalist, voyeuristic depiction of human physical violence. Yet conversely quite contemporary in the means of transmission and in the video's perceived emphasis on the motivations of those involved in the fights, in which each physical 'contest' was uploaded to the Internet via social media platforms – in this case social networking service MySpace.com – in an attempt to monetise the displays of overt hyper-masculine competitivism and aggression through attracting online viewers and thus advertisement royalties with the digitally mediatised and carefully edited spectacles of physical violence.

DOI: 10.4324/9781003276791-6

The example Ferrell et al. (2008) use is highly relevant to our discussion of the theoretical lineage between cultural criminology, sport and transgression, as aside from the fact that the incident discussed transgresses the categories of illegitimate violence/crime, mediatised spectacle of deviance and an arguably 'sporting' physical contest between the young men involved, the particular phenomenon they describe distinctly encapsulates numerous cultural thematic processes of the contemporary era that are pertinent to our discussion. With the amateur online 'fight sport' spectacle not only encapsulating and embodying but also negotiating and illuminating some of the various social, cultural and politico-economic forces at play can propel some individuals in contemporary Western societies to both take part in and consume as viewers, such forms of visceral inter-personal violence as entertainment or leisure through the highly visual framework of a digitally mediatised combat 'sport'.

The ever-fluid and frequently ambiguous boundary between 'sport' and 'violence', as this chapter seeks to illuminate, is just one area where the theoretical lens of cultural criminology can be exported into the sporting sphere. In multiple ways, such as the production and consumption of fight sport events, engaging and participating in the many differing but increasingly brutal combat contests that seek to find a contemporary point of equilibrium between the rationalised rule-bound sphere of sport and the disorderly, unsympathetic and hyper-aggressive realm of 'real' physical violence. So, to provide an understanding of the many instances of transgression and deviance that occur both within and around different sports, this chapter examines the potential uses of the critical criminological lenses to further understand the many instances of 'transgression' that percolate and sometimes proliferate the domains of contemporary sports and leisure. In doing so, we simultaneously accept Ferrell et al.'s (2008: 210) 'invitation' to join them in the 'free intellectual space', in order to illuminate and further understand the multiple and contested meanings of 'crime' and 'transgression' in the late-modern Western societies. Whilst Ferrell et al. (2008) touch upon pay-per-view boxing title fights and some 'extreme sports', they do not write *specifically* on the importance of sports as a field for cultural criminological inquiry; a challenge laid out through the overarching themes of this particular chapter.

Therefore, following an overview of the historical foundations, and theoretical and methodological frameworks of cultural criminology, and its close links to the concept of 'edgework', this chapter continues by examining the participation in various 'extreme sports' or 'fight sports', and the representation and consumption of hyper-violent, (often) hyper-masculine, spectacle sports such as Mixed Martial Arts (MMA), Bare-Knuckle Boxing (BKB) and the seemingly persistent recent growth in hyper-visual, mediatised spectacles of competitive, mostly amateur, sporting violence, such as 'Backyard Brawls' and the phenomenon of the so-termed 'Team Fight Championships'. As we conclude, considering the transgressive and deviant behaviours identifiable in sport, in addition to other risk-taking subcultures (Giulianotti, 2009) that are situated within sport and leisure fields, these behaviours can be more accurately interpreted and better understood through the critical lenses offered by cultural criminological frameworks.

The Rise of Cultural Criminology

This section provides a brief overview of cultural criminology's theoretical and methodological underpinnings – as well as its intellectual aims and aspirations – that are characterised by its 'melange of intellectual and disciplinary influences' (Ferrell, 1999: 399). Following Hayward and Young (2004: 259), cultural criminology refers to the 'placing of crime and its control in the context of culture; that is, viewing both crime and the agencies of control as cultural products – as creative constructs'. As they continue, cultural criminological approaches, at their core, emphasise the interactions between 'constructions upwards and constructions downwards' (ibid.). In brief, cultural criminology remains focussed on the diverse *meanings* of crime and how such meanings are generated, constructed or reinforced in relation to cultural processes (Ferrell et al., 2008). An individual's motivations for committing crimes are thus analysed in that individual's cultural context.

More broadly, cultural criminology continues critical criminology's departure from the positivist traditions situated in the social sciences and the study of crime (see Chapter 2), which remain predominantly concerned with causal explanations and official statistics but proceed with little or no engagement with human actors' motives, identities or existence (Prieur, 2018). Cultural criminology also 'focus[es] on failures of social control' (Groombridge, 2017: 88). Hence, the differences between cultural criminology and positivist criminology remain significant (Ferrell et al., 2004) and the former 'rejects the positivist notion of objectivity in favor of a focus on the meanings of symbols and styles within particular cultural and subcultural frameworks' (Phillips and Strobl, 2006: 305–306). However, this is not based upon an outright rejection of 'numerical summaries' and the 'hard practicalities of crime and crime control' (Ferrell et al., 2004: 4). Rather, it is because: 'in choosing any mode of analysis or representation, cultural criminologists remain conscious of pluralities of meaning and possibilities of alternative perception' (ibid.). Thus, Presdee (2000) writes that cultural criminologists aim to make sense of the ways in which cultural forms and expression become criminalised. With such aim in mind, cultural criminologists employ the '"evidence" of everyday existence, wherever it is found and in whatever form it can be found; the debris of everyday life is its "data"' (p. 16).

Ferrell et al. (2004) highlight that cultural criminology now has come to represent a significant alternative to conventional criminologies. As argued elsewhere, it was predominantly in the 1990s that cultural criminology, in itself, surfaced as a distinctive criminological perspective for the study of crime, crime control, representations and meanings (Ferrell and Hayward, 2018). By the early 2000s, Ferrell et al. (2004) could refer to a recent upsurge in academic contributions to this area of critical criminology. Taken together, this remains important to comprehend the emergence of cultural criminology.

However, cultural criminology did not emerge in an 'intellectual or historical vacuum' (Ferrell and Hayward, 2018: 19). The very origins – or the starting point – of cultural criminology may be linked back to the momentum that was ignited in the 1960s and 1970s with the emergence of Birmingham School and 'New Criminology' (see Chapter 2). Importantly, cultural criminology is influenced by the seminal work of the Hebdige (1979) and Hall and Jefferson (1976) which, collectively, emphasise the importance of subcultural identities and deviance in relation to themes of power, culture and social class. Cultural criminology must also be viewed as largely shaped by the important work of Jack Katz (1988), who offers an analysis which maintains that individuals are drawn into 'crime' due to its seductive, emotional and thrilling character. Thus, whereas the influential connections between cultural criminology, Katz's (1988) work and the Centre for Contemporary Cultural Studies (CCCS) in Birmingham remain central to understand cultural criminology's early beginnings, it was not until Ferrell and Sanders' landmark text *Cultural Criminology* (1995) that a more coherent approach emerged.

The emergence of cultural criminology was also characterised by a transatlantic convergence of North American and British criminological thought. Yet the strand distinctively integrated perspectives from cultural studies, sociology, critical theory and interactionist sociology into the study of crime and crime control (Ferrell, 1999). Hence, in his account of the historical, theoretical and methodological underpinnings of cultural criminology, Ferrell (1999: 396) explains that:

> At its most basic, cultural criminology attempts to integrate the fields of criminology and cultural studies or, put differently, to import the insights of cultural studies into contemporary criminology. Given this, much scholarship in cultural criminology takes as its foundation perspectives that emerged out of the British/Birmingham School of cultural studies, and the British 'new criminology'... of the 1970s.

In addition to the mentioned influences of cultural studies, Ferrell notes that insights from 'postmodernism' have been incorporated by cultural criminologists to assist the study of 'representation, image, and style' which sits central to cultural criminology (ibid.: 397). Additionally, cultural criminology is anchored in constructivist sociological perspectives such as symbolic interactionism that assist the understanding of the social and political construction of crime, deviance and crime control.

Moreover, the intellectual influences on cultural criminology also impact its methodological frameworks. Resultantly, to engage with the cultural context and meanings of crime and deviancy, Ferrell (1999) reminds us that cultural criminologists have tended to employ either ethnographic fieldwork or rely upon media or textual analyses. Such methodologies have been employed in the questioning of representations of crime and justice and the overreliance on 'official' government data (Phillips and Strobl, 2006). Accordingly, following the lead of Ferrell (1999), four broad areas of inquiry are associated with cultural criminology. These may be summarised as follows: *crime as culture; culture as crime; media constructions of crime and crime control* and, finally, the *politics of culture, crime, and cultural criminology*. Fundamentally, as this chapter proceeds, we seek to capture these (sometimes overlapping) areas of inquiry within the domains of sport and leisure.

Whilst we have already mentioned Ferrell et al.'s (2008: 210) invitation to the 'free intellectual space' of cultural criminology, it was more recently reiterated by Ferrell and Hayward (2018: 30) that cultural criminology should remain both 'open' and 'invitational'. Cultural criminology, they argue, 'remains to be continued' (ibid.). Therefore, having unpacked cultural criminology, its historical and disciplinary influences, its emergence and approaches, this chapter now seeks to partake in cultural criminology's continuation. Whilst we seek to revisit the theory of 'edgework' next – as closely related to cultural criminology – we will apply the relevant lenses to MMA and BKB as often-considered two commodified, violent, masculine and transgressive sports.

Edgework, Voluntary Risk-Taking and the Joy Transgression

Cultural criminology is underpinned by an approach to the study of crime, deviance and transgression which appreciates the relevant dynamic meanings and the relevant cultural context. Following this, we now will outline how the sociology of voluntary risk-taking and what is theorised as 'edgework' (Lyng, 1990) can be situated in sport, and subsequently employed by scholars working within the core premises of cultural criminology, who aim to better understand risk-taking and the search for sensation and excitement.

Stephen Lyng (1990) introduced the theory of edgework, which remains principally concerned with the explanation of voluntary risk-taking and 'about individuals "working an edge"' (Kidder, 2022: 183) and, in doing so, often risk their health and well-being. Significantly, there are important overlaps between 'edgework' and cultural criminology. Not only does the concept of 'risk' represent a 'fundamental feature' of criminology (see Anderson and Brown, 2010), but *crime-as-edgework* has been a prominent theme within cultural criminology, whereas the relevant socio-cultural contexts of 'crime' or illicit activities play an important role in edgework approaches to crime (Anderson and Brown, 2010). As Pauschinger (2020: 512) reminds us, 'edgework' originates from cultural criminology and the latter's 'phenomenology of emotions'. Indeed, the concept of edgework has been widely applied to specific illicit instances of transgression and crime (see Ferrell et al., 2001) such as drug experimentation. In such contexts, it may explain why: 'the seductive character of many criminal activities may derive from the particular sensations and emotions generated by the high-risk character of these activities' (Lyng, 2004: 360).

However, the edgework framework has also influenced the growing body of literature on risk-taking and the joy of transgression and pursuit of sensation in sport and leisure contexts (see e.g. Bunn, 2017; Kidder, 2022). In sport, edgework theory has been applied to extreme sports and activities such as parkour (Kidder, 2019), skydiving (Laurendeau, 2006), BASE jumping (Forsey, 2012), MMA (Channon, 2020; and discussed later) and white-water kayaking (Fletcher, 2008). As such, this section will revisit Lyng's theory of edgework, as specifically situated in sport, and pay attention to how edgework can connect understandings of micro-level practices (such as voluntary risk-taking) with wider, macro-level structures (Kidder, 2022). For Kidder (2022: 183), Lyng's edgework theory has 'significantly impacted cultural approaches to the study of risk'. At the time of writing, Lyng's (1990) seminal article has received over 1700 citations on Google Scholar, demonstrating the wide reach and purchase of his original edgework study. Subsequently, Lyng (2004, 2005) has also developed further his thesis on voluntary risk taking.

Edgework can explain why dangerous and potentially threatening situations appeal to individuals – or 'edgeworkers' – who are seeking to voluntarily explore the 'edges' of dangerous environments that pose existential risks and threats, despite the absence of material rewards for engaging in such activities. Such perspective is simultaneously 'strongly connected' to the cultural criminological recognition of emotions and attractions in the understanding of the 'roots of transgression, as the social structures within which they are embedded' (Pauschinger, 2020: 513). Further, as Anderson and Brown (2010: 551) write, cultural criminologists have 'widely invoked the edgework concept to describe crime as an act of cultural resistance and a site for the expression of personal agency'.

Lyng (1990) had originally observed an increase in the media attention dedicated to high-risk sport and leisure activities including 'hang gliding, skydiving, scuba diving [and] rock climbing' (p. 852). For Lyng, individuals' pursuit of experiences that could lead to personal injury or death emerged as a paradox considering the wider public agenda that remained preoccupied with risk minimisation and the reduction of risks to death and health. In this context, it remains imperative to briefly consider Beck's (1992) influential thesis on the risk society. In Beck's (1992) view, the scientific and technological progress of the modernity led to a society preoccupied with risks and their aversion: the 'risk society'. In the risk society, risks are increasingly de-localised, catastrophic and man-made. This shift, however, has had enormous political, societal and individual implications. On the individual level, it has meant that individuals face new sets of risks that sharpen the 'reflexivity of citizens towards the damaging and potentially disastrous effects of modernization' (Giulianotti, 2009: 550).

Furthermore, the eroding changes to the structures and traditional ties of family, class, ethnicity and gender in the new 'risk regime' also led to a shift away from the 'standard biographies' towards the 'do-it-yourself' biographies defined by less certainty and endless personal decision-making (Mythen, 2005: 132). So, returning to the concept of edgework, it is within this risk-infused and oriented everyday milieu enacted by the risk society that some individuals voluntarily search towards extreme risks. However, at the heart of this lies a quest for sensation, excitement and thrill that are some of the fundamental motives behind these experiences and activities. Following Lyng's (1990: 885) sociological explanation of voluntary risk-taking, this may be conceptualised as 'involving, most fundamentally, the problem of negotiating the boundary between chaos and order'.

Lyng's original theory can, according to Kidder's (2022) recent summary and update, be divided into three separate aspects, that is, (1) material practices, (2) embodied experiences and (3) supporting structures. Here, material practices refer to those activities and skills that are related to edgework. The embodied experiences, meanwhile, encompass what Lyng (1990) referred to as 'sensations'. This is the 'affective product of edgework's material practices' (Kidder, 2022: 187) and may involve the emotions of fear, thrill and dangers that 'edgeworkers' experience, for example, when a skydiver jumps from a plane. This is where a high-consequence activity is entered; and the 'outcome cannot be known in advance' but where the 'practitioner's usual perceptions of the world become altered' (p. 187). Lastly, the supporting structures refer to those connections between the micro-level practices of voluntary risk-taking and then the 'macro-level structures that sustain them' (ibid.: 188). Here, Kidder submits that:

> Lyng's (1990) original approach to the micro-macro link was a Marxian analysis of alienation combined with a Meadian perspective on the spontaneity of the "I." To be succinct, in contemporary Western societies, people are largely alienated at their jobs and feel little personal efficacy in their paid labour. So, it is in their leisure pursuits that dissatisfied workers find purpose and satisfaction. Because of the consequentiality of edgework practices and the need to acquire specific skills, voluntary risk offers a unique arena to engage in meaningful activity – namely, surviving what would otherwise kill or maim.
> *(ibid.: 188)*

In that sense, for individual edgeworkers, edgework 'serves a compensatory function in modern society' (Anderson and Brown, 2010: 546; see also Giulianotti, 2009). Following Lyng's lead, those individuals who engage in edgework do this to compensate for an alienated experience of 'deskilled and rationalized labor' (ibid.). On a basic level, working on the edge hence becomes a mean for thrill, satisfaction, personal agency and a temporary departure from the 'everyday' life.

As aforementioned, edgework theory has been applied to several sports and leisure activities and subcultures. For example, Ferrell et al. (2001) ethnographically examine BASE jumping in the US in the case of the Bridge Day event and deploy the edgework framework. As a recreational sport, BASE jumping refers to the activity of illegally parachuting from bridges, building, antennas and cliffs. It originally emerged as an 'underground, mostly illegal world of high risk and high adventure' (p. 180). Here, 'BASE' forms an acronym that describes those fixed objects that participants primarily jump from, which includes B (building), A (antennae), S (span/bridge) and E (earth/cliffs) (Green et al., 2020). Fundamentally, BASE jumping is predominantly an illegal activity that occurs at the nighttime since the participants, or jumpers, often climb over security fences, ignore no-trespassing signs and enter construction sites or famous landmarks (Ferrell et al., 2001).

Whilst often an illegal activity, the mentioned Bridge Day event represents a legal and annual one-day event where jumpers launch themselves from an 876-feet-high bridge and have seconds to deploy their parachutes or canopies, adapt their body position and flight path and land safely (Kerr and MacKenzie, 2020). Despite the background of a blurred illicit/licit activity and the obvious safety and legal risks, Ferrell et al. (2001) argue that the one-day events also give insight into the individual, collective meaning constructions and subcultural media productions. As they note, with the emergence of BASE jumping (as an activity) so has a BASE jumping subculture emerged, too. This subculture, they argue, 'provides the kinds of technical supports, informal guidelines, information on sites and security, measures of prestige and vocabularies of motive' (ibid.: 181). Ultimately, this renders BASE jumping both possible and meaningful. As argued:

> Whether launching themselves from the New River Gorge Bridge crowded with some 100,000 spectators, gliding into the gorge below, or touching down in the congested landing area at river's edge, jumpers on Bridge Day participate in the growing spectacle of their sport. Through their participation, they find themselves caught up in a complex, expanding spiral of mediated meaning. The jumpers can no more escape the gaze of the Bridge Day audience than they can escape the mediated dynamics that increasingly infuse and elongate their experience at Bridge Day and beyond.
> *(Ferrell et al., 2001: 183)*

The edgework approach lies close to cultural criminology. In this respect, this section has unpacked the intersections between Lyng's notion of edgework (1990, 2004, 2005) and sporting cultures and lifestyles with a specific reference to BASE jumping (Ferrell et al., 2001). As these examples prove, in late-modern societies preoccupied and shaped by risk and uncertainty (Beck, 1992; Bauman, 2000), voluntary risk-taking or liminal leisure – occurring in or as connected to sport – can provide risk-seeking individuals, or 'edgeworkers', with specific skills, purpose, satisfaction and meaning. To best understand this, however, a contextual appreciation is necessary. The importance of meaning behind what appears to be 'transgressive' or 'deviant' activities will be discussed further in the next section, in relation to MMA and other combat sports. However, as contended throughout this chapter, the critical analysis of the many transgressive and risky behaviours in sport can extend the criminology of edgework further in this regard.

To better understand the meanings of edgework, Kidder (2022) argues that there is a distinctive need for detailed and 'involved' examinations of how individuals frame their own actions. He writes that, 'studying the discursive frames used to account for edgework offers researchers new opportunities for understanding historical shifts in cultural interpretations about what constitutes danger and meaningful actions in relation to it' (p. 185). Meanwhile, Bunn (2017: 1319) holds that considerations of the applicability of edgework require 'a greater phenomenology of risk and risk-taking', which 'explores voluntary risks in its relationship with key safeties, dangers, and distinctions of day-to-day life'.

Here, the previously mentioned and advocated methodologies of cultural criminology, such as the 'new' and occasionally 'risky' ethnographies (see e.g. Armstrong, 1998; Wacquant, 1995), appear particularly constructive and inviting in order to further explore and comprehend the micro-macro processual relations between risk-taking within the realms of sport and leisure and the wider risk and transgressive cultures of late-modern 'Western' societies. And, moreover, how 'risk takers describe their experience at the edge as self-actualizing or self-determining, authentically real and creatively satisfying' (Lyng, 2004: 362) in the continuous quest for and negotiation of identity, (sub)cultural capital and social status, belonging, tradition and meaning.

MMA: History, Representations and Consumption

This section delves further into the social history, representation and global consumption of the sport of MMA – sometimes referred to as 'cage fighting' in popular-cultural commentary. It attempts to understand further its complex (sub-)cultural meanings and participants' motivations for their engagement with the sport. Whereas other combat sports, including boxing, have previously been studied by social scientists and immersive ethnographers (Sugden, 1985, 1996; Wacquant, 1995, 2004, 2011; Woodward, 2004, 2007; Jump, 2020), Spencer (2009) highlights that, up until the point of his publication, there had been very limited academic research on MMA. Notwithstanding, more recently, MMA has been dedicated to more critical scholarly attention, paralleled with the increased popularity of the sport globally (particularly the US-based MMA competition the Ultimate Fighting Championship (UFC)). To date, scholars of sport have, for example, explored MMA in relation to fighters' motivations and mental health (e.g. Sugden, 2021), philosophy (Holt and Ramsay, 2021), masculine identities (Channon and Matthews, 2015), 'edgework' (Channon, 2020), civilisation processes and spectacle (Sánchez García and Malcolm, 2010), and violence and pain (Andreasson and Johansson, 2019). As stated, the upsurge in academic recognition of MMA should be seen in light of the enhanced global popularity of the sport, both as a professional combat sport and in terms of wider public consumption through media and amateur participation, which grew rapidly throughout the 2010s (Sugden, 2021).

The sport of professional boxing, the more longstanding 'big brother' of MMA in fight sport terms, has within academic and popular discourse historically been considered *the* most violent sport. However, this conception has altered since the late 1990s, and particularly in more recent years, following MMA's rise on amateur and professional level (Spencer, 2009). Yet it remains crucial to underline here that versions of such extreme fighting or 'cage fighting' can be traced back to 648 BC and the 33rd Olympiad (Andreasson and Johansson, 2019) with many forms of sometimes competitive and punitive physical violence as a public spectacle existing in various degrees of prevalence in human societies globally throughout history.

Keeping this historical view of subjective public violence in mind remains imperative for elucidating further a greater understanding of the complex continuous interactions between local, national and international structural forces and individual agency involved in teasing out the theoretical explanations behind the recent rise in popularity of MMA at this particular point in history in the early twenty-first century. In addition, there are symbolic cultural meanings involved in the motivations for taking part in this sporting practice as either a novice, amateur or professional. These meanings relate to the paradoxical processual flows of social continuity and change and that are crucial in generating a more detailed academic understanding of the rise in popularity of MMA and other spectacle 'fight sports' using the critical cultural criminological lens outlined by Ferrell et al. (2008).

MMA refers to 'sport activities based on the combination of bare handed (as opposed to with weapons) oriental martial arts and Western combat sports' (Sánchez García and Malcolm, 2010: 40). The full-contact sport, which involves separate events for men and women, encompasses an:

> amalgam of un-armed combat styles though different forms of MMA placing different emphases on the specific combination of standing striking techniques (from disciplines such as boxing, karate, kick-boxing, kung-fu, taekwondo, thai-boxing, savate) and grappling techniques and fighting on the ground (from disciplines such as judo, Greco-Roman wrestling, sambo or Brazilian jiu-jitsu).
>
> *(Sánchez García and Malcolm, 2010: 40)*

Although a form of MMA, known as *Vale Tudo* or 'Anything Goes', existed in Brazil prior to the sport's professional introduction in the US, it is usually the US-based competition and marketing brand UFC that is generally credited for being most influential in the recent global rise of MMA as a sport and form of popular-cultural entertainment. The first UFC competition – UFC 1 – took place in Denver, Colorado, in 1993 – as a spectacle also broadcast around the world via pay-per-view television, and the subsequent introduction of a framework of unified rules of Mixed Martial Arts as an international professional sport was proposed, negotiated and agreed upon by various athletic commissions throughout the 2000s (UFC, 2021). These rules were then unanimously adopted by the Association of Boxing Commissions (ABC) on 30 July 2009. The goal of this 'new' form of sporting competition was, according to UFC's website (2021): 'to find "the Ultimate Fighting Champion" by staging a single-night tournament featuring the best athletes skilled in the various disciplines of all martial arts, including karate, jiu-jitsu, boxing, kickboxing, grappling, wrestling, sumo and other combat sports' (UFC, 2021). Thus, the winner of the tournament would be crowned the 'ultimate' fighting champion, whilst this seemingly served to test the 'usefulness' of different fight disciplines against one another, as much as the individual athletic abilities of the participants.

During MMA contests, fighters will typically compete in a ring or eight-sided caged-in area known as the octagon. Here, pain is inflicted on opponents and number of clean strikes, aggressiveness and fighting style scored by judges, and TKO match victories decided by 'punching, kicking, elbowing and kneeing their opponents into submission' (Spencer, 2009: 120). As such, risk and pain are commonly considered to lie at MMA's core, in addition to its inherent violent and transgressive elements (Sugden, 2021).

With the real risk of serious injury for competitors – and even the death of fighters (The Guardian, 2016; Sánchez García and Malcolm, 2010) – MMA has been surrounded by media and public controversy since its inception. This is much due to its 'sheer violence' and the mainstream descriptions of the sport as 'barbaric' and 'inhumane' (Andreasson and Johansson, 2019: 1183–1184) by external observers. Consequently, legislators and medical communities have previously called for a ban of the sport (ibid.). Indeed, professional MMA remains illegal in some countries, such as Norway, and has only recently been decriminalised in others, such as Canada in 2013.

Despite the amount of controversy, the UFC – the 'biggest' MMA organisation internationally in terms of television viewing figures, live crowd attendance figures, financial turnover, sponsorship revenues and prize money (for fighters) – has since its inception in 1993 evolved rapidly. The UFC has developed from a somewhat novelty martial arts tournament into a global mediatised spectacle that attracts millions of television viewers around the world and enormous crowds to its live shows (see Andreasson and Johansson, 2019). Indeed, the UFC, and the sport of MMA, have become a part of the contemporary consumer culture landscape of many nations globally (ibid.).

Currently, the sport's best fighters, such as Anderson Silva, Conor McGregor, Khabib Nurmagomedov and Randy Couture – to name just a few – enjoy the same contemporary celebrity status as the top athletes of other, more longstanding, professional sports such as the top athletes of the National Football League and English Premier League, numerous National Basketball Association (NBA) stars and many other sports personalities. Both their financial net-worth as athletes and the global pay-per-view television viewing figures of UFC events make this branch of contemporary MMA – despite the outlined controversies, violence and danger for participants in the octagon – one of the most popular sporting spectacles of the contemporary era. This simultaneously renders the representation and consumption of MMA a relevant site of inquiry for the cultural criminological engagement with the media's construction of crime, violence and deviancy more broadly (cf. Ferrell, 1999). MMA remains a hyper-violent and masculine sport which concurrently represents a popular form of entertainment in late-modern consumer societies.

It is here that one must pause and redraw the intellectual paradox between historic continuity and change and look to situate the global rise in popularity of MMA as a spectator and participatory sport at this particular point of history as set within the wider analysis of the evolution of late-modern 'Western' societies.

As notwithstanding the many public health horror stories spawned by the rapid industrial expansion of urban settlements in the global 'North' in the 1700 and 1800s, there is much historical data (e.g. Briggs et al., 1996; Gurr, 1981) to suggest that, in Europe particularly, overall levels of serious inter-personal and 'every day' violence have been gradually falling since the mid-fourteenth century. Conversely, despite a fall in overall levels of violence throughout the Modern Age, incidents of serious 'subjective' inter-personal violence have become confined to some of the most deprived urban locales in the most unequal nations. If one briefly adopts the philosophical viewpoints of Zizek (2008) and contemporary criminological scholars such as Hillyard et al. (2004) and Hall (2002), it could be argued that rather than disappearing from societies of the global 'North' throughout the Modern Age, that violence, disorder and harm more broadly have simply become woven into the structural fabric of increasingly unequal late-capitalist societies (see Chapter 7), less subjective and directly observable in day-to-day life, but potentially just as harmful in its cultural, social and public health impacts.

Young's (2011) notion of the aeitiological crisis is also of relevance here, when seeking to address a significant societal obsession with the consumption of violence as entertainment at a point in history where overall levels of 'actual' violence are low. In that, despite the supposedly 'healthy' free-market economies of neo-capitalist states, such as the UK and US, issues such as child poverty remain high in both nations, relative deprevation proliferates, secondary/high-school educational attainment rates in literacy and numeracy are decreasing, whereas life expectancy levels for certain social groups have recently stalled. As such, many working-class occupants of contemporary 'Western' societies, particularly in the UK and US, have repeatedly buffered the social storms of rampant deindustrialisation and infrastructure privatisation from the 1980s onwards, the impacts of the 2008/09 global financial crisis and the neoliberal austerity politics that followed, and most recently the socially harmful impacts of the COVID-19 pandemic.

Geo-politico-economic events that have seen real-term standards of living in the forms of wages, healthcare, welfare and education fall to their lowest points since the aftermath of the Second World War for many average citizens. Whilst at the same time, the ever-increasing gap between rich and poor gets wider and, overall, the national economy grows. Arguably, it is against this backdrop of recent social history that we see the starkest proliferation of hyper-rationalised deeply ingrained symbolic consumer culture, the recent growth in popularity of MMA and the returning popularity of other, arguably even more brutal fight sports such as BKB and the Team Fight Championships (TFC).

Consumer Culture, the 'Reorientation of the Western Super-Ego' and Representations of the 'Most Violent' Fight Sports

Bare-Knuckle Boxing (BKB) is boxing without the usage of boxing gloves or other padding on the participants' hands. The difference between this sport and unorganised street fighting is that the former adheres to a formal agreed upon set of rules accepted by the contest organisers, those officiating, those spectating or viewing and, of course, the participants involved (Juengel, 2003). Despite the introduction of the use of gloves to boxing contests, the practice of organised fight events where participants are either bare-fisted or wear rudimentary bandages as hand wraps is a phenomenon that has existed in both greater and lesser degrees across many different nations and/or geographical areas over time (Sugden, 1996).

One period of history where the sport of BKB observably grew in popularity in parts of the global 'North' was during the process of rapid industrialisation and urbanisation that occurred as a result of the industrial-scientific revolution in the 1700s and 1800s (Chill, 2017). There remains documentation of bare-knuckle bouts taking place during this period of history in Australia, North America and Europe, with notable regulatory developments emerging out of the UK in the form of the 'London Prize Ring' rules, published in 1838 – revised again in 1853, rules which governed both the sport of Boxing and BKB in Britain until they were superseded by the Marquess of Queensberry Rules in 1867 (Rodriguez, 2009). Both sets of rules were based upon those drafted by English BKB participant John 'Jack' Broughton in 1743, which introduced codes of conduct that remain key components to the organisation of professional Boxing to this day (ibid.). Laws such as no 'butting, gouging, scratching, kicking, hitting a man while down, holding the ropes, and using resin, stones or hard objects in the hands, and biting' (Rodriguez, 2009: 26) staunchly enforced in attempt not only to reduce the risk of serious injury to participants but also to formally outline an internationally recognised standard of 'fair play' for the sport.

BKB as a sport then declined in popularity alongside the increased regulation and growth in popularity of gloved Boxing in the late 1800s; however, the idea of this hyper-brutal practice increasing in prominence during times of rapid social change remains a key component to understanding the contemporary resurgence of the sport in the UK and USA in recent years. The increased formal regulation of sport more broadly largely occurred in the latter half of the nineteenth century (Dunning, 1971), and for over a hundred years the practice of BKB was forced underground, becoming increasingly associated during the twentieth century with illicit gambling and organised crime (Hobbs, 2013; White, 2015). Although never illegal in the UK, the practice of BKB became somewhat stigmatised and remained largely dormant in popular culture until very recently when the trademarked brand BKB TM made moves towards the formation of a national regulatory body covering the organisation of bare-knuckle events in Great Britain. Despite the British Board of Boxing Control (BBBC) publicly declaring no present desire to become involved in overseeing the practice, organisation and/or regulation of bare-knuckle boxing in the UK, BKB TM as a private governing body have outlined their own commercial vision for disseminating their rules and organisational format of this sport internationally under their sanctioned rules, officials, events and regulations (Bradshaw, 2018).

The United States' equivalent of the UK's BKB TM, concerned with governing the regulation of bare-knuckle boxing events in the USA, where the sport is illegal in some states but not others, has been trademarked as BKFC TM – The Bare-Knuckle Fighting Championship – and the company have laid out a similar vision for the sport to that of BKB TM in the UK. With BKFC overseeing upwards of 20 events across numerous States of the USA since BKFC 1 in 2018. Both self-proclaimed regulatory organisations in the United Kingdom and the USA and some external media commentators (i.e. Bradshaw, 2018; BKB TM, 2022; BKFC TM, 2022) have compared the origins and vision of both BKB TM and BKFC TM as organisations to that of the UFC in the early 1990s, and the highly brutal sport of organised BKB in recent years to that of MMA as a fight discipline in the 1990s and early 2000s. Although events sanctioned by each private organisational committee are observably growing in frequency, in media coverage, in digital online presence, and as spectator events – with one BKB TM event at the O2 Arena in London in 2018 attracting over 2,000 spectators – whether the popularity and prevalence of bare-knuckle boxing as an organised combat sport continues to grow internationally in the near future currently remains to be seen. As although to compare the still rather niche recent rise in popularity of BKB to that of MMA 20–30 years previously might seem like a gross exaggeration at this current moment in time, there are observable cultural similarities between the two phenomena, set within the wider evolution of late-modern 'Western' societies that can be analysed within the broader theoretical lineage of this chapter.

Indeed, the hyper-brutal, hyper-masculine, combat sports of MMA and BKB have both emerged (or re-emerged) as sporting entities at a particular point in history when, despite the structural inequalities outlined earlier, consumer culture remains rampant across all social strata. In 'Western' nations at least, symbolic consumerism is deeply woven into the cultural fabric of mainstream society (Hall et al., 2008), with both online and offline representations of culture and self, becoming based on the use of signs ever-increasingly blurring the boundaries between the simulated and the real (Baudrillard, 1993). Cohorts of young working-class men have long internalised gendered behaviours and identity performance that suggests an embodied ability to 'hold one's own' in instances of competitivism, conflict or aggression – whether verbal or physical (Connell, 2005; Hall et al., 2005; Winlow, 1999). However, in the period of heavy industry that dominated societies of the global 'North' between the late 1700s and mid-to-late-twentieth century, such culturally embodied traits and performative behaviours were largely internalised as a result of one's classed habitus (Bourdieu, 1984), subtly and subconsciously moulded in response to the physical realities of heavy manual labour, an ever-fluid but omnipresent threat of external international warfare, and a violently rigid social class system (Hall, 2000, 2002), whereas, throughout the rapidly evolving uncertain liquid-modern (Bauman, 1992) shifts in social order to the now post-structural, post-industrial societies of the 'West' (Harvey, 1990), young individuals who inhabit the lower ends of the ever-widening economic-social strata are culturally shaped to seek assurance, distinction and refuge in the comforting thralls of consumerism and the semiotic value of the sign (Baudrillard, 1993).

Therefore, to return to our main point of discussion, via the growth in consumption of increasingly violent fight sports events, whilst keeping in mind the shifting terrain of the broader 'Western' social order, we see the theoretical lens of cultural criminology outlined by Ferrell et al. (2008) as useful in explaining the (sub)cultures, behaviours and interactions that form around the participation in aggressive or risky practices such as extreme, adventure or combat sports, as well as a culturally ravenous appetite amongst sizeable sections of the populations of the global 'North' to consume representations of increasingly raw forms of fight 'sporting' practices broadcast online and via satellite TV, where one can both experience and perform deviance by proxy (Jewkes, 2015; Poulton, 2014; Rafter and Brown, 2011).

Such desire to continue to consume and share online ever more brutal forms of real violence, as well as the move towards the rationalisation and commercialisation of violent fight sports such as MMA and BKB in the United Kingdom and the United States as outlined earlier can be understood as part of a much broader social transition that has taken place within the hyper-rationalised consumer societies of the global 'North' over the last 40 years, where deregulation of the international financial markets has resulted in unprecedented wealth divides and economic insecurity for millions in the least protected of the 'Western' nations (Dorling, 2018; Hall et al., 2008), and much of the recent geo-politico landscape has been dominated by a chaotic mixture of individualist ego and nationalist-fighting rhetoric of elites. The political nihilism that has manifested in the minds of swathes of 'Western' citizens has led to a fatalistic attitude towards the world of work for many young people (Winlow and Hall, 2006; Winlow et al., 2017). A shift has sought to elevate further the internalised importance of symbolic consumerism for personal and collective identity formation, as well as giving those who submit to the new post-structural social order the illusion of the freedom of choice in the search for and negotiation of self-gratification, (sub)cultural capital, communal belonging, tradition and meaning. An increased self and collective submergence in both online and offline 'hyper-real' (Baudrillard, 1993) leisure settings can also be seen as an important cultural facet of late-modern society in this regard.

The increased participation in and consumption of violent fight sports, such as MMA and BKB, in contemporary 'Western' societies can be viewed as part of a larger move towards the transgressive consumption of brutal violence and quasi-sporting violent spectacles online. Hyper-visual mediatised spectacles of competitive, mostly amateur, 'sporting' violence, such as 'Backyard Brawls', 'Gloves Up, Guns Down' and the 'Team Fight Championships', are all recent examples of both online-media branding and hyper-masculine competitivisms through 'sporting' violence and liminal leisure that have grown in prominence in the last few years (Spruill, 2021; Vargas, 2019; Zuniga-West, 2015). And the private and public social media platforms of many young working-class men regularly contain short virally shared brutal fight videos, both of the sporting kind and those more vicious unorganised examples of material such as street brawls, football hooligan clashes, gun and knife attacks, 'gang' fights and torture. The symbolic sharing of such footage, along with the video clips of hyper-aggressive fight sport spectacles, can be seen as a product of contemporary neo-capitalist societies, not only because the global technological capabilities of the World Wide Web and the largely unregulated realms of contemporary social media platforms allow space for such material to circulate so widely but also because the insatious cultural desire amongst some sections of late-modern populations to consume these transgressive – somewhat voyeuristic – representations of shocking inter-personal violence and brutality creates a market space for such video material that generations capital, clicks and an associated realm of cultural symbolism.

The growth of participation in ever more violent fight sports and risky leisure activities on an amateur and professional level can perhaps not necessarily be separated from the, at first glance, highly different activities of sharing videos of the more shocking or brutal physical violence on social media. As ultimately all examples of such sporting participation, the symbolic cultural performances involved, the media representation of fight sport events, individual and collective consumption and the symbolism and cultural capital being a 'fan' or sharer of such content evokes, contribute towards the formation of transgressive identities for the self and social groups that exist as part of a much broader, uncertain and hyper-fluid cultural tapestry of late-modern 'Western' societies.

As already stated, central to the cultural criminological perspective is the engagement with the cultural meanings that are attached to sports or leisure practices and (sub)cultural consumption. As Raymen and Smith (2019: 117) suggest, it is within the 'transgressive forms of leisure and culture' which cultural criminologists see 'the battlefields in which the struggle for individual freedom, identity and self-expression against an allegedly oppressive moral culture would be fought'. Sporting subcultural practices such as MMA and BKB have often found themselves subject to much criticism as examples of violent, physically risky and transgressive combat sports. Concurrently, this calls for a greater theoretical understanding of why it is becoming increasingly popular to participate in and consume such sports. For example, between 2009 and 2020, the number of MMA gyms in the UK increased from 12 to 320 (Sugden, 2021). In such context, Sugden's (2021) 4-year-long ethnographic study of MMA fighters in North-West England provides us with an empirical understanding of the cultural context and meaning of the seemingly violent and transgressive MMA practice. Although Sugden primarily draws from the sociology of health literature and remains concerned with jiu-jitsu as a subsect of MMA, his main findings simultaneously uncover hidden meanings and subcultural practices of MMA participants that can both add to and compliment certain theoretical aspects of this current chapter.

For example, aside from the issues relating to symbolic identity performance and consumption of violence documented here, Sugden's (2021) ethnographic study into the sport found that a main motivation for investing time into MMA and accepting the physical risks involved relates positively to individual learning and development, mindfulness and coping. First, learning jiu-jitsu provides the opportunity for a journey of personal development, which again provides meaning to the participation in MMA. MMA thus served as an exit from 'unhealthy lifestyles', such as 'crime, drugs, and so on' (p. 6). Second, the fighters Sugden interacted with would often point towards the therapeutic value of jiu-jitsu, mentally and physically, and its ability to promote openness and kindness. Finally, the MMA gym and the training activities provided a space for coping with 'inner and external grievances' (p. 7) including stress, anxiety and depression. As such, MMA and other regulated fight sports can provide participants with a platform for mental health development that stretches beyond the gym and into the more time and space diffuse everyday life.

In that sense, although MMA gyms from an outsiders' point of view may 'appear as a playground for innate violence' (ibid.: 9), assisted by the previously popular/mediatised depictions of MMA, there is an important context that must be accounted for that can help us further understand this particular risk-filled subculture. In the age of what Bauman (2000) calls 'liquid modernity', uncertainty and confusion are omnipresent features, which again impacts individuals' sense of purpose and satisfaction (Lyng, 1990). Moreover, in the words of Ferrell and Hayward (2018: 20), as a consequence of late-modernity:

> Meaning and self-expression are sought in a world whose hyper-pluralism and cultural fluidity regularly overwhelm the self, and where new forms of surveillance and control make the concept of individual autonomy all but meaningless.

Therefore, sporting (sub)cultures that are commonly represented as and assumed to be transgressive, deviant, hyper-masculine and violent – such as MMA and BKB – simultaneously provide participants with a sense of meaning, belonging and status, as well as offering spaces for personal development – despite the obvious physical risks that participation entails. As such, we see how an engagement with the wider cultural context of deviant and transgressive sporting subcultures can arguably help us to understand the meanings and motivations behind the participation in these cultures and some of the ways in which young athletic working-class individuals can search for identity, meaning, belonging and status in the complex hyper-fluid tapestry of late-modern societies more broadly.

Summary

As Measham (2004: 213) maintains, '[c]ultural criminologists. . . are engaged in the conceptual development of the agency-structure debate and a reconsideration of the role of emotionality in criminality'. Thus, to summarise, cultural criminologists broadly approach 'crime' and 'crime control' in a cultural context (Hayward and Young, 2004). Following this perspective, which incorporates insights from cultural studies, sociology and subcultural theory, and has emerged as an alternative to positivist criminology, 'crimes' and the culture in which they occur (or are responded to) should not be separated. In relation to cultural criminology, it has been argued that 'as new intersections of crime and culture emerge from the inequities of late-modernity, cultural criminology remains to be continued' (Ferrell and Hayward, 2018: 30). Such a standpoint remains important, and the cultural criminological lenses have here been cross-pollinated with the insights offered by 'edgework' theory (Lyng, 1990). Collectively, the frames offered from these insights have been employed to make sense of transgression, voluntary risk-taking, violence and sensation-seeking in sport and the consumption of sport, throughout this chapter.

As situated within the continuation of cultural criminology (Ferrell and Hayward, 2018), this chapter has applied its relevant lenses to the domain of ('extreme') sport and leisure contexts and activities. By doing so, we have sought to illustrate the fluid and ambiguous boundaries between sport, violence and transgression as expressions of personal agency in a complex late-modern age. More specifically, in this chapter, this was explored through a critical discussion of MMA and BKB – as two highly controversial sports – and the consumption of these two hyper-visual, highly symbolic, commodified and mediated sporting practices. The argument we present holds that transgressive behaviours in sport and leisure – and the individual motivations and meanings involved – can be better understood through the application of the conceptual relations and methodological underpinnings deriving from cultural criminology, which appreciates the post-structural, hyper-rationalised, macro-consumer cultures that such sports have emerged and are practiced within.

References

Anderson, L. and Brown, M. (2010) 'Expanding horizons of risk in criminology', *Sociology Compass* 4(8): 544–554.

Andreasson, J. and Johansson, T. (2019) 'Negotiating violence: Mixed martial arts as a spectacle and sport', *Sport in Society* 22(7): 1183–1197.

Armstrong, G. (1998) *Football Hooligans: Knowing the Score*, Oxford: Berg.

Baudrillard, J. (1993) *Symbolic Exchange and Death*, London: Sage.

Bauman, Z. (1992) *Mortality, Immortality and Other Life Strategies*, Cambridge: Polity Press.

Bauman, Z. (2000) *Liquid Modernity*, Cambridge: Polity Press.

Beck, U. (1992) *Risk Society: Towards a New Modernity*, London: Sage.

BKB TM. (2022) 'BKB', available from www.bkbworld.co.uk [accessed 01/22].

BKFC TM. (2022) 'BKFC', available from www.bareknuckle.tv [accessed 01/22].

Bourdieu, P. (1984) *Distinction: A Social Critique of the Judgement of Taste*, London: Routledge.

Bradshaw, L. (2018) 'The rise of bare-knuckle boxing in London', *The Culture Trip*, available from: https://theculturetrip.com/europe/united-kingdom/england/london/articles/the-rise-of-bare-knuckle-boxing-in-london/ [accessed 01/22].

Briggs, J., Harrison, C., McInnes, A. and Vincent, D. (eds.) (1996) *Crime and Punishment in England*, New York: Palgrave Macmillan.

Bunn, M. (2017) 'Defining the edge: Choice, mastery and necessity in edgework practice', *Sport in Society* 20(9): 1310–1323.

Channon, A. (2020) 'Edgework and mixed martial arts: Risk, reflexivity and collaboration in an ostensibly "violent" sport', *Martial Arts Studies* (9): 6–19.

Channon, A. and Matthews, C.R. (2015) '"It is what it is": Masculinity, homosexuality, and inclusive discourse in mixed martial arts', *Journal of Homosexuality* 62(7): 936–956.

Chill, A. (2017) *Bare-Knuckle Britons and Fighting Irish: Boxing, Race, Religion and Nationality in the Eighteenth and Nineteenth Centuries*, Jefferson: McFarland & Company, Inc.

Connell, R.W. (2005 [1995]). *Masculinities*, Cambridge: Polity Press.

Dorling, D. (2018) *Peak Inequality: Britain's Ticking Timebomb*, Bristol: Policy Press.

Dunning, E. (eds.) (1971) *The Sociology of Sport*, London: Cass.

Ferrell, J. (1999) 'Cultural criminology', *Annual Review of Sociology* 25(1): 395–418.

Ferrell, J. and Hayward, K.J. (2018) 'Cultural criminology continued', *Alternative Criminologies* (Eds. P. Carlen and L. Ayres Franca), Oxon/New York: Routledge, pp. 17–33.

Ferrell, J., Hayward, K.J., Morrison, W. and Presdee, M. (2004) 'Fragments of a manifesto: Introducing cultural criminology unleashed', *Cultural Criminology Unleashed* (Eds. J. Ferrell, K.J. Hayward, W. Morrison and M. Presdee), London: Glasshouse, pp. 1–9.

Ferrell, J., Hayward, K.J. and Young, J. (2008) *Cultural Criminology: An Invitation*, London: Sage.

Ferrell, J., Milovanovic, D. and Lyng, S. (2001) 'Edgework, media practices, and the elongation of meaning: A theoretical ethnography of the bridge day event', *Theoretical Criminology* 5(2): 177–202.

Ferrell, J. and Sanders, C.R. (eds.) (1995) *Towards Cultural Criminology*, Boston: Northeastern University Press.

Fletcher, R. (2008) 'Living on the edge: The appeal of risk sports for the professional middle class', *Sociology of Sport Journal* 25(3): 310–330.

Forsey, C. (2012) *Men on the Edge: Taking Risks and Doing Gender Among BASE Jumpers*, Winnipeg: Fernwood Publishing.

Giulianotti, R. (2009) 'Risk and sport: An analysis of sociological theories and research agendas', *Sociology of Sport Journal* 26(4): 540–556.

Green, A., Gardner, D. and Legg, S. (2020) 'An exploration of the emotional experience of BASE jumping', *Sport in Society*: 1–15.

Groombridge, N. (2017) *Sports Criminology: A Critical Criminology of Sports and Games*, Bristol: Policy Press.

The Guardian. (2016) 'Portuguese MMA fighter João Carvalho dies after TKO in Dublin', available from: www.theguardian.com/sport/2016/apr/12/mma-fighter-joao-carvalho-dies-dublin-tko [accessed 01/2022].

Gurr, T.R. (1981) 'Historical trends in violent crime: A critical review of the evidence', *Crime and Justice* 3: 295–353.

Hall, S. (2000) 'Paths to Anelpis: 1: Dimorphic violence and the pseudo-pacification process', *Parallax* 6(2): 36–53.

Hall, S. (2002) 'Daubing the drudges of fury: Men, violence and the piety of the "hegemonic masculinity" thesis', *Theoretical Criminology* 6(1): 35–61.

Hall, S. and Jefferson, T. (1976) *Resistance Through Rituals*, London: Hutchinson.

Hall, S., Winlow, S. and Ancrum, C. (2005) 'Radgies, gangstas, and mugs: Imaginary criminal identities in the twilight of the pseudo-pacification process', *Social Justice* 32(1): 100–112.

Hall, S., Winlow, S. and Ancrum, C. (2008) *Criminal Identities and Consumer Culture: Crime, Exclusion and the New Culture of Narcissism*, Devon: Willan Publishing.

Harvey, D. (1990) *The Condition of Postmodernity: An Enquiry into the Origins of Cultural Change*, London: Wiley-Blackwell.

Hayward, K.J. and Young, J. (2004) Cultural criminology: Some notes on the script', *Theoretical Criminology* 8(3): 259–273.

Hebdige, D. (1979) 'Subculture and style', *The Cultural Studies Reader* (Eds. S. During), London: Routledge, pp. 429–438.

Hillyard, P., Pantazis, C., Tombs, S. and Gordon, D. (eds.) (2004) *Beyond Criminology: Taking Harm Seriously*, London: Pluto.

Hobbs, D. (2013) *Lush Life: Constructing Organised Crime in the UK*, Oxford: Oxford University Press.

Holt, J. and Ramsay, J. (eds.) (2021) *The Philosophy of Mixed Martial Arts: Squaring the Octagon*, Oxon/New York: Routledge.

Jewkes, Y. (2015) *Crime and the Media: Key Approaches to Criminology* (3rd Edition), Oxford: Blackwell.

Juengel, S.J. (2003) 'Bare-knuckle boxing and the pedagogy of national manhood', *Studies in Popular Culture* 25(3): 91–110.

Jump, D. (2020) *The Criminology of Boxing, Violence and Desistance*, Bristol: Bristol University Press.

Katz, J. (1988) *Seductions of Crime: The Moral and Sensual Attractions in Going Evil*, New York: Basic Books.

Kerr, J.H. and Houge Mackenzie, S. (2020) '"I don't want to die. That's not why I do it at all": Multifaceted motivation, psychological health, and personal development in BASE jumping', *Annals of Leisure Research* 23(2): 223–242.

Kidder, J.L. (2019) 'Risk in lifestyle sports: The case of parkour', *The Suffering Body in Sport* (Eds. K. Young), Bingley: Emerald Publishing, pp. 39–53.

Kidder, J.L. (2022) 'Reconsidering edgework theory: Practices, experiences, and structures', *International Review for the Sociology of Sport* 57(2): 183–200.

Laurendeau, J. (2006) '"He didn't go in doing a skydive": Sustaining the illusion of control in an edgework activity', *Sociological Perspectives* 49(4): 583–605.

Lyng, S. (1990) 'Edgework: A social psychological analysis of voluntary risk taking', *American Journal of Sociology* 95(4): 851–886.

Lyng, S. (2004) 'Crime, edgework and corporeal transaction', *Theoretical Criminology* 8(3): 359–375.

Lyng, S. (2005) 'Edgework and the risk-taking experience', *Edgework: The Sociology of Risk Taking* (Eds. S. Lyng), New York: Routledge, pp. 17–49.

Measham, F. (2004) 'Drug and alcohol research: The case for cultural criminology', *Cultural Criminology Unleashed* (Eds. J. Ferrell, K.J. Hayward, W. Morrison and M. Presdee), London: Glasshouse, pp. 207–218.

Mythen, G. (2005) 'Employment, individualization and insecurity: Rethinking the risk society perspective', *The Sociological Review* 53(1): 129–149.

Pauschinger, D. (2020) 'Working at the edge: Police, emotions and space in Rio de Janeiro', *Environment and Planning D: Society and Space* 38(3): 510–527.

Phillips, N.D. and Strobl, S. (2006) 'Cultural criminology and kryptonite: Apocalyptic and retributive constructions of crime and justice in comic books', *Crime, Media, Culture* 2(3): 304–331.

Poulton, E. (2014) 'The hooligan film factory: Football violence in high definition', *Football Hooliganism, Fan Behaviour and Crime* (Eds. M. Hopkins and J. Treadwell), London: Palgrave Macmillan.

Presdee, M. (2000) *Cultural Criminology and the Carnival of Crime*, London/New York: Routledge.

Prieur, A. (2018) 'Towards a criminology of structurally conditioned emotions: Combining Bourdieu's field theory and cultural criminology', *European Journal of Criminology* 15(3): 344–363.

Rafter, N. and Brown, M. (2011) *Criminology Goes to the Movies*, New York: New York University Press.

Raymen, T. and Smith, O. (2019) 'Deviant leisure: A critical criminological perspective for the twenty-first century', *Critical Criminology* 27(1): 115–130.

Rodriguez, R.G. (2009) *The Regulation of Boxing: A History and Comparative Analysis of Policies*, Jefferson, NC: McFarland and Co.

Sánchez García, R. and Malcolm, D. (2010) 'Decivilizing, civilizing or informalizing? The international development of mixed martial arts', *International Review for the Sociology of Sport* 45(1): 39–58.

Spencer, D.C. (2009) 'Habit (us), body techniques and body callusing: An ethnography of mixed martial arts', *Body & Society* 15(4): 119–143.

Spruill, L. (2021) '"Gloves up, Guns down" movement in Detroit provides safe outlet for settling issues: Organization addressing gun violence in communities', available from: www.clickondetroit.com/news/local/2021/08/18/gloves-up-guns-down-movement-in-detroit-provides-safe-outlet-for-settling-issues/ [accessed 01/22].

Sugden, J.P. (1985) 'The exploitation of disadvantage: The occupational sub-culture of the boxer', *The Sociological Review* 33(1): 187–209.

Sugden, J.P. (1996) *Boxing and Society: An International Analysis*, Manchester: Manchester University Press.

Sugden, J.T. (2021) 'Jiu-jitsu and society: Male mental health on the mats', *Sociology of Sport Journal* 1: 1–13.

UFC. (2021) 'History of UFC', available from: www.ufc.com/history-ufc [accessed 01/2022].

Vargas, T. (2019) 'Are backyard brawls a solution to gun violence? Inside the fight club that lets two people with a grudge pummel each other to resolve their grievances', *The Independent*, available from: www.independent.co.uk/independentpremium/long-reads/fight-club-brawl-gun-violence-virginia-streetbeefs-a9133256.html [accessed 01/22].

Wacquant, L.J. (1995) 'Pugs at work: Bodily capital and bodily labour among professional boxers', *Body & Society* 1(1): 65–93.

Wacquant, L.J. (2004) *Body and Soul: Notebooks of an Apprentice Boxer*, Oxford: Oxford University Press.

Wacquant, L.J. (2011) 'Habitus as topic and tool: Reflections on becoming a prizefighter', *Qualitative Research in Psychology* 8: 81–92.

White, P. (2015) *The Legends of Bare-Knuckle Boxing: The History & the Champions*, CreateSpace Independent Publishers.

Winlow, S. (1999) 'Badfellas: An ethnography of crime, tradition and changing masculinities in a Northern City', Doctoral thesis: Durham University, available from: http://etheses.dur.ac.uk/1115/ [accessed 09/19].

Winlow, S. and Hall, S. (2006) *Violent Night: Urban Leisure and Contemporary Culture*, Oxford: Berg.

Winlow, S., Hall, S. and Treadwell, J. (2017) *The Rise of the Right: English Nationalism and the Transformation of Working-Class Politics*, Bristol: Policy Press.

Woodward, K. (2004) 'Rumbles in the jungle: Boxing, racialization and the performance of masculinity', *Leisure Studies* 23(1): 5–17.

Woodward, K. (2007) *Boxing, Masculinity and Identity*, London: Routledge.

Young, J. (2011) *The Criminological Imagination*, Cambridge: Polity Press.

Zizek, S. (2008) *Violence: six sideways reflections*, London: Profile Books.

Zuniga-West, D. (2015) 'Team fighting championship is too brutal for the United States – for now', *Vice*, available from: www.vice.com/en/article/gq8agb/team-fighting-championship-is-too-brutal-for-the-united-statesfor-now-000 [accessed 2022].

7
SPORT AND SOCIAL HARMS – QATAR AND WORLD CUP 2022 IN FOCUS

Crimes of the Powerful (2)

Introduction

On 2 December 2010, Qatar won their bid to host the 2022 FIFA men's World Cup (World Cup) finals. From the outset, it was clear that preparations for this sport mega-event would entail the construction of nine and expansion of three stadiums. Given that the country's manual labour force is largely made up of migrant workers, the news that the State of Qatar would recruit construction workers from across the world was unsurprising. However, in September 2013, European media sources reported that many migrant workers were mistreated under affordances of the 'Kafala' system in Qatari law. As a result of mistreatment, some migrant workers died: by February 2021, it was reported that 6,500 migrant workers from India, Pakistan, Nepal, Bangladesh and Sri Lanka had died in Qatar since it was awarded the World Cup (Pattisson and McIntyre, 2021).

This context presents an opportunity to explore and elaborate on the critical criminological 'social harms' perspective (see Cain and Howe, 2008; Canning, 2017; Friedrichs and Schwartz, 2007; Hillyard et al., 2004, 2005; Hillyard and Tombs, 2007, 2021; Hillyard, 2015; Leighton and Wyatt, 2021; Matthews and Kauzlarich, 2007; Pemberton, 2007) given that many of the actions that created this situation were 'legal' in national and – often – international law. In this chapter, we use this theory to critically analyse the context in which 'abuses' of migrant workers are building stadia and infrastructure in readiness for the 2022 World Cup by principally drawing upon Hillyard and Tombs' (2004, 2005, 2007) work. However, we add to this by blending in conceptual ideas offered within 'relational sociology' (Cleland et al., 2018; Crossley, 2011; Donati, 2010, 2013, which draws some inspiration from Simmel, 1950) to search for the allocation of 'responsibility' for these 'abuses' and the empirical work of Carson (1970a, 1970b, 1971, 1974, 1979, 1980, 1982, 1985a, 1985b) to consider how legislation that workers and reform

DOI: 10.4324/9781003276791-7

into future practices might be 'regulated', and by whom/what. The argument we present across this chapter is that the story of the migrant construction workers in Qatar is a significant example of social harms suffered in and through sport but that other examples can be found across a transnational and neoliberal world.

Unpacking 'Zemiology': 'Social Harms' and Criminal Law

Our specific understanding of 'zemiology' or a 'social harm-centred' approach to understanding 'criminality' has four theoretical roots. First, from the 1968 National Deviancy Conference (NDC) 'breakaway' group, which some, such as Mooney (2011, 2019), see as the birth of 'critical criminology', we take the notion of questioning *power* and *power relations*. To elaborate, in *The New Criminology* (1973), the first book co-authored by three members of this breakaway group, Ian Taylor, Paul Walton and Jock Young, it is argued that 'crime' – as the acts that become 'criminalised' through legal systems – tend is not the callous or greedy act of predatory individuals but a consequence of the contradictory circumstances in which (especially poor) people find themselves. Thus, for Taylor et al. (1973), criminological research must take on board the 'structural analysis of the forces conducive to crime and disorder' (ibid.: 263) rather than failing to grasp 'crime as human action, as reaction to positions held in an antagonistic social structure, but also as action taken to resolve those antagonisms' (ibid.: 236). In other words, they argue that criminal justice systems tend to be flawed in their selection and labelling of actions as 'criminal', instead of drawing attention to how the crimes of the working class are more easily detected than those of the more powerful groups in society. 'Crime' and 'criminalisation' when set against 'harm' become expressions of power – a concept that needs to be more closely unpacked both within and beyond the critical criminological canon and can range from positions with state connections to those with economic influence (Box, 2002; Crewe, 2012; Scraton, 2007) – that protects the 'powerful' and potentially penalises the 'powerless'.

Second, research, by 1968 NDC breakaway group member W.G. (Kit) Carson, points towards exploring issues of *regulation* and *individuals' regulatory power* from a social harms perspective, particularly asking questions about what 'regulation' might consist of, who those 'regulators' are and what authority they have to regulate in a transnational economy. To do this, Carson's work on 'white-collar crime' through, first, his research on the nineteenth-century Factory Acts and how these permitted child labour exploitation and the broader epidemic injuries of workers (Carson, 1970a, 1970b, 1971, 1974, 1979, 1980, 1985a) and, second, his investigation into occupational difficulties in the petroleum industry which specifically included the management's disregard for common safety regimes, in the quest to maximise operational time efficiencies and, thus, 'profit' (Carson, 1982, 1985b). Carson argued that the role of the individual regulator, as a key social actor, is worth analysis. In some instances, such as those related to the Factory Acts, Carson focussed on the mechanisms such as legislation – and the regulation of such mechanisms – that potentially allow, by not outlawing, exploitation and harm. In this work, Carson

(1970a) forms a critical appreciation of Sutherland's research into 'white-collar crime' (see Chapter 3) but argued that expanding his discussions to include socially injurious behaviour that is prohibited through criminal law potentially focussed on the individuals involved rather than legislatures. Carson understands that one such area in which these ideas are illuminated is Factory Acts and legislation, which are mainly directed towards regulation of employers' occupational roles. He points out that a prolonged time period of 150 years in the UK, the 'state' gradually increased the level of its intervention in the workplace by stipulating the minimum standards of safety, health and welfare which factory-owners should uphold.[1] Conversely, this takes him to his concern with individual social actors who are regulators, the inspectors. Thus, whilst such legislation appears to protect the 'powerless', changes to the law render 'crime' ambiguous – meeting 'standards' is open to vast inspectional discretion, leaving workers subject to 'harm' and potentially tragic ramifications. Therefore, the live questions are presented about who regulates provisions, and what might be deemed to be permissible under such inspections. Carson suggests that many processes in the enforcement of safety policies are not unique to the Factory Inspectorate and discusses these in other contexts, most notably in *The Other Price of Britain's Oil* (1982). This book is concerned with the hidden costs of death and injury through workplace neglect, accidents and the spread of disease amongst North Sea offshore workers that emerged in the extraction of oil. Carson (1982) pointed out that successive British governments had failed to institute the necessary controls to sufficiently safeguard men and women working on oil rigs instead of prioritising the maximisation of profit, even viewing the loss of life as inevitable in the excuse of the lack of implementation of basic safety arrangements. In common with his analysis of the Factory Acts, the questions of regulation are turned to, primarily, the government for failing to create sufficiently robust legislation to protect workers and secondarily, the individual inspectors whose discretion in regulating working practices in North Sea oil rigs allowed the loss of significant numbers of life. Brannigan and Pavlich (2007) suggest that in both contexts Carson researched offences that lost lives and caused 'harm' frequently unquestioned in legal systems. Thus, for Carson, key questions in discussions around responsibility for social harm (including its avoidance) emerge from the roles of regulation and regulators.[2]

Third, Hillyard *et al.* refresh these ideas in both *Beyond Criminology: Taking Harm Seriously* (2004) and *Criminal Obsessions: Why Harm Matters More Than Crime* (2005). In common with Taylor et al. (1973), Hillyard et al. (2004, 2005) call for the ontological basis of 'crime' to be questioned but advance this argument by suggesting that the epistemological understanding of 'harm' be rethought to be given analytical primacy. By doing this, Hillyard and Tombs (2004, 2005) make two key points that inform our discussion of zemiological understanding of workplace injustices for migrant construction workers in Qatar. First, Hillyard (2015: 39) recognises the difficulty in setting the *parameters of 'social harm'* in utilising the zemiological approach, suggesting they should be rethought in a broad sense. To be sure, Hillyard and Tombs (2004, 2005) argue that social harm might encompass a multitude of other expressions such as *physical harms* (which may include premature death, injury through medical treatments, motor vehicle accidents, injury or death through paid or unpaid 'work', hate crime attacks, etc.); widening the notion of *financial and economic harm* to incorporate activities, that may not be 'illegal' in many Western judicial systems, to include – for instance – poverty caused by property/cash loss emanating from pension and mortgage 'mis-selling', mis-appropriation of funds by government, malpractice by private corporations and private individuals, increased prices through cartelisation and price-fixing, and redistribution of wealth and income from the poorer to the richer through regressive taxation and welfare policies (Hillyard and Tombs, 2004: 19, 2005: 14). Hillyard and Tombs believe that widening the parameters financial or economic harm beyond 'criminality' recognises the personal and social effects of poverty and unemployment. In addition, Hillyard and Tombs recognise that although *affective harms*, such as those relating to emotional and psychological states, are difficult to measure or attribute to causation, they should not be precluded from an understanding of social harm. Thus, 'social harm' can be broad ranging in its impacts and consequences, and should not automatically follow prescriptions offered through nationally or internationally bound criminal law, but this might mean it is difficult to identify, detect and measure. Second, in the analysis of the arrangement of social harms, Hillyard and Tombs (2004, 2005) point out that their approach frees up the narrow and – often – individualistic notions of 'responsibility' that are given in criminal justice systems. Thus, unpicking the myriad of market, state, political and – often – neoliberal forces is important in deciding *the allocation of responsibility*. In turn, Hillyard and Tombs (2004, 2005) and Tombs and Whyte (2010) argue that any responses to social harms need the emergence of debates about policy response, resources allocated to finding a solution to the situation and a clear position of the order of priority to do this; as such it is counter to the unilateral power afforded from the criminal justice system to 'non-representative elites' who preside over the accused individuals. The zemiological approach can be taken as a challenge to the codification of power afforded by the criminal justice system that may reflect capitalist and 'elite' interests, which makes the criminalisation of lower-class citizens easier – irrespective of the 'harm' created by their actions – than those higher up a social structure (Hillyard and Tombs, 2004, 2005; see also Slapper and Tombs, 1999; Tombs and Whyte, 2015; Whyte, 2007).

Fourth, we interpret responsibility for such social harms through a lens offered by 'relational sociology' (Cleland et al., 2018; Crossley, 2011; Donati, 2010, 2013; Tilly, 2002; White, 2008). Donati (2010: 6) points out that in this approach a 'society' is only the sum of its relations, thus presenting that 'society is not a space "containing" relations, or an arena where relations are played. It is rather the very tissue of relations (society "is relation" and does not "have relations")'. Crossley (2011) and Donati (2010, 2013) both see Georg Simmel (1950) as laying a foundation for relational sociology by seeking to write a 'grammar of social life' through considering the impact of group size on a relationship's characteristics and processes. Simmel (1950) argues that dyadic – those with only two members – relationships qualitatively differ from other group sizes as both actors are confronted by only each other and not the wider collective. In turn, should one of the actors leave that relationship, its interaction ends? Dyadic relationships do not attain a super-individual life that exists above the individuals involved. This lack of super-individual structure intensifies the absorption of the participants in their dyadic relationship making the dependence of the whole on each partner obvious. In triadic (three actor relationships) and larger networks of relations, group duties and responsibilities can be delegated, but in the dyad each actor is immediately and directly responsible for any collective action –actor neither can deny responsibility by shifting it to the group nor hold the group responsible for what s/he has done or failed to do. The turn to this theory prompts us to ask questions about relational positions in the development of social harms in sport, and it is to this literature that we now turn.

Social Harms and Sport

From small-scale participation to the hosting and operating of mega-events, sport is a site where the social harms that Hillyard and Tombs (2004, 2005) outline may operate. Despite this, the analytical lens it affords has not been widely used in research in this area. Indeed, the anomaly to this trend comes from Hillyard (2015: 26) when he states:

> A month before Christmas a close friend was ice-skating with her daughter on an open-air ice rink. She fell and broke her arm in two places after hitting a rough patch on the ice. She was off work for a number of days and spent many hours in hospital. Subsequently, she discovered that five people that week had broken their arms after falling on the same rink. It was obvious that a combination of too many skaters and lack of maintenance were key elements in the 'accidents'. There is no legal requirement that these falls are 'notified' to a central government department and published on a regular basis. They will form part of some set of 'accident' statistics but will receive very little media attention when published. Now imagine the uproar if five people had been attacked in a city centre on five separate occasions and all had their arms broken. There would be a public uproar demanding that the Chief Constable do something about it.

In this instance, it is the sport participation of recreational ice-skating that provides the context for Hillyard to make his point about the banal existence of social harm. He argues that an important element that is used to distinguish between events that incur 'harm' is whether the outcome was intended, or not. Slipping on ice, whilst skating, is constructed as 'accidents' whereas attacks are not. Thus, in the case of 'accidents', the responsibility lies with the individual although the owners may not have – in the example Hillyard provides – kept the surface smooth, prohibited overcrowding and so on. Therefore, just because harm is not 'intended' does not mean that it does not exist or that the individuals who take part are culpable.

Rather, for Hillyard, the situation is still harmful because of potential lapses in regulation.

A clear example in which social harm was accidentally created was 1989's Hillsborough Stadium disaster in which 97 Liverpool fans died during and after their team's F.A. Cup semi-final against Nottingham Forest (see Chapter 5). Successive governments' positions across a 23-year period were that supporters largely culpable for the disaster (see Scraton, 2016), adding to the affective harms experienced by those who survived the accident or the families of those who died in it, the government-endorsed Hillsborough Independent Panel produced a report that changed the official narrative in September 2012. The new narrative found that the safety of fans admitted to the terrace at the Leppings Lane end of the ground was 'compromised at every level' (*The Report of the Hillsborough Independent Panel*, 2012: 6). This included aspects ranging the condition of the turnstiles, the management of the crowd, alterations to the terrace, the construction of gated the 'pens' in which fans were held, the placement of the crush barriers and the access to the fateful central pens via a tunnel with a one in six gradients. What is more, it also found that a serious crush occurred on the same terrace during the 1981 FA Cup semi-final between Tottenham Hotspur and Wolverhampton Wanderers in which 'many people were injured and fatalities narrowly avoided' (*The Report of the Hillsborough Independent Panel*, 2012: 6).

Social harm in sport is not always as extreme in the cases of the Hillsborough Stadium disaster or the deaths of migrant construction workers in Qatar (as we discuss), or as banal as the case of a broken arm through ice-skating. Like the sports-related violence Young (2012, see Chapter 1) recounts, social harm could be *everywhere* in sport: the athlete who suffers serious – including sporting career-ending – injuries (Gaston, 2014; Roderick, 2006; Roderick and Collinson, 2020; Young, 1993); the emotional hurt family members may experience through their relative – who is an athlete – having to relocate to gain employment (Carter, 2011; Roderick, 2012); the Russian state-sponsored homophobia that the IOC did not challenge with any conviction in before and during the 2014 Sochi winter Olympic games (Lenskyj, 2014; Travers and Shearman, 2017; Van Rheenen, 2014; Zeigler, 2014), and the multitude of abuses that young people might experience in silence in their desire to 'make it' in sport (Brackenridge, 1997; Ohlert et al., 2021; Tomlinson and Yorganci, 1997). We elaborate upon these conceptual touchstones in our analysis of social harm in sport, specifically drawing upon the death and mistreatment of migrant construction workers in Qatar who are building the stadium and enhancing the physical infrastructure of the country in readiness for the 2022 FIFA World Cup, but before doing that we elaborate on the specifics of this case study.

Qatar and the 2022 FIFA World Cup

As with any case study, the context is important to tease out the social processes that can be generalised (David, 2006). The State of Qatar has complicated history after previously laying under Bahrani rule (1783–1868) and then Ottoman rule (1871–1916), until its partitioning in the aftermath of the First World War (Fromherz, 2012). In 1916, it fell under British protectorate before gaining independence in 1971. This history is further complicated by it being officially founded whilst part of the Ottoman Empire, in 1878 (McCoy, 2014), but since it gained full independence has been ruled by an absolute monarchy, meaning that its current head of state, Emir Tamim bin Hamad Al Thani (whose family have been ruling the country since 1825), has unrestricted political power of its sovereign state and its people (Ulrichson, 2014). According to Ulrichson (2014), Qatar's population was recorded as 1.8m people in 2013, of which 278,000 were Qatari citizens – of which a majority adhere to the strict Wahhabi interpretation of Islam – and 1.5m expatriates.[3] The global significance of Qatar arises not from the size of its population but through its natural gas/oil reserves and its large sovereign wealth fund, Qatar Investment Authority (QIA). Indeed, Qatar is the world's richest country per capita (*World Atlas Factbook*, 2014) and is recognised as a 'high income economy' by the World Bank (reflecting its wealth per capita), which stems from its position of having the world's third-largest natural gas and oil reserves.

Qatar is one of 12 members of the Organization of the Petroleum Exporting Countries (OPEC) on account of its proven oil reserve of 15bn barrels (it is speculated that the actual figure it has in reserve might be 10bn barrels), whilst its gas fields account for around 5 per cent of the global resource, making it the third biggest contributor in the world (Kamrava, 2013). It currently yields a peak of 500,000 barrels (80,000 m^3) per day although these production levels are predicted to fall as its fields will be mostly depleted by 2023, and Qatar's National Vision 2030 has prepared for this by making investment in renewable resources a major goal for the country (Kamrava, 2013). This transnational economic power has been underlined by the formation of QIA in 2005, which specialises in making foreign investment – particularly in the United States, Europe and the Asia Pacific global regions – through its Qatar Holding investment arm with the country's sovereign wealth fund. In 2013, QIA, with assets of $115bn [USD], was ranked twelfth amongst the richest sovereign wealth funds in the world (Ulrichson, 2014). In 2014, QIA had investments around the world that included fashion brand Valentino, engineering firm Siemens, London's The Shard, Heathrow Airport, Sainsbury's supermarket and luxury department store, Harrods and jewellers, Tiffany (Ulrichson, 2014). The Qatari banking sector managed to escape the direct impact of the global subprime fallout and in the global banking sector QIA has investments in Barclays Bank, Santander Brasil, Bank of America and the Agricultural Bank of China along with car manufacturers Volkswagen (Kamrava, 2013).

In the field of sport, QIA owns the financial rights to Paris Saint-Germain football club. Indeed, association football is the most watched sport in Qatar despite it never having qualified for a World Cup finals although the country has held the AFC Asian Cup finals twice, in 1988 and 2011.[4] Reiche (2015) points out that these are amongst the 85 major sports events that have been held in the country since 1988 in a list that includes the Women's Tennis Association regularly holds its Qatar Ladies Open (annually) and its Tour Championships (in 2008, 2009 and 2010) in the country; from 2002, an annual cycling Tour of Qatar has taken place and, in March 2013, the country became the first in the Middle East to host a Motocross Grand Prix. On 2 December 2010, Qatar won their bid to host the 2022 World Cup finals, entailing the building of nine new stadiums and the expansion of three existing stadiums for this event and making it the first World Cup finals to be held in the Middle East. Whilst Qatar's winning bid to host the tournament was enthusiastically greeted enthusiastically in the Persian Gulf global region, it immediately became the source of controversy elsewhere in the world especially Europe and North America. These concerns initially centred on four issues, which we now explain.

First, chiming loudly with the white-collar criminality in sport, there were concerns about the ways in which Qatar achieved sufficient votes to win the right to host the tournament (see Chapter 3 for a full discussion). Second, the Constitution of Qatar (signed in 2003) outlines Sharia law to be the main source of legislation in the country. The legality of alcohol consumption is therefore slippery. Thus, although some luxury hotels are allowed to sell alcohol to non-Muslim customers, the Constitution permits flogging to be used as punishments for alcohol consumption. This raises two points: first, a culture that surrounds World Cup finals (although not *the* culture that surrounds them) is a 'party' of football supporters in which the consumption of alcohol is highly significant (Stott and Pearson, 2007; Pearson, 2012). The absence of – or a severe reduction in – alcohol would change the nature of the experience for some supporters. Second, from the 1978 World Cup, FIFA has sought commercial 'partners' to sponsor its major tournaments. Given the 'party' associated to the tournament and the rise of official 'fan zones'/'fan parks' at such events that serve as ways of monitoring and controlling supporters' behaviour (Frew and McGillivray, 2008; McGillivray and Frew, 2015; Lee Ludvigsen, 2021; Millward, 2009; Rookwood, 2021), there is an increased market incentive for alcohol companies to fulfil the role as 'partners' for commercial reasons at both the 'fan zones' (where their products may be the only ones that are permitted to be consumed) and the advertising opportunities afforded through worldwide television broadcasts. At the 2014 World Cup, larger manufacturer, Budweiser was a 'second tier' World Cup 'partner' and it voiced concern at the 2022 being held in Qatar, principally wrapping this in a discourse of concern about the processes in which it was awarded the tournament (Blitz, 2014) after it and FIFA had previously pressured Brazil into temporary legislative reform regarding the sale of alcohol in stadiums during its tournament (Oleaga, 2014).

Third, there is academic debate about the shape and extent of homophobia – recognising its multiple levels and various forms – in football (Cashmore and Cleland, 2012; Caudwell, 2011). However, previous Myrtle Beach Football Club defender, Anton Hysén, and ex-L.A. Galaxy Football Club winger Robbie Rogers are two rare examples of openly gay current professionals. In Qatar, homosexual acts between adult females and adult males are illegal.[5] In the days that followed the news that Qatar would host the 2022 World Cup, questions were posed about the impact this might have on gay participants, officials and supporters. Sepp Blatter responded to such questions by 'joking' that 'they [LGBT+ fans] should refrain from any sexual activities' (quoted in *The Guardian*, 2010). This response did not quell concerns about the harms that may come to homosexual men and women visiting Qatar in a fashion about not dissimilar concerns ahead of the treat of gay athletes, officials and supporters at the Sochi 2014 winter Olympic Games (see Travers and Shearman, 2017; Van Rheenen, 2014; Zeigler, 2014).

Fourth, in February 2015, it was confirmed that the tournament would have to be moved from its 'normal' June and/or July slot, which suits the 'off season' in Western Europe elite divisions that contribute the highest number of football players that compete in the tournament (Millward, 2013), to November and December. This decision was ushered by average June/July daytime temperatures that can exceed 50°C (120°F), which are widely held to be too hot to play football, to the extent that FIFA medical chief Jiri Dvorak described the 'highly critical risk' to players, officials and fans attending a World Cup in Qatar between June and August (Conway, 2014). If it would be held in June/July, and without extreme cooling systems, it is possible that our later discussions about some of the social harms that stadium construction workers face could be extended to understand the physical dangers that even highly paid football players (and variably paid officials) face in partaking in the event.

A legitimate question, however, is why Qatar might seek to gain by hosting sport mega-events, such as the 2022 World Cup. After all, it has to spend in the region of $100bn [USD] on infrastructure projects to support the World Cup. This includes the construction of nine state-of-the-art stadiums, $20bn [USD] worth of new roads, $4bn [USD] for a causeway connecting Qatar to Bahrain, $24bn [USD] for a high-speed rail network, hotels with 55,000 rooms and a new airport to accommodate fans, players and officials (Pattisson, 2013). There are at least three potential answers to this question.

First, as discussed in Chapter 5, sports mega-events come imbued with legacy promises. Following from the summer Olympic Games that Barcelona hosted in 1992, a longstanding legacy is the opportunity to project a subjectively desirable image of the host city/nation/people/industry to large pockets of the world through global media coverage of the tournament, which may result in increased tourism to the host location in subsequent years (Roche, 2000). In 2003, *The Times* ran a report that said Qatar was seeking to 'shake off its bland image' and join 'the hunt for the tourist dollar' by targeting an increase in visitors and holidaymakers from the UK, Germany, France, Switzerland, Italy, Russia, Belgium, the Netherlands, Luxembourg, Scandinavian countries, Australia, Japan and India (Graham-Hart, 2003: 2). Subsequently, in 2005, the state-owned Qatar Tourism and Exhibitions Authority (QTEA) announced a 5-year plan to boost the number of visitors from 964,000 as of 2007 to 1.5m by 2010 (Reiche, 2015). To do this, in 2008 the state allocated $17bn [USD] in a 'tourism development' fund that would be largely spent on hotels, exhibition spaces and other infrastructure, increasing visitor accommodation by 400 per cent from the point of announcement (in 2008) to 2012 (Arlidge, 2012). On top of this, legislation was passed to relax business regulation to increase private sector activities, therefore diversifying the local economy away from its dependence upon oil production. Second, Qatar has the 17th largest prevalence of obesity in the world, and Reiche (2015) argues that its sovereign leaders might feel that the sense of occasion of holding major sports tournaments in the country might inspire higher levels of physical activity, thus improving the nation's health.[6] Third, Brannagan and Giulianotti (2014, 2015) and Reiche (2015) feel that Qatar's appetite to grow its profile in sport and particularly to host the 2022 World Cup is part of an attempt to leverage 'soft power' in the Middle East global region and across the world at large. Indeed, Reiche (2015) points out that Qatar's neighbours, Iran and Saudi Arabia are both considerably bigger in metrics including physical size and military size. He points out that this may concern actors within its sovereign government given that in 1990, Kuwait –another small, oil-rich nation – was invaded by neighbouring Iraq therefore, a way that Qatar can increase its global significance to boost its 'national security'[7] is to leverage 'soft power' by developing a reputation and image utilising the global media gaze offered by sport mega-events. This reputation could be damaged by media and political stories that are held to be undesirable in other areas of the world, as highlighted by the 'harms' potentially caused in the accounts described earlier and – notably – in the case of the Kafala system and the treatment of guest construction workers, as we now discuss.

The Kafala System and the Unfolding of Story of Construction Workers' 'Social Harm'

Around 1.2m foreign workers are resident in Qatar; and these mostly hail from India, Pakistan, Bangladesh, Nepal, Indonesia and the Philippines (Kamrava, 2013). This figure makes up around 94 per cent of the labour force, mostly employed in low-skilled trades. Qatar is one of six countries that is a member of the geo-political Cooperation Council for the Arab States of the Gulf group, commonly also known as the Gulf Cooperation Council (GCC), where the use of the 'Kafala system' is normalised. Although Qatar underwent labour law reforms which saw the Kafala system officially abolished in the country in 2020, there are concerns that many of its practices remain legally in operation in the country (Pattisson, 2020).

Bajracharya and Sijapati (2012) explain the Kafala system to be a principle of sponsorship that is based on obligations in the treatment and protection of foreign guest workers. Historically, this involved the host assuming responsibility for the safety and protection of foreigners and guests (Murray, 2013; Pessoa et al., 2015). However, over time, its practices became contra to the original meaning, becoming principally used to provide the central governments of the GCC countries with the means of regulating labour flow into their respective countries (Bajracharya and Sijapati, 2012). Under today's Kafala system, workers' contracts are a minimum of 2 years in which their visa and legal status are tied to the sponsor, or the Kafil (Pessoa et al., 2015). Bajracharya and Sijapati (2012) point out that this means that the sponsor is required to take full economic and legal responsibility for the worker, including the worker's recruitment fee, medical examination and issuance of national identity card (known as an 'iqama'), upon arrival in the GCC countries. Under these circumstances, the Kafil has complete control over the mobility of the worker, removing his/her free agency and making him/her completely dependent on his/her sponsor since an employee cannot transfer employment or even leave the country without an exit visa from his/her sponsor. Given this power imbalance, guest workers in GCC countries are often subjected to occupational social harms such as low salaries, long working hours and physical, verbal, sexual and psychological abuses with such actions 'legal' in national and international criminal justice systems as they are not covered by labour laws and their work (Bajracharya and Sijapati, 2012). On top of this, since migrant workers are unable to exercise their rights and freedoms, they form a global 'invisible working class'; and their lack of visibility makes them more difficult to scrutinise and regulate their working conditions.

Under such circumstances, the Kafala system might be thought to be a form of forced labour. Although the social harms perspective disaggregates 'harm' and criminal justice systems, legal positions are not entirely insignificant. Thus, it is important to point out that there are potentially at least two international legal obligations that might be cited when referring to violations of international law because of the Kafala system. First, there are the principles set out by the International Labor Organization (ILO). Hudspeth (2014) says that the ILO has two fundamental conventions that practices facilitated by the Kafala system might break: a) the 1930 ILO Convention No. 29 Concerning Forced or Compulsory Labor that outlaws governments allowing forced labour and slavery to take place in their country; and b) the Abolition of Forced Labor Convention, 1957 (No. 105) that suggests that conditions that allow forced labour should be penalised. Second, and on these grounds, the International Trade Union Confederation (ITUC) successfully filed a complaint against Qatar through the ILO's Committee on human rights (Hudspeth, 2014). Beyond this, pressure groups such as *Human Rights Watch* and *Amnesty International* both claim that there are numerous other violations that amount to forced labour and trafficking (Hudspeth, 2014) but – whilst the 'social harm' emanating from such practices is accepted – the legality of these claims is not entirely established by any international law.

Nine months before the award of the right to host the 2022 World Cup to Qatar, Deepak Adhikari (2010) published an article on the Kafala system in *The Kathmandu Post*. He reported the story of Nepalese migrant workers who had died whilst working in GCC countries but whose bodies were only returning home some months after they had passed away. Adhikari suggested that on an average day, two dead Nepalis return in coffins from destinations they have migrated to for economic reasons, with at least 600 Nepalis dying in the Gulf countries in 2009. He pointed out that there are a myriad of reasons why so many Nepalese migrant workers die but attributes many to lack of 'pre-departure orientation' (leading to 'road accidents'), a lack of good accommodations, unhealthy lifestyles whilst away from home, high workloads, depression, and 'unbearably hot temperatures', many of these lead to heart failure but are ultimately reducible to the 'sponsorship' of other humans that Kafala system facilitates. The large circulation figures and the publication of the story in English lead to stories of the conditions experienced circulating amongst networks that were primarily concerned with human rights issues, if not representatives of the 209 FIFA representatives that voted on the hosting of the World Cup.

The *International Trade Union Confederation (ITUC)* responded in May 2011 with a report that focussed on the dangerous working conditions migrants from Nepal, Somalia, the Philippines and Sri Lanka experience on arrival in Qatar and the United Arab Emirates. *ITUC (2011)* points out that the Kafala system permitted restrictive rules on labour rights, preventing the development of effective trade unions for migrants and denying the right to strike or collectively negotiate for better conditions. The report insisted on improvements to workers' rights stating that FIFA and the Qatari authorities create the reform and that those international companies seeking lucrative contracts connected to the World Cup boycott it if their claims were not met. This report was followed by similar others, such as those by *Human Rights Watch* (in June 2012), *Business for Corporate Responsibility* (in October 2012), *Amnesty International* (in November 2013), *Engineers Against Poverty* (in January 2014), and follow-up reports by *ITUC* (in March 2014) and *Amnesty International* (in November 2014). All shared similar concerns, shedding light on the social harms and poor working conditions that were afforded to migrant construction workers in Qatar that were largely owing to the Kafala system.

Social Harms and Migrant Workers in World Cup 2022 Infrastructure Development

Amongst his 18 'cells' of sports-related violence, Young (2012: 90) discusses the possibility of 'offences against workers and the public', which takes in those actions that include mentally, physically and/or sexual forms of human rights violations, such as those experienced by under-age workers in sports-related 'sweat shop' industries located in global South countries including Malaysia, China, Pakistan and Indonesia. He outlines that such workers may suffer further abuse from their powerful bosses, who they fear (see also Donnelly, 2008; Kerr et al., 2020; Sage, 1999). This is the cell Young (2012) identifies that corresponds most closely with the 'social harms' experienced by migrant construction workers in Qatar. Hillyard and Tombs (2004, 2005) describe social harm as being a broad-ranging concept that may include multiple dimensions but does not automatically focus upon the prescriptions provided by nationally or internationally bounded criminal law. Thus, it focusses on accidental and purposeful damage caused to people and communities away from the power encryption of legislation. The Kafala system and the mistreatment of migrant workers may not be 'illegal' but it does create 'social harm'. In the process of sensitising an international public consciousness to the issues faced by migrant construction workers, the INGOs tell the stories of migrant workers, and in doing so highlighting a number of abuses to which they are subjected. These can be divided into seven categories that migrant workers have negatively experienced: i) deceived about the nature of the work; ii) deceived about the terms of the work; iii) housed in squalid conditions; iv) provided with insufficient food and water; v) made to work excessively long hours; vi) insufficiently protected by health and safety provisions; and vii) prevented from leaving the country. We advance the social harms' perspective by mapping these onto four dimensions operating in Qatar: *physical*, *financial/economic*, *affective/psychological* and *cultural safety*. We now unpack these dimensions.

The most serious social harm that World Cup 2022 infrastructure and stadia construction workers may experience is their loss of life. Estimates on how many migrant workers will lose their lives have varied but ITUC claimed that at least 7,000 might before the tournament commences (Quirke, 2015) and Pattisson and McIntyre (2021) claimed 6,500 had between 2010 and 2021. Loss of life falls under the umbrella of *physical* dimensions of social harms, a category that the critical media sources and INGOs reports find might also include issues such as work-related injury, poor provisions and protections for health and safety, excessive working hours, insufficient/unsuitable food and water supplies, squalid housing conditions and limited access to healthcare in relation to migrant construction workers in Qatar.

A pressure that many construction companies in Qatar experience is that the projects they are building are sizeable, complex and have ambitious completion dates. The hot weather conditions often do not favour fast completion deadlines, whilst the workforce is drawn from a wide range of countries with workers speaking different native languages. In such circumstances, Amnesty International (2013: 41) argues that under such conditions, 'robust health and safety procedures are vital' but the INGOs find that these tend to be sacrificed in order to complete the work in shorter time periods. Indeed, reports offered by Amnesty International and ITUC are replete with such evidence. For instance, a Nepalese worker told its researchers that 'On the construction site [in Doha] I fainted because of exhaustion – because of the heat and working in the sun' (quoted in Amnesty International, 2013: 41), whilst, during its data collection period, Amnesty International researchers were informed about two incidents where employers refused to take injured migrant workers to hospital. One worker had been injured in a workplace accident, and the other had collapsed on site due to the heat. Similarly, Raju told ITUC researchers that:

> I had been working in Doha for four years . . . it was raining that day. The work was going very fast. We had no safety glasses. I was hit in the eye with a nail. After the accident the foreman told me to go outside. I came back to the labour camp. I was in a lot of pain and couldn't see, so some friends took me to the emergency room. The doctor told me I had damaged my retina. I cannot see out of my left eye and it is difficult to work.
>
> *(Raju, 27, Nepalese Construction Worker in Qatar quoted in ITUC, 2014: 13)*

This story appears not to be an isolated case with Doha-based Filipino construction worker Jago reporting: 'One of my concerns is safety at work. My employer does not provide any boots or other safety equipment, not even a uniform' (quoted in ITUC, 2014: 11). Thus, equipment and other provisions to reduce the risk of injury may not be provided by some employers. Once a construction worker suffers injury, some companies do not provide sufficient support – for instance, Amnesty International (2013: 43) recorded a male Sri Lankan construction worker recounting a story where his employer reported that he 'did nothing' for a colleague who dislocated his shoulder to the point that fellow workers 'got a taxi to get him and another injured guy treated at the hospital. We paid for the taxi, not the company, and he had to pay for his own hospital fees' (Sri Lankan construction worker, quoted in Amnesty International, 2013: 43). In some instances, it seems that employers will dock workers' pay if they are ill or injured. The ground on which this may be permissible is that Article 82 of the State of Qatar's Labour Law requires that employees prove their illness with a note from a doctor approved by their employer. However, several workers in Doha said that their employers would only accept a doctor's note from Hamad hospital, 15 kilometres away from the Industrial area, which makes it very difficult for sick/injured workers to travel. The penalty that workers might incur for an unapproved absence from work varied between 1 and 4 days' pay (Amnesty International, 2013: 43). Potentially even more severe, Amnesty International (2013) found two workers from separate companies who alleged that when they got badly injured, the companies cancelled their residence permits and sent them home, rather than paying for them to be treated in Qatar on their corporate insurance policy.

Beyond the pressures to work when ill/injured, construction workers may be made to work excessive hours, with many giving in excess of 60 hours over a 6-day week, the maximum allowed under national Labour Law. Some of those who worked excessive hours told Amnesty International (2013: 44) that they were willing to work hours in excess of the Labour Law maximum for the correct rate of overtime payment. However, many reported that they were under remunerated for their endeavours. Qatari regulations ban outdoor work in areas exposed to the sun between 11.30 am and 3 pm. Yet, Amnesty International (2013: 44) report cases where migrant construction workers were forced into unbroken 12-hour labour shifts that ignored these regulations. In such conditions, a supply of drinking water is needed. However, Amnesty International (2013) found evidence to suggest that this was forthcoming on all sites, illustrating this point by recounting a narrative given by a group of Sri Lankan men who said that such provision on their site was inadequate, with 3,000 construction workers sharing only one water tanker which was not properly cooled, leaving it boiling hot in the afternoon.

Beyond poor working conditions, a second set of *physical* social harms that are evident relates to the accommodation that migrant workers are required to live in during their stay, as directed by the terms of the Kafala system. Particular problems in this respect were highlighted by Pattisson in *The Guardian* (2013), Amnesty International (2013) and the ITUC (2014) and included the overcrowding of rooms – involving 10–15 migrant workers sleeping in the same space – including some workers having to sleep without a bed; missing/non-functioning air conditioning in those rooms which made sleeping in the hot conditions very difficult; poor sanitisation which included overflowing sewage and the covers to septic tanks left open; workers' compounds not cleaned with bathrooms and kitchens not properly maintained; and a lack of basic provisions such as power and running water. In common with Carson's (1982) research into the conditions British North Sea oilrig workers endured in the 1970s, overcrowding and poor sanitisation placed the workers at risk of disease and illness. On top of this, some migrant workers experience further *physical* social harm by being insufficiently fed by their Kafil:

> We were working on an empty stomach for 24 hours; 12 hours' work and then no food all night. When I complained, my manager assaulted me, kicked me out of the labour camp I lived in and refused to pay me anything. I had to beg for food from other workers.
>
> *Ram Kumar Mahara, 27, Nepalese migrant worker in Qatar (quoted in Pattisson, 2013: 2)*

The State of Qatar has not accepted responsibility for exerting these harms, claiming them to be the companies who sponsor the migrant construction workers should show a greater degree of corporate responsibility towards their workers – which, in return, will yield greater productivity (Simmel, 1950). For instance, Stefan Van Dyke, a member of the Qatar 2022 welfare committee stated:

> Once the worker lives well and eats well, he works well. We had to get the contractors to buy into the process and there is a return on their investment. We are being told that they are seeing a lower rate of absenteeism . . . Some of the difficulties the contractors have is to visualise the standard [we want].
>
> *(quoted in Booth and Pattisson, 2014: 1)*

Quite clearly issues of *physical* social harms are recognised, but responsibility over whose duty is passed between sponsoring employees, the agents involved in recruiting workers and the government of Qatar. These themes continue in the *financial/economic* dimensions of social harm in World Cup construction projects in Qatar. In this domain, issues coalesce around three main points: first, the underpayment of wages to migrant workers by their Kafil, second, the withholding of wages by such employers and third, the total failure to recompense overseas workers for their labour. Indeed, Booth and Pattisson (2014) highlight workers' underpayment by pointing out that despite the physical harms stadium construction workers endure many earn as little as 45p per hour, or £4.90 per day. At this level and other levels of remuneration, Amnesty International's (2013: 33–34) report is replete with accounts from migrant workers who have been deceived about their levels of pay and then told that there is no appeal or arbitration process to support such individuals. However, an unnamed representative from a Doha-based Embassy of a labour-sending country told Amnesty International (2013: 41) that:

> Non-payment of wages is the most common complaint . . . For example yesterday 80 workers came in having not been paid . . . . When we send people back [to their home country] they tend not to have received their salaries for three, four, five or six months.

Beyond late pay, some migrant workers were quoted in both Amnesty International (2013) and ITUC (2014) reports as stating that their wages had not been paid at all. This appeared to emerge for four reasons: first, when the construction companies were not paid for the jobs, they completed some failed to pay their employees, as such passing on the impact of commercial non-payment. Second, a spokesman for The Supreme Committee for Delivery and Legacy admitted that there had been 'challenges with calculation of overtime pay and hours' specifically around overtime rates and right to be paid at all for working those extra hours and that the committee was responding to these issues with its own inquiry (quoted in Booth and Pattisson, 2014). Third, as earlier noted, Amnesty International (2013) and ITUC (2014) both found issues where migrant workers had been docked multiple days' pay for each day of holiday or illness leave. Fourth, delayed and non-payment can be a form of control that the Kafil have over their sponsored employees and a Nepalese construction worker at the Lusail City marina complex told *The Guardian* journalists the company he was employed by 'kept two months' salary from each of us to stop us running away (quoted in Pattisson, 2013). Under pressure exerted from the INGOs, the state of Qatar approved a law in February 2015 that enforced employer payment of wages by direct bank deposit, with the intention of reducing the likelihood of late and non-payment (Dorsey, 2015; Kovessy, 2015); however, migrant workers had already been subjected to some of the *financial/economic* social harms that Hillyard and Tombs (2004, 2005) outline.

In some cases, *financial/economic* social harms might become manifest as additional *emotional/psychological* social harms (Hillyard and Tombs, 2004, 2005). This proved to be the case amongst some migrant construction workers. For instance, Amnesty International (2013: 40) argued that the impact of late payment and non-payment of wages is devastating for some migrant workers with large numbers stating they had taken on loans with high rates of interest (sometimes with annual rates of up to 36 per cent) in their home country. Beyond repayment of loans, many migrant workers were emotionally distressed that the impact of their late/non-payment might mean that their families — often wives and children — would be evicted from their homes back in the countries where the workers were based (Amnesty International, 2013: 21). Therefore, a letter from a group of workers to their Kafil construction firm read: 'Due to pending salaries we are facing huge financial crisis to manage our daily routine expenses as well as our family commitments. This is leading us to series of mental stress' (quoted in Amnesty International, 2013: 40). On top of *emotional/psychological* social harms induced by late/

non-payment of wages, many migrant workers reported to the INGOs that they felt upset, depression and severe psychological distress caused by the treatment they had received and their sense of powerlessness in the resolution of their situations (Amnesty International, 2013: 6).

These social harms extend into the domain of *cultural safety*. In particular, migrant workers' cultural safety might be endangered under Kafala system in Qatar where, under the Sponsorship Law, employers are required to give permission to each migrant worker that wants to leave the country. The employer's power to restrict workers' freedom of movement has a profound psychological effect on workers, who throughout their working career in Qatar are always aware that their employers have the ability to prevent them from going home. The National Human Rights Committee noted such 'negative practices' of sponsors 'unjustifiably denying employees their right to obtain exit permits to leave the country' (quoted in Amnesty International, 2013). What is more, the conditions ushered by the Kafala system mean that, first, employers who do not pay fines on expired residence permits of migrant workers (that may have expired for a range of reasons) will block the workers' exit of the country and second, under the State of Qatar Labour Law Article 57, a Kafil is defined as the route through which workers acquire legal tickets to travel back to their home country. If the Kafil does not purchase this ticket, the employee is officially 'trapped' in Qatar. All of this leave such workers powerless in deciding how the legality and duration of their stay in Qatar (Amnesty International, 2013; ITUC, 2014). On top of this, the Kafala system means that the Kafil effectively 'owns' the right to employ the migrant worker in Qatar, which means it is effectively impossible for him/her to change employer without its approval. In the process of operating the Kafala system, some employers reportedly confiscated passports, which was in breach of the State of Qatar's World Cup organisers' worker welfare standards that state: 'The contractor shall ensure that all workers have personal possession of their passports and other personal documents' (cited in Booth and Pattisson, 2014), nevertheless concrete evidence of management acting on behalf of the Kafil had to be found to criminalise such actions making punishment – as with many crimes of the powerful – difficult to enforce (Tombs and Whyte, 2003).

Power and Politics in Reforming Migrant Workers' Rights

Despite highlighting acute social harms, INGOs such as *Human Rights Watch*, *Business for Corporate Responsibility*, *Amnesty International*, *Engineers Against Poverty* have no direct power to change national or international law. Amnesty International (n.d.) claims to be 'a global movement of more than 7m people' that 'reach[es] almost every country in the world' making its potential to mobilise significantly but, like the other INGOs, all it can do is 'call for' solutions and reform and apply 'pressure' (with little reference or consistency as to where such pressure will be most suitably applied). However, INGOs can raise public awareness of issues that are deemed unjust. After *ITUC*'s first report and those by *Human Rights Watch* and *Business for Corporate Responsibility*, journalist Pete Pattisson broke the story to a mainstream audience through an article titled 'Revealed: Qatar's World Cup "slaves"' on 25 September 2013. This was significant for two reasons: first, *The Guardian*'s average daily circulation figures that year were around 250,000 (Greenslade, 2014) with most copies sold in the UK but second, and potentially most important, its website receives in the region of 77.9m unique browsers per month from across the world (*MediaWeek*, 2013). *The Guardian* recorded that individual article had been shared almost 100,000 times by February 2015. The online storage of article was accompanied by a short video, a discursive section that drew in over 1,600 readers' comments and gave rise to an ongoing section titled 'Modern Slavery in Focus' that is supported by INGO *Humanity United* and includes issues related to the Kafala system as a core focus.

In a similar vein to the INGO reports, Pattisson's newspaper article stated that 'dozens' of Nepalese workers had died in the construction of the country's infrastructural development in preparation for the World Cup (later adding that the figure was 44 between 4 June and 8 August), whilst 'thousands more are enduring labour abuses' (Pattisson, 2013: 1). On 23 December 2014, the Nepalese foreign employment promotion board had declared that 157 of its workers in Qatar had died between January and mid-November 2014, of these 67 were attributable to sudden cardiac arrests, 8 to heart attacks and 34 deaths recorded as workplace accidents (Gibson and Pattisson, 2014). In common with the social harms highlighted by the four INGOs, *The Guardian*'s original report drew attention to a) evidence of labour that could be considered to be 'forced' to work on the Qatari infrastructure, b) allegations from Nepalese men that they had not been paid for months and had their salaries retained to stop them running away, c) some workers on other sites reporting that employers routinely confiscated their passports and refused to issue ID cards, which gave them a status of illegal aliens, d) labours reporting being denied access to free drinking water in the desert heat and e) approximately 30 Nepalese seeking refuge at their embassy in Doha to escape the brutal conditions of their employment. This report named the Lusail City development as one such place where such poor working conditions were taking place, and implied that the Lusail City Real Estate Development Company (LCREDC) was guilty of imposing the treatment afforded by the Kafala system. Two months later, in November 2013, *Amnesty International* named SEG construction, a contracting company concerned with engineering and construction work that is based in Beirut (Lebanon) but serves projects across the Middle East and its subcontractors in Qatar, the Floridian construction company Krantz, as corporate actors that were key perpetrators in creating such 'harms' against Nepalese and other migrant workers. The INGO and newspaper reports drew 'official' responses to the stories, which were published in *The Guardian*'s online special report (25 September 2013). Specifically, these came from LREDC, the UK-domiciled consulting engineers and architecture company, Halcrow, The Qatar 2022 Supreme Committee (Q22) and The Qatar Labor Ministry.

Relationships in the situation that has caused the social harm to migrant construction workers in Qatar are not dyadic. Rather, the number of state and corporate actors involved is multiple. The mistreatment and death of migrant construction workers is deemed unacceptable but – as Simmel (1950) argued in groups that are made up of more than two social actors – responsibility for change is diffuse. Thus, LREDC opened its account by stating that it would not tolerate breaches of labour or health and safety law and that 'all of our subcontractors are legally obliged to meet, as a minimum, Qatar labour law' (LREDC spokesman quoted in *The Guardian*, 2013). In fact, beyond this it pledged an expectation that all of its subcontractors 'to go beyond the law in the protection of individual employees both in health and safety and labour law'. It stated that it was 'extremely concerned at the allegations' pointing out that it 'employs, directly and via subcontractors, over 20,000 people' who are 'each valued' (LREDC spokesman quoted in *The Guardian*, 2013). Most notably, LREDC attempted to remove themselves from any culpability by placing the 'blame' on an individual subcontractor. 'Responsibility' is relational; lost in the passing of 'blame' in relationships that stretch beyond the dyadic (Simmel, 1950). In line with the questions that Carson encourages social researchers to ask, they first, failed to inform readers of the system of regulation it – as the parent company – has over its subcontractors and second, if regulation *does* take place, of the relationship between the social actors who perform those duties and those in key positions in both the parent company and the subcontractors. Halcrow attempted to remove itself in a similar fashion by declaring:

> Our supervision role of specific construction packages ensures adherence to site contract regulation for health, safety and environment. The terms of employment of a contractor's labour force is not under our direct purview. We, at Halcrow, ensure that our staff are compensated fairly according to industry standards and are provided with training on skills necessary to conduct their work efficiently, including training on health, safety and sustainability.
>
> *(Halcrow statement quoted in The Guardian, 2013)*

One hundred fifty-seven migrant workers were still recorded as having died through health issues connected to poor working conditions in 2014; the actual figure had the potential to be even higher when those who were not recorded or not recorded to have died were taken into account. The Q22, the 'talented and creative team' that are made up of 'more than 40 nationalities' (*Qatar 2022 Supreme Committee*, n.d.) who are locally responsible for the organisation of the event announced itself to be 'deeply concerned with the allegations . . . [and] considers this issue to be of the utmost seriousness' (Q22 statement quoted in *The Guardian*, 2013). Ultimately, its defence against the allegations was that it would work with 'international NGOs, including Human Rights Watch and Amnesty International' and have been 'informed that the relevant government authorities are conducting an investigation into the allegations' (Q22 statement quoted in *The Guardian*, 2013), deferring judgement to the country's sovereign power. The Qatar Labor Ministry responded by answering a number of questions that were posed by *The Guardian*, and whilst – akin to Q22 – it showed concern at the loss of life, took no responsibility for them. For instance, when asked why so many young Nepalese construction workers were dying of heart problems in Qatar, its response was: 'This question would be better suited for the relevant health authorities or the government of Nepal'. Across its responses, it showed why the treatment of migrant workers in its country was legal in its own national legislation. 'Responsibility' was passed between state and corporate actors in the complex relationships (Simmel, 1950). However, the issue stands that the Kafala system and its adoption into Qatari law means that their treatment of migrant workers was deeply harmful but not 'illegal'.

In November 2013, this was followed up by the European Parliament passing an emergency resolution condemning the abuse of migrant workers in Qatar. This resolution 'called' on the Qatari government to reform and uphold its labour laws and reminded FIFA 'that its responsibility goes beyond the development of football and the organisation of competitions' (*European Parliament Emergency Resolution*, 2013: 5). However, two major obstacles were placed in the way of this request: first, the European Parliament is made up of 751 members elected from the 28 Member States of the enlarged European Union. These members represent a diversity of views, and the proposed resolutions are democratically decided upon. As such, for this motion to be passed, Christian Democrat and Conservative voting blocs enforced the removal of a clause calling for Qatar to abolish the Kafala sponsorship system (Gibson, 2013b). Second, as a European postnational structure, it has minimal powers in directly influencing law and politics in non-European countries, such as Qatar (Delanty and Rumford, 2005). Thus, it can also 'call for' or 'request' change rather than enforcing it. Also in November 2013, a United Nations (U.N.) Special Rapporteur mission into human rights of migrants in Qatar stated that: 'The mandate of the Special Rapporteur covers all countries, irrespective of whether a State has ratified the International Convention on the Protection of the Rights of All Migrant Workers and Members of Their Families, of 18 December 1990' (*United Nations Human Rights*, 2013). However, when it delivered its report in April 2014, it criticised the abuse of migrant workers, but its first recommendation was that the Qatari government and legal system should: 'Effectively implement existing legislation, prosecute violations and impose appropriate sanctions on companies and individuals who violate the rights of migrants' (*United Nations Human Rights*, 2013: 17) when much of the mistreatment was legally permitted by the laws afforded by the Kafala system. Beyond its first recommendation, others emerged that may offer alternative hope for change. For instance, amongst other suggestions it recommended that Qatar should:

- 'Abolish the Kafala system and replace it with a regulated open labour market, where the work permit allows the worker to change employer' (*United Nations Human Rights*, 2013: 17);

- 'Refrain from detaining individuals for the sole reason of having absconded from their employer. End the systematic detention of migrants awaiting deportation and always explore alternatives to detention' (*United Nations Human Rights*, 2013: 20); and
- 'Provide migrants with information about their rights and how to access them. This could be done, inter alia, by disseminating the Workers' Rights Book of the National Human Rights Committee, both in migrant-sending countries and in Qatar' (*United Nations Human Rights*, 2013: 20).

The Qatari state would implement in much the way that the UK government implemented the Factory Acts and health and safety reform on North Sea oil rigs in Carson's analysis. Indeed, he found that any changes to the law might mean meeting such 'standards' is open to vast inspectional discretion, continuing to leave workers subject to 'harm' and potentially tragic ramifications. Even if an external intergovernmental organisation, such as the U.N. levered social change to the legality and operation of the Kafala system in Qatar, live questions are presented about who would regulate the new provisions, and what might be deemed to be permissible under such inspections.

However, space exists for another corporate actor to take some responsibility for the relationships that ultimately subject many migrant construction workers to social harm, and thus take responsibility for ensuring that these do not happen in the future. That actor is FIFA. By awarding Qatar the rights to host World Cup 2022, FIFA legitimised the way in which the Kafala system is often used in the country, knowing that one of the post sport mega-event 'legacies' it would leave would be stadia and infrastructure developments that would have to be built in advance of 2022 (Ganji, 2016; Millward, 2017). However, FIFA president at the time of the award of the World Cup finals to Qatar, Sepp Blatter, did not hold a consistent position on his organisation's role and responsibilities in this situation. After the story about some of the social harms migrant workers in Qatar were subjected to break through in *The Guardian*, Sepp Blatter warned that FIFA cannot 'turn a blind eye' to the deaths of the migrant construction workers but also stated that: 'I am going to Qatar now and we will put the situation of Qatar with the situation we are facing with *their responsibility* [our emphasis]. We have plenty of time concerning Qatar but it is 2022, it is in nine years [away]' (quoted in Gibson, 2013a). Quite clearly from his quote, FIFA is not accepting responsibility for these harms, allocating this to the State of Qatar – only accepting responsibility for the sport mega-event, to be held in 2022. On 2 December 2014, he followed up this sentiment by reiterating that employers of migrant workers in Qatar 'are responsible for their workers and not FIFA' (quoted in *The Guardian*, 2014). However, less than 2 months later, at the Asia Cup Final on 31 January 2015, Blatter stated with reference to holding the 2018 tournament in Russia – where, as with the Sochi 2014 Winter Olympic Games, state-sponsored homophobia exists (see Lenskyj, 2014) – and the 2022 tournament in Qatar:

> 2 December 2010, I will never forget this date where we have made the decision for two World Cups, which was wrong . . . I will tell you, that human

rights and other rights will be part of the basic conditions to organise the competition. That will be new for the next World Cup – the World Cup 2026.

(quoted in The Independent, 2015)

In this statement, Blatter did not take responsibility for the death and other abuses of migrant construction workers in Qatar but recognises the issues, claiming a legacy of the tournament on FIFA will be that in future a strong record in upholding human rights will be necessary for a country to win the right to host a World Cup. How rigidly this promise is kept is unknown as are the ways in which such records will be judged, and who will do that judging. Blatter's replacement, Gianni Infantino, has been largely uncritical of Qatar, hailing 'significant progress' in reforms to workers' welfare on issues which, as discussed later in this chapter, INGOS such as Amnesty International, see differently.

Regulating Regulation and Regulators: DLA Piper and the Quest for Reform of the Kafala System

Following the critical media coverage, pressure group appeals, postnational/intergovernmental recommendations, and – potentially – growing unease from FIFA's commercial partners, the sovereign Qatar government commissioned the multinational global law firm, DLA Piper to investigate claims of migrant workers' abuse and methods for effective reform of its system. This report was sent to the government in April 2014 and then made available to the public through Engineers Against Poverty the following month. DLA Piper was critical of the 'extrapolation of statistics in the press' about work-related injury and deaths (DLA Piper, 2014: 77), noting that 964 migrant workers from Nepal, India and Bangladesh had died in 2012 and 2013. Of these, 246 died from 'sudden cardiac death' (p. 90), 35 died from falls with 28 committed suicide. It suggested that these deaths were separate from work-related injuries, which accounted for only a small number of deaths. However, the report criticised the Kafala system, arguing it to be 'no longer the appropriate tool for the effective control of migration' (DLA Piper, 2014: 44).

Beyond this claim, DLA Piper made 62 'recommendations' to the government of Qatar under the umbrella of 'overall key' areas, 'sponsor transfers', 'exit visas', 'passports' and the 'charge of absconding'. In the first of these categories, the report recommended that the State of Qatar conduct 'a wide-ranging and comprehensive review of the Kafala system' (DLA Piper, 2014: 8) which would decide 'whether *certain aspects* [our emphasis] of the system should be abolished or phased out over time' (DLA Piper, 2014: 8). Quite clearly, this 'recommendation' placed responsibility for reform upon the Qatar government rather than an external agency – leaving significant manoeuvrability over what aspects would be reformed, whilst by March 2015 there was no clear timetable as to when any changes would be enforced despite the Labor Minister Abdullah bin Saleh Al Khulaifi promising that reforms would be implemented 'as quickly as possible' a year earlier (Kovessy,

2015). Second, under the banner of 'sponsor transfer', DLA Piper recommended that employers and sponsors who are found to have abused the Kafala system and/or Qatari Labour laws should have their right to employ migrant labour removed. As Carson (1982) notes, responsibility for recording any abuses would fall on individual inspectors from the State of Qatar's Labour Department. Thus, for 'social harm' to be recorded as abuse, the action would have to be deemed illegitimate through the Kafala system – which can be interpreted to permit such action – or illegal through national legislation *and* that action would have to be detected and reported as such by individual inspectors. The likelihood of a major sponsor being found 'guilty' and having its right to do so revoked could be small. Third, DLA piper recommended that the 'exit-visa' system should be internally reviewed by the Qatari government. In particular, it asked the State of Qatar 'review and reconsider the necessity of an exit visa under the Kafala sponsorship system' and that migrant workers should be given two key 'rights'. Specifically, these were the right to a) 'apply to the Ministry of Interior for the issuance of an exit visa' (DLA Piper, 2014: 9); b) the right to 'clear information as to their rights and access to representation by the Labour Relations Department (in the Ministry of Labour and Social Affairs) in the event the migrant worker believes a request for an exit visa has been unjustly refused' (DLA Piper, 2014: 57). These 'rights' gave responsibility to the migrant workers to ask for clarity on their position rather than compelling the sponsoring firms to upfront provisions for the individuals. Fourth, DLA Piper recommended that employers 'be required' to make available secure storage items in which migrant workers can keep items such as passports and that the 'Labour Inspection Department should make enquiries as to the whereabouts of migrant workers' passports during the course of inspections' (DLA Piper, 2014: 58). Once again, the onus of responsibility is placed on individual inspectors' shoulders but DLA Piper's report states that this recommendation 'should be enforced vigorously' (DLA Piper, 2014: 58). Fifth, under the banner of 'Charge of Absconding' DLA Piper called for clarification on the proper application, framework and appropriate supervision of the sponsorship termination mechanism and argued that migrant workers should be afforded the due process of law, specifically including the right not to be unlawfully detained (DLA Piper, 2014: 58), reinforcing the emphasis on the inspectorate to successfully identify then record 'injustices' or 'violations' of workers' rights. Gibson (2014) pointed out that the State of Qatar claimed that the number and frequency of inspections of construction sites had increased but DLA Piper (2014) argued better training for inspectors, more powers afforded to them, more interpreters for worker interviews and more transparency in the process was needed. Carson (1982) reminds us that – historically – inspectorate powers have not always been best utilised. For regulatory mechanisms to be successful, they must be consistent, robust and preferably beyond the level of social actors' subjective judgements (Carson, 1982).

Above all else, DLA Piper deferred to the State of Qatar's Ministry of Interior in noting that the government department had 'already reviewed the current system and proposed reforms aimed at reducing the risk of restricting migrant workers' freedom of movement are already being implemented' (DLA Piper, 2014: 55). McGeehan's (2014) response, published in *The Guardian*, was lukewarm. On the one hand, he commended DLA Piper for 'leaving the Qatari government in no doubt as to the problems that exist and what it can and should do to fix them'. On the other hand, he was critical of its outcomes on three counts. First, he pointed out the DLA Piper's failure to recommend an immediate abolition of Qatar's exit-visa system, revealing that instead the recommendation was for the system to be phased out over time, ignoring that the exit-visa system as it stands may not be legal in the eyes of international law. Second, he disapproved of DLA Piper's 'light-touch regulation' approach to the critical issue of enforcing labour standards, suggesting that laws and regulations only have an impact when they are supported by sanctions. Third, McGeehan (2014) posited that the enforcement mechanisms DLA Piper outlined were not strong enough. In particular, McGeehan (2014) asks:

> Is blacklisting really an appropriate penalty for Qatari recruitment agents who swindle migrant workers out of thousands of dollars, leaving them heavily indebted and vulnerable to forced labour? An electronic payment system will detect the non-payment of wages, but strong punishment for offenders is sorely lacking. So how will wage payment be enforced?

McGeehan's (2014) concern was that DLA Piper's recommendations might not be acted upon.

In Chapter 3, Jennings' (2011) work was utilised to outline that when IOC reform commission was formed by its President Antonio Samaranch. To do so, he called in his associates including former FIFA President Joao Havelange, former U.S. Secretary of State Henry Kissenger and global public relations company, Hill & Knowlton. Similarly, when FIFA President Sepp Blatter responded to public pressure and sponsors' concerns by appointing external chairs to its 'Ethics Committee', it also approached Kissenger who was not only an associate of Samaranch but also Blatter. The external regulators that were recruited were those connected to senior individuals in the organisation rather than those that were clearly removed from it. According to Foster (2013), DLA Piper had previous connections to the Qatari government on account of it receiving 'more than $300,000 (£186,000) in lobbying fees this year [2013] from Al Jazeera America', which is a 'private institution of public utility' which means it remains close to the sovereign power in the State of Qatar.

DLA Piper (2014) initially claimed that from May 2014, the 2022 Supreme Committee and the Qatar Foundation would adopt standards for contractors to treat migrant construction workers. However, Dorsey (2015) posits that by February 2015 the State of Qatar had so far failed to enshrine those standards in national legislation, with its implementation being only 'minor changes' such as obliging employers to pay wages and salaries by bank transfer. What is more, Dorsey also suggested that the increase in numbers of labour inspectors tasked with enforcing existing rules and regulations – as recommended by DLA Piper – had been only very small, undermining the credibility Qatar's willingness to reform. Therefore, critical questions that could be raised are 'did DLA Piper make recommendations that were genuinely *external* given its connection to the State of Qatar?', 'how can these recommendations be enforced/inspected?', 'what sanctions – if any – can be placed on whom/what if these recommendations are not acted upon?' and 'what role does the individual inspectorate have in ensuring recommendations are carried out?' Even after the analysis offered here, we can only guide towards these questions rather than locating such answers such is the obfuscated nature of the field.

Outlook and Developments: One Year to Go

On 21 November 2021, a date marking the tournament's one-year-to-go milestone, a countdown clock for the 2022 World Cup was unveiled during a spectacular launch in Doha.[8] At the time of writing, less than a year before the Qatar World Cup, the final planning phases have been marked by important developments. Perhaps most notably, in February 2021, an investigative analysis by Pattisson and McIntyre (2021) in *The Guardian* claimed that over 6,500 migrant workers had died since Qatar was awarded the World Cup. The report drew upon data gathered from the embassies of India, Nepal, Bangladesh, Sri Lanka and Pakistan, and *The Guardian*'s investigative journalists also drew attention to the 'lack of transparency, rigour and detail in recording deaths in Qatar' (ibid.). For instance, it was noted that 80 per cent of the deaths of Indian migrant workers were categorised as 'natural deaths' (ibid.). Pattisson and McIntyre's analysis found that death records commonly are not categorised in terms of occupation or workplace, but that it still remains likely that many of the workers died whilst working on World Cup infrastructure projects. Indeed, as Nick McGeehan from FairSquare Projects stated, '[a] very significant proportion of the migrant workers who have died since 2011 were only in the country because Qatar won the right to host the World Cup' (quoted in *The Guardian*, 2021a). In August 2021, some of *The Guardian*'s revelations were corroborated by the publication of an Amnesty International (2021a) report which also emphasised Qatar's failure to investigate, remedy and prevent the deaths of migrant workers that often are attributed to 'natural causes' or 'cardiac arrest', rather than to working conditions.

Crucially, whilst there have been reforms in Qatar between 2015 and 2021, including the introduction of a minimum wage for workers and a new labour law that removed the mentioned kafala system (Amnesty International, 2020), Amnesty International's conclusion state that these, by themselves, are unlikely to prove sufficient in the absence of additional legislation:

> Recent reforms introduced in May 2021, as part of the wider programme of reforms introduced recently by the Qatari government, are important and will offer workers greater protection from heat if fully enforced. But the new regulations will remain insufficient unless further legislation is introduced,

including to mandate rest periods in proportion to the climatic conditions and the nature of work undertaken.

(Amnesty International, 2021a: 51)

Indeed, as late as November 2021, Amnesty International reported that the country's labour reforms had stalled and that: 'time [was] running out', if the authorities intended to 'deliver on promises to abolish the abusive "kafala" sponsorship system and better protect huge numbers of migrant workers' (Amnesty International, 2021b). Furthermore, Amnesty International's (2021a) report calls for FIFA to take responsibility. For example, it recommends that FIFA and national football associations administrating or participating in the World Cup take actions including the commissioning of an independent review of the Supreme Committee's (Qatar's body in charge of planning and delivering the World Cup infrastructure) 'incident investigation procedure and the reports it prepares on all deaths on projects under its purview, with a particular focus on the 35 deaths that the Supreme Committee has classified as "non-work-related" to date' (ibid.: 54). The INGO also recommended that FIFA carried out an 'independent, thorough and transparent investigation' into all migrant worker deaths and ensured that procedures for adequate compensation for families of the deceased were established (ibid.).

As the opening of Qatar's World Cup has approached in time, the country's issues of human and workers' rights have also been criticised by commentators, pundits and athletes. For example, in the qualifying rounds for the 2022 World Cup, Germany, the Netherlands and Norway bore t-shirts drawing attention to Qatar's human rights record. Norway's national team entered the pitch for their fixtures against Gibraltar and Turkey with t-shirts stating 'Human Rights On and Off the Pitch' (*The Guardian*, 2021a). Furthermore, in an extraordinary congress meeting, the Norwegian FA also voted on whether the national team should boycott the 2022 World Cup if the side qualified, after massive calls for action from several Norwegian elites and grassroots clubs and the Norwegian Supporters Alliance (NSA). As a statement from the NSA (2021) fan movement said: 'a boycott will set a precedent for the future and give a clear indication of limits for FIFA and host nations'. However, a boycott of the World Cup was, in the end, voted down.

So, 1 year before the 22nd edition of the World Cup is launched in Qatar, concerns surrounding the country's human and workers' rights records, free speech and discriminatory laws perpetuate. In November 2021, two journalists investigating the working and living conditions for migrant workers were reportedly arrested in Qatar (*The Guardian*, 2021b), whilst the equality campaign Kick It Out in tandem with members from Stonewall, Football Supporters' Association (FSA), Football vs. Homophobia and Sports Media LGBT+ recently established a Qatar 2022 working group seeking to work for LGBTQ+ inclusion at the World Cup (Kick It Out, 2021). Thus, whilst commentators, journalists, INGOs, activists and fan movements have succeeded in drawing increased attention to the human and social costs of this World Cup edition, the harms experienced by the migrant workers and, importantly, the lack of accepted responsibilities for these still co-exist alongside unfulfilled promises of reform.

Summary: Social Harms, Zemiology and Sport

Between 21 November and 18 December 2022, Qatar will house the largest football mega-event in the world. And, by employing the case of the controversial Qatar's 2022 World Cup which – at the time of writing – is 12 months away in time, this chapter has cross-pollinated ideas from 'zemiology' (Hillyard et al., 2004, 2005; Hillyard and Tombs, 2007; Canning and Tombs, 2021) with central conceptual touchstones deriving from 'relational sociology' (Cleland et al., 2018; Crossley, 2011; Donati, 2010, 2013). This chapter has principally been concerned with the treatment of migrant construction workers at stadium construction project for the World Cup and the conditions in which they operate and live. As we have argued, the social realities of the migrant stadium construction workers in Qatar, the Kafala system and the associated human rights abuses discussed earlier collectively serve as a powerful exemplar of the social harms that are suffered in modern-day sport. Such an argument carries an enormous significance because, ultimately, this echoes the wider social harms that can be situated across the neoliberal world and that are inflicted by corporations and governments. The study of social harms – zemiology – has emerged as a critique of criminology's restricted scope vis-à-vis the meanings of 'crime' and we have, throughout this chapter, extended Hillyard et al.'s (2004, 2005) and Hillyard and Tombs' (2007) theories into the domain of sport, in which such propositions possess a considerable purchase. Additionally, this chapter has drawn upon the work of Carson (1970a, 1970b, 1971, 1974, 1979, 1980, 1982, 1985a, 1985b) to examine the theme of 'responsibility' in context of the abuses discussed earlier. By connecting to Carson's work, this chapter has provided a contemporary update and context in which to further consider his arguments around regulation, finding that regulating those regulators continues to be of key significance.

Essentially, questions may be asked about the implications beyond the Qatar 2022 World Cup. Whereas the analysis offered earlier has centred primarily on the case of Qatar, the relationships between social harms, sport and sport mega-events must now be further explored in order to advance the boundaries of what may be considered the critical criminology of sport. Indeed, we have touched upon Sochi's 2014 Winter Olympics and Russia's 2018 World Cup with reference to issues of homophobia and the treatment of LGBTQ+ supporters, athletes, journalists and officials and as the 2020s proceeded, social harms could again emerge in peripheries of the mega-events that pop up around global cities. As this chapter has demonstrated, 'the relationship between sport and harm is nuanced, complex and diffuse' (Francis, 2012: 15) and we may also look towards other recent or forthcoming sport mega-events to reaffirm such notion. For example, the Tokyo 2020 Summer Olympic Games was, as Chapter 8 reflects on, staged during the public health crisis of COVID-19 causing potentially serious health risks for, inter alia, athletes, staff, residents and the city's health workers.

Meanwhile, in the summer of 2028 the Olympic torch relay will conclude in Los Angeles. The two cases are important for critical criminological investigations into the relationship between social harm and sport. With regard to Los Angeles's forthcoming sporting spectacle, such investigations could, more specifically, address the treatment and displacement of homeless populations across the city (see Boykoff, 2020). In their article in *The Nation*, Zirin and Boykoff (2021) observe that Los Angeles' unhoused population is currently in the region of 60,000 and is expected to rise by 36 per cent by 2023. However, as Los Angeles continue to 'remake the city in time for the games', this has resulted in police crackdowns, displacement and evictions of 'undesirable' populations residing in the city's Echo Park neighbourhood. Indeed, as evidence from the mega-cities of London and Vancouver (Kennelly and Watt, 2011) illustrate, such urban sanitising practices are not new and occur over several years. Thus, and looking beyond Qatar's 2022 World Cup, the insights from 'zemiology' offer a lens through which we can understand how such issues are experienced locally and 'on-the-ground', adding to our understanding of how sport, states and corporations create, amplify or preserve 'social harms'.

Notes

1. Tombs and Whyte (2010) argue that these conditions were degraded in the UK under policies made by the 'New' Labour government.
2. These themes were additionally picked up by Tombs and Whyte (2003) in research exploring the regulation of 'criminality' that predates the coining of the 'social harms' or 'zemiological' approach.
3. According to 2013 figures, Indians make up the largest expatriate community in Qatar, contributing 545,000 people to the national population of 1.8m. On top of this, 2013 figures show there are 341,000 Nepalis, 185,000 Filipinos, 137,000 Bangladeshis, 100,000 Sri Lankans and 90,000 Pakistanis to be amongst its residents.
4. The AFC Asian Cup is an international football tournament run by the Asian Football Confederation (AFC) in which teams representing Asian FIFA members compete. The winning team becomes the champion of Asia.
5. Article 296 of Qatar's current Penal Code (Law 11/2004) stipulates imprisonment between 1 and 3 years for sodomy between men. This Article does not address sexual acts between women although, gay or bisexual women living in Qatar could face criminal charges for violating other public morality laws, such as the ban on fornication.
6. This is despite the UK government suggesting that a legacy of the summer 2012 Olympic Games (held in London) might be a 'healthier' and 'more active' nation – a promise that has not been delivered according to most measures (see www.bbc.co.uk/news/education-20358298).
7. See Chapter 5 for the 'Welsh School's' criticisms of this notion of 'security'.
8. See: www.youtube.com/watch?v=-QWy2R55fb0 [accessed 12/2021].

References

Adhikari, D. (2010) 'A casket of dreams: Deaths of Nepali migrants overseas', *Migrant Rights*, 26 March, available from: www.migrant-rights.org/research/a-casket-of-dreams-deaths-of-nepali-migrants-overseas/ [accessed 1/2022].

Amnesty International. (2013) 'The dark side of migration: Spotlight on Qatar's construction sector ahead of the world cup', London.

Amnesty International. (2020) 'Qatar: New laws to protect migrant workers are a step in the right direction', available from: www.amnesty.org/en/latest/news/2020/08/qatar-annoucement-kafala-reforms/ [accessed 01/2022].

Amnesty International. (2021a) 'In the prime of their lives: Qatar's failure to investigate, remedy and prevent migrant workers' deaths', available from: www.amnesty.nl/content/uploads/2021/08/MDE-22.4614.2021-In-the-prime-of-their-lives-migrant-worker-deaths-in-Qatar_FINAL.pdf?x53918 [accessed 12/2021].

Amnesty International. (2021b) 'Qatar: Labour reforms have stalled, with old abuses resurfacing – new report', available from: www.amnesty.org.uk/press-releases/qatar-labour-reforms-have-stalled-old-abuses-resurfacing-new-report [accessed 01/2022].

Amnesty International. (n.d.) 'No extra time: How Qatar is still failing on workers' rights ahead of the world cup', London.

Arlidge, J. (2012) 'A new Washington in the desert sands', *The Sunday Times*, 12 February, p. 23.

Bajracharya, R. and Sijapati, B. (2012) 'The kafala system and its implications for Nepali domestic workers', *Centre for the Study of Labour and Mobility – Policy Brief*, 1, available from: www.ceslam.org/docs/publicationManagement/Kafala_Nepali_Domestic_Workers_Female_Migration_Eng.pdf [accessed 8/2015].

Blitz, R. (2014) Budweiser piles pressure on Fifa over Qatar claims', *Financial Times*, available from: www.ft.com/content/a5535284-efe2-11e3-9b4c-00144feabdc0 [accessed 01/2022].

Booth, R. and Pattisson, P. (2014) 'Qatar world cup stadium workers earn as little as 45p an hour', *The Guardian*, 29 July, available from: www.theguardian.com/global-development/2014/jul/29/qatar-world-cup-stadium-workers-earn-45p-hour [accessed 7/2015].

Boykoff, J. (2020) *Nolympians: Inside the Fight Against Capitalist Mega-Sports in Los Angeles, Tokyo and Beyond*, Nova Scotia: Fernwood.

Box, S. (2002) *Power, Crime and Mystification*, London: Routledge.

Brackenridge, C. and Kirby, S. (1997) 'Playing safe: Assessing the risk of sexual abuse to elite child athletes', *International Review for the Sociology of Sport* 32(4): 407–418.

Brannagan, P.M. and Giulianotti, R. (2014) 'Qatar, global sport, and the 2022 FIFA world cup', *Leveraging Legacies from Sports Mega-Events* (Eds. J. Grix), Basingstoke: Palgrave Pilot, pp. 154–165.

Brannagan, P.M. and Giulianotti, R. (2015) 'Soft power and soft disempowerment: Qatar, global sport and football's 2022 world cup finals', *Leisure Studies* 34(6): 703–719.

Brannigan, A. and Pavlich, G. (eds.) (2007) *Governance and Regulation in Social Life: Essays in Honour of WG Carson*, Abingdon: Routledge.

Cain, M. and Howe, A. (2008) 'Introduction: Women, crime and social harm: Towards a criminology for the global age', *Women, Crime and Social Harm: Towards a Criminology for the Global Age* (Eds. M. Cain and A. Howe), London: Bloomsbury Publishing.

Canning, V. (2017) *Gendered Harm and Structural Violence in the British Asylum System*, London: Routledge.

Canning, V. and Tombs, S. (2021) *From Social Harm to Zemiology: A Critical Introduction*, Abingdon: Routledge.

Caudwell, J. (2011) '"Does your boyfriend know you're here?" The spatiality of homophobia in men's football culture in the UK', *Leisure Studies* 30(2): 123–138.

Carson, W.G. (1970a) 'White-collar crime and the enforcement of factory legislation', *The British Journal of Criminology* 10(4): 383–398.

Carson, W.G. (1970b) 'Some sociological aspects of strict liability and the enforcement of factory legislation', *Modern Law Review* 33(4): 396–412.

Carson, W.G. (1971) 'White collar crime and the enforcement of factory legislation', *Crime and Delinquency in Britain* (Eds. W.G. Carson and P. Wiles), London: Martin Robertson & Company.

Carson, W.G. (1974) 'Symbolic and instrumental dimensions of early factory legislation: A case study in the social origins of criminal law', *Crime, Criminology and Public Policy: Essays in Honour of Sir Leon Radzinowicz* (Eds. R. Hood), London: Heinemann.

Carson, W.G. (1979) 'The conventionalization of early factory crime', *Journal of the Sociology of Law* 7(1): 37–60.

Carson, W.G. (1980) 'Early factory inspectors and the viable class society', *International Journal of the Sociology of Law* 8(2): 187–191.

Carson, W.G. (1982) *Other Price of Britain's Oil: Safety and Control in the North Sea*, London: Martin Robinson Press.

Carson, W.G. (1985a) 'Hostages to history: Some aspects of the occupational health and safety debate in historical perspective', *The Industrial Relations of Occupational Health and Safety* (Eds. B. Creighton and N. Gunningham), Sydney: Croom Helm.

Carson, W.G. (1985b) 'Technology, safety and law: The case of the offshore oil industry', *Social Responses to Technological Change* (Eds. A. Brannigan and S. Goldenberg), London: Greenwood Press.

Carter, T. (2011) *In Foreign Fields: The Politics and Experiences of Transnational Sport Migration*, London: Pluto.

Cashmore, E. and Cleland, J. (2012) 'Fans, homophobia and masculinities in association football: Evidence of a more inclusive environment', *The British Journal of Sociology* 63(2): 370–387.

Cleland, J., Doidge, M., Millward, P. and Widdop, P. (2018) *Collective Action and Football Fandom: A Relational Sociological Approach (Palgrave Series in Relational Sociology)*, Basingstoke: Palgrave.

Conway, R. (2014) 'Qatar 2022 world cup: When will tournament take place?' *BBC Sport*, 5 November, available from: www.bbc.co.uk/sport/0/football/29915163 [accessed 1/2022].

Crewe, B. (2012) *The Prisoner Society: Power, Adaptation and Social Life in an English Prison*, Oxford: Oxford University Press.

Crossley, N. (2011) *Towards Relational Sociology*, Abingdon: Routledge.

David, M. (2006) *Case Study Research*, London: Sage.

Delanty, G. and Rumford, C. (2005) *Rethinking Europe: Social Theory and the Implications of Europeanization*, Abingdon: Routledge.

Dorsey, J. (2015) 'The 2022 world cup: A potential monkey wrench for change', *History of Sport* 31(4): 1739–1754.

Donati, P. (2010) *Relational Sociology: A New Paradigm for the Social Sciences*, Abingdon: Routledge.

Donati, P. (2013) 'Relational sociology and the globalized society', *Applying Relational Sociology: Relations, Networks, & Society* (Eds. F. Dépelteau and C. Powell), Basingstoke: Palgrave.

Donnelly, P. (2008) 'Sport and human rights', *Sport in Society* 11(4): 381–394.

DLA Piper. (2014) 'Migrant labour in the construction sector in the state of Qatar', available from: www.engineersagainstpoverty.org/documentdownload.axd?documentresource id=58 [accessed 11/2014].

European Parliament Emergency Resolution. (2013) 'Qatar: Situation of migrant workers (2013/2952(RSP)', 21 November, available from: https://eur-lex.europa.eu/legal-content/GA/TXT/?uri=CELEX:52013IP0517 [accessed 1/2022].

Foster, P. (2013) 'Qatar accused of fudging "independent" inquiry into migrant world cup workers', *The Telegraph*, 22 November, available from: www.telegraph.co.uk/news/

worldnews/middleeast/qatar/10468716/Qatar-accused-of-fudging-independent-inquiry-into-migrant-World-Cup-workers.html [accessed 7/2015].

Frew, M. and McGillivray, D. (2008) 'Exploring hyper-experiences: Performing the fan at Germany 2006', *Journal of Sport & Tourism* 13(3): 181–198.

Francis, P. (2012) 'Sport and harm: Peter Francis introduces the themed section for this issue', *Criminal Justice Matters* 88(1): 14–15.

Friedrichs, D.O. and Schwartz, M.D. (2007) 'Editors' introduction: On social harm and a twenty-first century criminology', *Crime, Law and Social Change* 48(1): 1–7.

Fromherz, A.J. (2012) *Qatar: Rise to power and influence*, London: Bloomsbury Publishing.

Ganji, S.K. (2016) 'Leveraging the world cup: Mega sporting events, human rights risk, and worker welfare reform in Qatar', *Journal on Migration and Human Security* 4(4): 221–259.

Gaston, L. (2014) 'The rugby players association's benevolent fund: A sociological study of the development of a social integration discourse in rugby football', PhD thesis: Durham University.

Gibson, O. (2013a) 'World cup 2022: Football cannot ignore Qatar worker deaths, says Sepp Blatter', *The Guardian*, 4 October, available from: www.theguardian.com/football/2013/oct/04/world-cup-2022-fifa-sepp-blatter-qatar-worker-deaths [accessed 1/2022].

Gibson, O. (2013b) 'Qatar abuse of migrant workers condemned by European parliament', *The Guardian*, 21 November, available from: www.theguardian.com/football/2013/nov/21/qatar-abuse-migrant-workers-condemned-eu [accessed 1/2022].

Gibson, O. (2014) 'Qatar government admits almost 1,000 fatalities among migrants', *The Guardian*, 14 May, available from: www.theguardian.com/world/2014/may/14/qatar-admits-deaths-in-migrant-workers [accessed 8/2015].

Gibson, O. and Pattisson, P. (2014) 'Death toll among Qatar's 2022 world cup workers revealed', *The Guardian*, 23 December, available from: www.theguardian.com/world/2014/dec/23/qatar-nepal-workers-world-cup-2022-death-toll-doha [accessed 1/2022].

Graham-Hart, J. (2003) 'Qatar joins the hunt for the tourist dollar', *The Times*, 27 December.

Greenslade, R. (2014) 'ABC figures show papers' efforts to stem circulation decline', *The Guardian*, 10 October, available from: www.theguardian.com/media/greenslade/2014/oct/10/abc-figures-show-papers-efforts-to-stem-circulation-decline [accessed 1/2022].

The Guardian. (2010) 'Sepp Blatter says gay fans "should refrain" at 2022 world cup in Qatar', 14 December, available from: www.theguardian.com/football/2010/dec/14/blatter-gay-fans-qatar-world-cup#:~:text=When%20asked%20about%20the%20issues,2022%2C%20there%20will%20be%20no [accessed 1/2022].

The Guardian. (2013) 'Qatar world cup 'slaves': The official response', 25 September, available from: www.theguardian.com/global-development/2013/sep/25/qatar-world-cup-official-response [accessed 1/2022].

The Guardian. (2014) 'Sepp Blatter: Qatar world cup workers' welfare is not Fifa's responsibility', 2 December, available from: www.theguardian.com/football/2014/dec/02/sepp-blatter-fifa-responsibility-workers-qatar-world-cup [accessed 1/2022].

The Guardian. (2021a) 'Norway players take human rights stand before world cup qualifier', available from: www.theguardian.com/football/2021/mar/24/norway-players-take-human-rights-stand-before-world-cup-qualifier [accessed 01/2022].

The Guardian. (2021b) 'Norwegian journalists reporting on world cup workers arrested in Qatar', available from: www.theguardian.com/world/2021/nov/24/norwegian-journalists-reporting-labourers-qatar-world-cup-arrested [accessed 01/2022].

Hillyard, P. (2015) 'Criminal obsessions: Crime isn't the only harm', *Criminal Justice Matters* 102(1): 39–41.

Hillyard, P. and Tombs, S. (2004) 'Beyond criminology?' *Beyond Criminology: Taking Harm Seriously* (Eds. P. Hillyard, C. Pantazis, S. Tombs and D. Gordon), London: Pluto.

Hillyard, P. and Tombs, S. (2005) 'Beyond criminology?' *Criminal Obsessions: Why Harm Matters More Than Crime* (Eds. P. Hillyard, C. Pantazis, S. Tombs, D. Gordon and D. Dorling), London: Crime and Society Foundation.

Hillyard, P. and Tombs, S. (2007) 'From "crime" to social harm?' *Crime, Law and Social Change* 48(1–2): 9–25.

Hillyard, P. and Tombs, S. (2021) 'Beyond criminology?' *The Palgrave Handbook of Social Harm* (Eds. P. Davies, P. Leighton and T. Wyatt), Basingstoke: Palgrave Macmillan.

Hillyard, P., Pantazis, C., Tombs, S. and Gordon, D. (eds.) (2004) *Beyond Criminology: Taking Harm Seriously*, London: Pluto.

Hillyard, P., Pantazis, C., Tombs, S., Gordon, D. and Dorling, D. (2005) *Criminal Obsessions: Why Harm Matters More Than Crime*, London: Crime and Society Foundation.

Hudspeth, B. (2014) 'Literature review on Kafala System in Saudi Arabia and Qatar', available from: www.academia.edu/9669734/UNFINISHED_Literature_review_on_Kafala_System_in_Saudi_Arabia_and_Qatar [accessed 1/2022].

The Independent. (2015) 'Qatar world cup 2022: Fifa president Sepp Blatter's human rights vow', 31 January, available from: www.independent.co.uk/sport/football/news-and-comment/qatar-world-cup-2022-fifa-president-sepp-blatters-human-rights-vow-10016003.html [accessed 7/2015].

International Trade Union Confederation. (2011) 'Hidden faces of the gulf miracle', May.

International Trade Union Confederation. (2014) 'The case against Qatar', March.

Jennings, A. (2011) 'Investigating corruption in corporate sport: The IOC and FIFA', *International Review for the Sociology of Sport* 46(4): 387–398.

Kamrava, M. (2013) *Qatar: Small State, Big Politics*, New York: Cornell University Press.

Kerr, G., Kidd, B. and Donnelly, P. (2020) 'One step forward, two steps back: The struggle for child protection in Canadian sport', *Social Sciences* 9(5): 68.

Kick It Out. (2021) 'Kick it out announces Qatar 2022 working group to drive LGBTQ+ inclusion at world cup', available from: www.kickitout.org/news/kick-it-out-announces-qatar-2022-working-group-to-drive-lgbtq-inclusion-at-world-cup [accessed 01/2022].

Kennelly, J. and Watt, P. (2011) 'Sanitizing public space in Olympic host cities: The spatial experiences of marginalized youth in 2010 Vancouver and 2012 London', *Sociology* 45(5): 765–781.

Kovessy, P. (2015) 'Qatar labor minister: No timetable for implementing kafala reforms', *Doha News*, 17 March, available from: http://dohanews.co/qatar-labor-minister-no-timetable-for-implementing-kafala-reforms/ [accessed 1/2022].

Lee Ludvigsen, J.A. (2021) 'Between security and festivity: The case of fan zones', *International Review for the Sociology of Sport* 56(2): 233–251.

Leighton, P. and Wyatt, T. (2021) 'The case for studying social harm', *The Palgrave Handbook of Social Harm* (Eds. P. Davies, P. Leighton and T. Wyatt), Basingstoke: Palgrave Macmillan.

Lenskyj, H.J. (2014) *Sexual Diversity and the Sochi 2014 Olympics: No More Rainbows*, Basingstoke: Palgrave Pivot.

Matthews, R.A. and Kauzlarich, D. (2007) 'State crimes and state harms: A tale of two definitional frameworks', *Crime, Law and Social Change* 48(1): 43–55.

McCoy, L. (2014) *Qatar*, London: Simon and Schuster.

McGeehan, N. (2014) 'Qatar report on migrant workers criticises treatment of staff', *The Guardian*, 14 May, available from: www.theguardian.com/global-development/2014/may/14/qatar-report-migrant-workers-staff [accessed 1/2022].

McGillivray, D. and Frew, M. (2015) 'From fan parks to live sites: Mega events and the territorialisation of urban space', *Urban Studies* 52(14): 2649–2663.

MediaWeek. (2013) 'Mail online and Guardian lead record highs for newspaper sites in January', 22 February, available from: www.mediaweek.co.uk/article/1171927/mail-online-guardian-lead-record-highs-newspaper-sites-january [accessed 1/2022].

Millward, P. (2009) 'Glasgow Rangers supporters in the city of Manchester: The degeneration of a "fan party" into a "hooligan riot"', *International Review for the Sociology of Sport* 44(4): 381–398.

Millward, P. (2013) 'Spatial mobilities, football players and the world cup: Evidence from the English premier league', *Soccer & Society* 14(1): 20–34.

Millward, P. (2017) 'World cup 2022 and Qatar's construction projects: Relational power in networks and relational responsibilities to migrant workers', *Current Sociology* 65(5): 756–776.

Mooney, J. (2011) 'Finding a political voice: The emergence of critical criminology in Britain', *The Handbook of Critical Criminology* (Eds. W. DeKeseredy and M. Dragiewicz), London: Routledge, pp. 13–31.

Mooney, J. (2019) *The Theoretical Foundations of Criminology: Place, Time and Context*, Abingdon: Routledge.

Murray, H.E. (2013) 'Hope for reform springs eternal: How the sponsorship system, domestic laws and traditional customs fail to protect migrant domestic workers in GCC countries', *Cornell International Law Journal* 45: 461.

NSA. (2021) 'Statement from Norwegian football supporters', available from: www.fotballsupporter.no/tag/supporters/ [accessed 01/2022].

Ohlert, J., Vertommen, T., Rulofs, B., Rau, T. and Allroggen, M. (2021) 'Elite athletes' experiences of interpersonal violence in organized sport in Germany, the Netherlands, and Belgium', *European Journal of Sport Science* 21(4): 604–613.

Oleaga, M. (2014) 'FIFA world cup sponsors: Budweiser partnership changing alcohol bans in Brazil, Russia 2018, Qatar 2022', *Latin Post*, available from: www.latinpost.com/articles/15443/20140623/fifa-world-cup-sponsors-budweiser-partnership-changing-alcohol-bans-brazil.htm.

Pattisson, P. (2013) 'Revealed: Qatar's world cup "slaves"', *The Guardian*, 25 September, available from: www.theguardian.com/world/2013/sep/25/revealed-qatars-world-cup-slaves [accessed 1/2022].

Pattisson, P. (2020) 'New labour law ends Qatar's exploitative kafala system', *The Guardian*, 1 September, available from: www.theguardian.com/global-development/2020/sep/01/new-employment-law-effectively-ends-qatars-exploitative-kafala-system [accessed 1/2022].

Pattisson, P. and McIntyre, N. (2021) 'Revealed: 6,500 migrant workers have died in Qatar since world cup awarded', *The Guardian*, 23 February, available from: www.theguardian.com/global-development/2021/feb/23/revealed-migrant-worker-deaths-qatar-fifa-world-cup-2022 [accessed 1/2022].

Pearson, G. (2012) *An Ethnography of English Football Fans: Cans, Cops and Carnivals*, Manchester: Manchester University Press.

Pemberton, S. (2007) 'Social harm future(s): Exploring the potential of the social harm approach', *Crime, Law and Social Change* 48(1): 27–41.

Pessoa, S., Al Neama, R. and Al-Shirrawi, M. (2015) 'Migrant workers in Qatar: Documenting their current situation', UREP Project 5–9–71, Final Report, available from: www.academia.edu/2411481/Migrant_Workers_in_Qatar_Documenting_their_Current_Situation [accessed 7/2015].

Qatar 2022 Supreme Committee. (n.d.) 'Message from the secretary general', available from: www.sc.qa/en/about/message-from-secretary-general [accessed 7/2015].

Quirke, J. (2015) 'ITUC: "7,000 construction workers will die in Qatar before 2022 world cup"', *Global Construction Review*, 18 December, available from: www.globalconstructionreview.com/ituc-7000-construction-work8e8r8s-die-qatar-2022/ [accessed 1/2022].

Reiche, D. (2015) 'Investing in sporting success as a domestic and foreign policy tool: The case of Qatar', *International Journal of Sport Policy and Politics* 7(4): 489–504.

The Report of the Hillsborough Independent Panel. (2012) 12 September, available from: www.gov.uk/government/publications/the-report-of-the-hillsborough-independent-panel [accessed 1/2022].

Roche, M. (2000) *Mega-Events: Olympics and Expos in the Growth of Global Culture*, London: Routledge.

Roderick, M.J. (2006) *The Work of Professional Football: A Labour of Love?* Abingdon: Routledge.

Roderick, M.J. (2012) 'An unpaid labor of love: Professional footballers, family life, and the problem of job relocation', *Journal of Sport and Social Issues* 36(3): 317–338.

Roderick, M.J. and Allen Collinson, J. (2020) '"I just want to be left alone": Novel sociological insights into dramaturgical demands on professional athletes', *Sociology of Sport Journal* 37(2): 108–116.

Rookwood, J. (2021) 'Diversifying the fan experience and securitising crowd management: A longitudinal analysis of fan park facilities at 15 football mega events between 2002 and 2019', *Managing Sport and Leisure*: 1–19.

Sage, G.H. (1999) 'Justice do it! The Nike transnational advocacy network: Organization, collective actions, and outcomes', *Sociology of Sport Journal* 16(3): 206–235.

Scraton, P. (2007) *Power, Conflict and Criminalisation*, London: Routledge.

Scraton, P. (2016) *Hillsborough: The Truth*, London: Mainstream Publishing.

Simmel, G. (1950) 'Quantitative aspects of the group', *The Sociology of Georg Simmel* (Eds. K.H. Wolf), London: Free Press.

Slapper, G. and Tombs, S. (1999) *Corporate Crime*, Harlow: Longman.

Stott, C. and Pearson, G. (2007) *Football 'Hooliganism': Policing and the War on the 'English Disease'*, London: Pennant Books.

Taylor, I., Walton, P. and Young, J. (1973) *The New Criminology: For a Social Theory of Deviance*, London: Routledge & Kegan Paul Books.

Tombs, S. and Whyte, D. (2003) 'Unmasking the crimes of the powerful', *Critical Criminology* 11(3): 217–236.

Tombs, S. and Whyte, D. (2010) 'A deadly consensus: Worker safety and regulatory degradation under New Labour', *The British Journal of Criminology* 50(1): 46–65.

Tombs, S. and Whyte, D. (2015) *The Corporate Criminal: Why Corporations Must Be Abolished*, Abingdon: Routledge.

Tomlinson, A. and Yorganci, I. (1997) 'Male coach/female athlete relations: Gender and power relations in competitive sport', *Journal of Sport and Social Issues* 21(2): 134–155.

Tilly, C. (2006 [2002]) *Stories, Identities and Political Change*, New York: Rowman & Littlefield Publishers.

Travers, A. and Shearman, M. (2017) 'The Sochi Olympics, celebration capitalism, and homonationalist pride', *Journal of Sport and Social Issues* 41(1): 42–69.

Ulrichson, K.C. (2014) *Qatar and the Arab Spring*, London: C. Hurst & Co.

United Nations Human Rights. (2013) 'Special rapporteur on the human rights of migrants', available from: www.ohchr.org/EN/Issues/Migration/SRMigrants/Pages/SRMigrantsIndex.aspx [accessed 1/2022].

Van Rheenen, D. (2014) 'A skunk at the garden party: The Sochi Olympics, state-sponsored homophobia and prospects for human rights through mega sporting events', *Journal of Sport & Tourism* 19(2): 127–144.

White, H. (2008) *Identity and Control: How Social Formations Emerge*, Princeton: Princeton University Press.

Whyte, D. (2007) 'The crimes of neo-liberal rule in occupied Iraq', *The British Journal of Criminology* 47(2): 177–195.

World Atlas Factbook. (2015) '2014–15', New York: Central Intelligence Agency.
Young, K. (1993) 'Violence, risk, and liability in male sports culture', *Sociology of Sport Journal* 10(4): 373–396.
Young, K. (2012) *Sport, Violence and Society*, Abingdon: Routledge.
Zeigler, C. (2014) 'How we blew it in Sochi: The LGBT community took a shot at anti-gay laws in Russia and missed the Olympic-sized target', *QED: A Journal in GLBTQ Worldmaking* 1(3), available from: https://muse.jhu.edu/article/557325 [accessed 1/2022].
Zirin, D. and Boykoff, J. (2021) 'The Olympic battle for echo park', *The Nation*, available from: www.thenation.com/article/society/olympics-echo-park/ [accessed 01/2022].

8
CONCLUSION
(Even) Further Towards a Critical Criminology of Sport

This book marks a vibrating moment in the formulation and intellectual making of a critical criminology of sport. This chapter will conclude *Sport and Crime: Towards a Critical Criminology of Sport* by summarising our main arguments and by reflecting upon how the outlined aims presented in Chapter 1 have been met throughout this book's main chapters. In this chapter, we also outline an emerging research agenda in the field of the criminology of sport.

Our overarching argument – from the aggregated discussions in the preceding chapters – is twofold. First, we contend that the application of critical criminological theory offers much to the various social scientific studies of sport, but that this canon of work has been mostly hitherto, and inexplicably, overlooked. It seemed that 'never the twain shall meet' but the reality has been proven to be different in this book. Here, we offer a history of critical criminology that could have previously intertwined with the social scientific study of sport but had largely remained separate (Chapter 2) and then five distinctive forms of critical criminology and have pioneered in their applications to sport (Chapters 3–7). The social scientific study of sport gains much from the guiding principles deriving from the concepts and perspectives of critical criminology. However, the second dimension of our overall argument is that critical criminology gains much from this conversation too. Brought in from the margins, updates are given to its approaches in the context of empirically rich areas of social life where legalities and rules are bent and broken, and deviance is prominent. This contribution is significant to sport, criminology and other social scientific subdisciplines such as the sociology of sport given that a distinctive 'criminology of sport', to date, has remained theoretically and empirically underdeveloped, despite the recently generated and much welcomed momentum that can be identified in the field (see Groombridge, 2017; Corteen, 2018; Jump, 2020; Georgoulas, 2013). And, particularly so, when juxtaposed to the sociology of sport (Dunning, 2004; Seippel, 2018) and sports law (Parrish,

2003; Thornton, 2011) which both, as distinctive subdisciplines, have predominantly tackled topics related to 'crime', 'social control' and 'deviance' in sport thus far. We call on other social scientists interested in sport and/or criminology to follow us in bringing the two together within a rigorously theorised critical frame.

However, we contend that 'sport' and 'crime' – both separately and in tandem – are culturally and politically important aspects of the present-day social and public life. Beyond academic spheres too, the *sport–crime* connections remain significant in political and bureaucratic quarters, in the media and in popular culture. Indeed, at the time of writing, streaming-service Netflix's 2021 true crime documentary series titled '*Bad Sport*' has recently been released. The series revolves around high-profile stories of 'sport' and 'crime', including incidents of murder, drug smuggling and corruption. Simply put, '[s]port and crime possess the power to stir emotion and arouse debate; most people have opinions on both' (Armstrong and Hodges-Ramon, 2015: 1). Thus, we insist that the study of crimes in sport matters and must be seriously engaged with.

This book's key arguments rest firmly upon our employment of critical criminological lenses. As applied throughout the book, we have consciously intended to showcase the applicability of these in sport. Indeed, this connects with Groombridge (2017: 155) who, in his assessment of the way forward for sports criminology, suggested that '[s]ports criminology might overlap with cultural criminology, crime and media perspectives and corporate crime, but other approaches are possible too'. The considerable arsenal of compatible theoretical tools available and located within the critical criminological projects underpins the foundations for this book.

To summarise, our in-depth investigation of sport commenced with a discussion which explored the origins, emergence and various meanings of 'critical criminology' (Chapter 2). Here, we situated sport's marginal position within critical criminology and the subsequent necessity for a broadened understanding of 'crime', 'criminality' and 'deviance' in sport, beyond merely football and 'hooliganism', which have represented two popular entrances to the study of 'crime' or 'deviance' in modern sport. Throughout the chapters, we have utilised critical approaches including 'white-collar crime' as applied to the business and management practices that have developed over time in FIFA and IOC, to explore the 'crimes' of the 'powerful' in sports (Chapter 3). We then borrowed and used ideas of 'governmentality' to explore sport-based interventions (SBIs) as youth crime reduction tools (Chapter 4); and Critical Security Studies (CSS) to examine the intensified post-9/11 'security' and 'safety' complexes at sport mega-events, the contested meanings of 'security' and governance more widely across sport. Further, we borrowed insights from cultural criminology to understand instances of violence, risk-taking and 'transgression' in sport (Chapter 6), before we finally returned to the 'crimes' of the 'powerful' and explored 'social harms' in the case of Qatar's 2022 World Cup's stadium construction projects (Chapter 7).

Throughout this book's chapters, these criminological approaches have consequently been employed to make better sense of a range of contemporary and pressing sporting practices, behaviours, institutions, sports-based interventions, sport mega-events and sports consumption. In this respect, we may also claim to have responded to Atkinson and Young's (2008) important call where they encouraged scholars to turn towards and make better use of criminological theory for an improved understanding of sport's wide array of social issues. Fundamentally, the critical approaches utilised in this book have successfully demonstrated how sport's power relations, as intrinsically connected to and co-existing with the wider political economy and state apparatuses, can legitimise, construct and reproduce inequalities, mechanisms of social control, 'harms'; preserve existing power structures and criminalise certain 'deviant' behaviours, groups or actions.

Emerging Lines of Research

Our drawing together of sport and critical criminology is far from complete, and we end this book by outlining an emerging research agenda. As we stated in Chapter 1, this research agenda is inter-disciplinary by nature but mainly directed towards a continued engagement with, and advancement of the critical criminology of sport and the wider relationships between sport and crime. Therefore, in order to strive for a maximisation of the potential of the criminology of sport, we first encourage researchers and students to be both methodologically and theoretically versatile and open-minded, in relation to emerging and digital ways of data gathering and analysis, and non-Western theoretical propositions. Notwithstanding, there are specific critical criminological lenses or branches that this book has not made full use of, which researchers could indeed engage with, in the context of sport. Similarly, there are some emerging issues that have merely been discussed in brief or passing throughout, which require increased attention from social scientists. Upon proceeding, we emphasise that both 'green criminologies' and 'feminist criminologies' have the potential to assist our understanding of 'crimes', 'harms' and 'violence' across sport. We also reflect on the impact of the catastrophic COVID-19 pandemic and how this crisis is relevant to the criminology of sport. However, important to acknowledge, at the time of writing, the pandemic is still ongoing, and its full impacts are still yet to play out.

With regard to 'green criminology' (see, for example, Lynch, 1990; Ruggiero and South, 2013; Brisman and South, 2019), this theory and its perspectives are, in broad terms, concerned with how the wider social and political dynamics, including powerful states or corporations, commit 'crimes' against and cause 'harms' to the environment. However, these 'crimes' and 'harms' may again impact both human and non-human life (Brisman and South, 2019). As an emerging branch of critical criminology from the 1990s and onwards, Lynch et al. (2018: 319) recently noted that 'green criminology remains a "youngster" relative to other forms of criminology'. Moreover, as Groombridge (2017) points out, green criminology has paid limited attention to sport. This raises questions around whether or, more exactly, *where* 'green criminological' perspectives may enhance the social understanding of sport.

For example, Wilson and Millington (2020) argue that sport mega-events have a range of potential negative impacts on the environment, including new sporting facilities, the destruction of natural vegetation, the alteration of wetland and maintenance of golf courses (regarding the latter, see Millington and Wilson, 2016). Undoubtedly, developments over the last two decades within sport invite the application of green criminological perspectives. In a time where climate change features centrally on the political and global risk agendas and presents, as Beck (2016: 40) wrote, a 'moment of metamorphosis', sport governing bodies have not remained detached and have subsequently sought to adapt its environmental practices (Ross and Leopkey, 2017), at least so, in its charters, public discourses and rhetoric. As Boykoff (2016: 145) writes, the 1992 Earth Summit in Rio de Janeiro undoubtedly influenced IOC, which since the build-up to the 2000 Sydney Summer Olympics has started to embrace 'the rhetoric of ecology'. As Boykoff contends, '[f]or Olympic honchos, green was the new green: Claiming the mantle of environmental sustainability meant positive public relations, and big bucks as well' (ibid.). Hence, since 2014, 'sustainability' has been one of the key pillars of the Olympics (Karamichas, 2021). A similar green turn may also be found in FIFA's discourses and regulations (Death, 2011).

Currently, Olympics-related 'legacy' promises made in the bidding process (see Chapter 5) have increasingly come to encompass or revolve around environmental sustainability. However, these aspirations or promises – in a similar fashion to other mega-event 'legacy' promotional discourses – do not always, necessarily or automatically materialise. Often, there are significant discrepancies between promises and the actual impacts. In the case of Rio de Janeiro's successful Olympic bid, Boykoff (2016: 231) highlights how the 'environment' and 'sustainability' turned into buzzwords that dominated the bidding books. This involved a promise to plant 24m trees in relation to the Rio Olympics in 2016; a promise which was substantially downsised as the mega-event approached in time (ibid.). Moreover, controversies concerning the contagious and unclean water at the Olympic rowing and canoeing venues emerged 1 year before the event, when it was reported that the water could threaten the health and safety of Olympic athletes and local residents (ibid.). Furthermore, Boykoff observes how Rio's Olympic golf course was 'built on an ecologically sensitive marshland' (p. 234) inside the Marapendi Nature Reserve, which was the home to a number of threatened species.[1] The politics and housing practices of sport mega-events arguably present interesting cases for the critical examinations of environmental crimes or harms.

More recently, Boykoff and Gaffney (2020) display how the connection between environmental harms and sport mega-events emerged in the Tokyo's bid and preparation for the 2020 Olympics (staged in 2021). They note that the 2020 Olympics, even before it had been staged, represented an 'ecological crisis', and employ the concept of 'greenwashing' to describe the trend where sports' governing bodies seemingly are:

> displaying concern for the environment and claiming credit for providing solutions while in reality doing the bare minimum, if anything, to make

material ecological gains – anesthetizes the public to the environmental impacts of the Olympics . . . Greenwashing reminds us to forget that elite sport is a consumer choice, a sharp-clawed tentacle of global capital that leaves indelible marks on cities and citizens, ecosystems, and our collective future.

(ibid.: 5–6)

Furthermore, in light of Tokyo 2020, Karamichas (2021) argued that it is time to reflect on how more sustainable editions of the Olympics may be staged, in relation to construction projects, displacements and CO_2 emissions linked to international air travelling. Ultimately, we argue that such reflections may benefit from insights located in the green criminologies. In a nutshell, green criminologists view ecological destruction in the context of capitalist projects which can boost 'green crimes' (Lynch et al., 2018). Here lies a significant inter-connected triad: between capitalism, environments and sport mega-events. Sport mega-events leave gigantic footprints on the environment and their cities' built and urban environments.

Increasingly, there is also a tendency that sport mega-events' hosting rights are awarded to countries located in the 'Global South', and these events are typically associated with higher construction spending (see Graeff and Knijnik, 2021). Thus, researchers should explore sport governing bodies and governments' rhetoric related to ecology and environments in bidding books and discourses; how 'environmental crimes' and 'harms' might be induced by the housing of sport mega-events and their construction projects; and how (misleading) 'greenwashed' promises might create or amplify 'harms' on humans and non-humans. In this vein, the 'green criminologies' may be particularly useful. Yet as Brisman and South (2019) note, green criminology may also be integrated with other criminological lenses, such as cultural criminology, which we addressed in Chapter 6.

Potentially, there are also distinct possibilities for extending feminist criminological work by using sports as an entrance for critical analysis. Concerning feminist criminologies, these can, for example, be employed to explore how representations of 'deviant femininity' (Heidensohn, 1996) emerge in the contested cases of 'sex-testing' or 'gender-verification' in sport, and how this has been regulated or policed by sports federations. Indeed, the high-profile case of Caster Semenya – a South African black female athlete – encapsulates this. Semenya was subject to gender testing following suspicion that she was a man (Nyong'o, 2010) following the 800-meter event at the International Association of Athletics Federations (IAAF) 2009 World Championships, which she won (Cooky et al., 2013). Reportedly, the gender-verification tests Semenya was subjected to were ordered due to Semenya's 'deep voice', 'muscular build' and rapid athletic improvements – and the case of Semenya was surrounded by media controversy (ibid.), as was the case of Indian athlete Pinki Pramanik. Questions around Pramanik's gender emerged when she was accused of rape by a woman she lived with (Mitra, 2014) and was arrested and subjected to a gender determination test (BBC, 2012). Broadly, feminist criminologies may contribute towards a strengthened understanding of the harms experienced by women in sport, and the wider structural conditions that enabled, for example, the two cases we mentioned.

Then, in terms of emerging issues within the 'crime' and 'sport' nexus, the various impacts of the catastrophic COVID-19 pandemic in sport remain imperative to address from criminological perspectives. At the time of writing, a commitment to a critical study of the visible and invisible impacts and issues related to COVID-19 should be at the forefront of a manifold of social sciences. And so, the COVID-19 pandemic also requires a critical criminological reimagination. In that respect, COVID-19 has generated a set of pressing questions, and the state responses to the pandemic have resulted in new types of 'state harm' and served, in some cases, to amplify pre-existing inequalities (see Coleman and Mullin-McCandlis, 2021; Sim and Tombs, 2021). The impacts of the pandemic on 'crime' and 'criminalisation' in sport, however, are yet to be fully addressed by scholars. This is much understandable, considering the recency of the pandemic, unfolding in the early days of 2020, and the fact that its medium- and long-term impacts still are yet to emerge in full. Whereas this section cannot cover all areas of this multifaceted crisis, we can still provide some tentative examples that may help us in locating the relation between COVID-19, sport and crime.

The pandemic led to the widespread suspension of sport across the world (Lee Ludvigsen, 2022). A number of sport mega-events and sporting competition were, in the early months of 2020, postponed or cancelled. Upon the discussions of the return of English football in May 2020, however, it was noticeable that criminalising discourses of football fans emerged when the prospects of fans gathering outside stadiums (and thereby failing to abide by social distancing rules and legislation) – where games were played behind 'closed doors' – were framed as an obstacle to football's return, despite limited evidence that fans, in fact, would gather outside stadia they had no access to (Reddy, 2020). This implies how a set of new discourses of regulation and control have emerged in line with pandemic developments. Another postponed sporting event included the aforementioned 2020 Olympics in Tokyo. However, already before the COVID-19 outbreak in early January 2020, this sport mega-event had been surrounded by controversies due to high radiation levels around the Olympic spaces and venues; the Games taking place in the aftermath of the 2011 earthquake and tsunami; and the host city's high heat (Boykoff and Gaffney, 2020). Notwithstanding, the controversy extended with IOC's decision to postpone the event for a year (Weed, 2020) – as there were no guarantees that the pandemic would be under control for its new dates between 23 July and 8 August 2021.

As the Games' new dates approached in time, concerns from residents in the country were expressed about staging the Olympics. Reportedly, 80 per cent of Tokyo's residents opposed the staging of the Olympics, with the Olympics drawing athletes from all around the world. Whilst overseas visitors were banned from attending the event, the Olympic commenced whilst Tokyo remained in a state of emergency due to the coronavirus transmission levels. Indeed, this even led some athletes to withdraw from the competition, and domestic fans were unable to visit the arenas. During the competition, reports emerged of hundreds of COVID-19 cases that were linked to the Olympics and the Olympic village (BBC, 2021).

In the context of COVID-19, the staging of sport mega-events, indeed, raises important questions in relation to host communities' and athletes' health and safety, and how sport mega-events like the Olympics can cause 'harms' to the 'less powerful' populations or social groups, who have the Olympic spectacle imposed on their lives and spaces, thereby potentially impacting their health in the pandemic's context. Regardless, wider questions around 'state harms', 'harms' and 'responsibility' (cf. Sim and Tombs, 2021), and the wider impacts of COVID-19 are not exclusive to sport mega-events and span other sport contexts including the closure of gyms and leisure centres, and exactly which 'sports' or activities that were forced into suspension and which sports that were allowed to continue despite the widespread restrictions on social gatherings in several regions.

Furthermore, Chapter 5 discussed 'surveillance' in sport and how 'security legacies' in the form of new practices, techniques and technologies may remain in place and impact host communities following an event's days. As Hutchins and Andrejevcic (2021: 375) warn us, the context of new health screening technologies may, in the response to COVID-19, work to preserve the desired consumption *during* the sporting events, for then to accelerate 'the broader deployment of crowd monitoring and control technologies beyond the walls of the stadium' after the relevant event. The responses to COVID-19, the monitoring of movement and social contact open up important and critical questions surrounding such monitoring technologies' accuracy (see Fussey et al., 2021), objectivity and processes of categorisation and social sorting (Lyon, 2007).

In the contexts of the pandemic and 'Covid-criminology', this connects with wider ideas of governmentality and social control in the 'post-pandemic' world, and especially what Shoshana Zuboff (2019) famously called 'surveillance capitalism'. Here, individuals' personal and behavioural data are collected, analysed and used by capitalist corporate powers in their pursuit of profits and occasionally shared with state apparatuses (ibid.). In this sense, the health crisis may represent a moment to concretise new modes of state power (cf. Foucault, 2008 [1977]) that are used to control or regulate populations or social groups. This, again, calls into question issues concerning privacy, consent and democracy. In light of the COVID-19-related public/private surveillance initiatives, these remain highly problematic. As is the case in the wider society, the new monitoring technologies and modes of regulation and criminalisation in the exceptional pandemic age are likely to emerge within sports or even be piloted in sports settings (Hutchins and Andrejevcic, 2021; Lee Ludvigsen, 2022). Hence, by drawing inspiration from Bigo (2016), the examination of the issues mentioned earlier can benefit greatly from in-depth conversations between criminologists and scholars of critical security studies (Chapter 5) and surveillance studies (see Lyon, 2007). This would simultaneously preserve the critical criminological tradition speaking to cross-disciplinary interventions and dialogues.

★★★

So, to make a final return to our central argument developed over the course of this book, we contend that the application of critical criminological lenses *sits* and *should sit* at the forefront of contemporary sport. In that respect, this book has made an important step and contribution further towards a 'criminology of sport', and we have shed a new light on a range of empirical settings, some of which have received limited attention in the earlier literature. Furthermore, this chapter's research agenda merely reaffirms our position regarding sport's relevance for the contemporary criminological project. Yet the research agenda simultaneously confirms how there still are a number of unexplored areas within the mentioned criminology of sport, both theoretically and in the context of recent and emerging issues, or crises, such as COVID-19. Whereas we have provided a significant and timely addition to the existing scholarship (Groombridge, 2017; Atkinson and Young, 2008; Blackshaw and Crabbe, 2004) and proceeded to focus on how theories and insights of critical criminology possess an extraordinary explanatory potential for understanding 'crime', 'harm', 'criminalisation', social justice and 'deviance' in sport, the potential of a critical criminology of sport is still yet to be maximised. Fundamentally, as Chapter 2 indicated, critical criminology theory has undergone and is likely to undergo further revisions, extensions and development in its future intellectual journey. Therefore, firmly within the scope of the continued criminological (re)imagination (cf. Young, 2011), we argue that sport should feature centrally. As a final point, we contend that ensuring this remains an intellectually intriguing and potentially rewarding future challenge for scholars of criminology and sport alike.

Note

1 Boykoff (2016) also reminds us that Rio de Janeiro already was home to two golf courses before the 2016 Olympics.

References

Atkinson, M. and Young, K. (2008) *Deviance and Social Control in Sports*, Champaign, IL: Human Kinetics.
Armstrong, G. and Hodges-Ramon, L. (2015) 'Sport and crime', *Oxford Handbooks Online*: 1–24.
BBC. (2012) 'The degradation of Pinki Pramanik', available from: www.bbc.co.uk/news/world-asia-india-18704298 [accessed 10/2021].
BBC. (2021) 'Tokyo 2020: What's happening to Covid during the Olympics?' available from: www.bbc.co.uk/news/57556978 [accessed 10/2021].
Beck, U. (2016) *The Metamorphosis of the World*, Cambridge: Polity Press.
Bigo, D. (2016) 'Rethinking security at the crossroad of international relations and criminology', *British Journal of Criminology* 56(6): 1068–1086.
Blackshaw, T. and Crabbe, T. (2004) *New Perspectives on Sport and 'Deviance': Consumption, Performativity and Social Control*, London: Routledge.
Boykoff, J. (2016) *Power Games: A Political History of the Olympics*, London: Verso.

Boykoff, J. and Gaffney, C. (2020) 'The Tokyo 2020 games and the end of Olympic history', *Capitalism Nature Socialism* 31(2): 1–19.

Brisman, A. and South, N. (2019) 'Green criminology and environmental crimes and harms', *Sociology Compass* 13(1): 1–12.

Coleman, R. and Mullin-McCandlish, B. (2021) 'The harms of state, free-market common sense and COVID-19', *State Crime Journal* 10(1): 170–188.

Cooky, C., Dycus, R. and Dworkin, S.L. (2013) '"What makes a woman a woman?" Versus "our first lady of sport" a comparative analysis of the United States and the South African media coverage of Caster Semenya', *Journal of Sport and Social Issues* 37(1): 31–56.

Corteen, K.M. (2018) 'A critical criminology of professional wrestling and sports entertainment', *The Popular Culture Studies Journal* 6(1): 138–154.

Death, C. (2011) '"Greening" the 2010 FIFA world cup: Environmental sustainability and the mega-event in South Africa', *Journal of Environmental Policy & Planning* 13(2): 99–117.

Dunning, E. (2004) 'Sociology of sport in the balance: Critical reflections on some recent and more enduring trends', *Sport in Society* 7(1): 1–24.

Foucault, M. (2008 [1977]) '"Panopticism" from "discipline & Punish: The birth of the prison"', *Race/Ethnicity: Multidisciplinary Global Contexts* 2(1): 1–12.

Fussey, P., Davies, B. and Innes, M. (2021) '"Assisted" facial recognition and the reinvention of suspicion and discretion in digital policing', *The British Journal of Criminology* 61(2): 325–344.

Georgoulas, S. (2013) 'Social control in sports and the CCTV issue: A critical criminological approach', *Sport in Society* 16(2): 239–249.

Graeff, B. and Knijnik, J. (2021) 'If things go South: The renewed policy of sport mega events allocation and its implications for future research', *International Review for the Sociology of Sport*: 1–18.

Groombridge, N. (2017) *Sports Criminology: A Critical Criminology of Sports and Games*, Bristol: Policy Press.

Heidensohn, F. (1996) *Women and Crime* (2nd Edition), London: Macmillan.

Hutchins, B. and Andrejevcic, M. (2021) 'Olympian surveillance: Sports stadiums and the normalization of biometric monitoring', *International Journal of Communication* 15: 363–382.

Jump, D. (2020) *The Criminology of Boxing, Violence and Desistance*, Bristol: Bristol University Press.

Karamichas, J. (2021) 'Tokyo 2020: How did the latest Olympics rank against other for sustainability?' available from: https://theconversation.com/tokyo-2020-how-did-the-latest-olympics-rank-against-others-for-sustainability-165359 [accessed 10/2021].

Lee Ludvigsen, J.A. (2022) *Sport Mega-Events, Security and Covid-19: Securing the Football World*, London/New York: Routledge.

Lynch, M. (1990) 'The greening of criminology: A perspective on the 1990s', *The Critical Criminologists* 2(3): 1–12.

Lynch, M.J., Stretesky, P.B. and Long, M.A. (2018) 'Green criminology and indigenous/native peoples: The treadmill of production and the killing of indigenous environmental activists', *Theoretical Criminology* 22: 318–341.

Lyon, D. (2007) *Surveillance Studies: An Overview*, Cambridge: Polity Press.

Millington, B. and Wilson, B. (2016) *The Greening of Golf: Sport, Globalization and the Environment*, Manchester: Manchester University Press.

Mitra, P. (2014) 'Male/female or other: The untold stories of female athletes with intersex variations in India', *Routledge Handbook of Sport, Gender, and Sexuality* (Eds. J. Hargreaves and E. Anderson), New York: Routledge, pp. 384–394.

Nyong'o, T. (2010) 'The unforgivable transgression of being Caster Semenya', *Women & Performance: A Journal of Feminist Theory* 20(1): 95–100.

Parrish, R. (2003) *Sports Law and Policy in the European Union*, Manchester: Manchester University Press.

Reddy, M. (2020) 'Fans have been leading lights in their communities, not louts waiting to disrupt football's return', *The Independent*, available from: www.independent.co.uk/sport/football/premier-league/pl-project-restart-when-fans-behind-closed-doors-a9509581.html [accessed 10/2021].

Ross, W. and Leopkey, B. (2017) 'The adoption and evolution of environmental practices in the Olympic Games', *Managing Sport and Leisure* 22(1): 1–18.

Ruggiero, V. and South, N. (2013) 'Green criminology and crimes of the economy: Theory, research and praxis', *Critical Criminology* 21(3): 359–373.

Seippel, Ø. (2018) 'Topics and trends: 30 years of sociology of sport', *European Journal for Sport and Society* 15(3): 288–307.

Sim, J. and Tombs, S. (2021) 'Narrating the coronavirus crisis: State talk and state silence in the UK', *Justice, Power and Resistance* 4(1): 1–28.

Thornton, P.K (2011) *Sports Law*, Boston: Jones & Bartlett Publishers.

Weed, M. (2020) 'The role of the interface of sport and tourism in the response to the COVID-19 pandemic', *Journal of Sport & Tourism* 24(2): 79–92.

Wilson, B. and Millington, B. (eds.) (2020) *Sport and the Environment: Politics and Preferred Futures*, Bingley: Emerald Group Publishing.

Young, J. (2011) *The Criminological Imagination*, Cambridge: Polity Press.

Zuboff, S. (2019) *The Age of Surveillance Capitalism: The Fight for the Future at the New Frontier of Power*, London: Profile Books.

INDEX

9/11 attacks 93, 104

activity-tracking vest 110
Adhikari, Deepak 154
ad hominem stories 77
Adidas 46–48, 50–51, 54, 57–58, 68; French division of 47; as global brand 51; sport business and marketing practices at 58
aeitiological crisis 134
affective harms 147
African Football Confederation (CAF) 66
Ahmad, Ahmad 66
Al Khulaifi, Abdullah bin Saleh 165
amateur 'fight videos' 123
Amnesty International 154–160, 162, 165, 168–169
Andersen, Jens Sejer 65–66
Andrade, Castor 56, 67
Anouma, Jacques 62
anti-doping organisations 111
anti-social behavior 8, 108; amongst young people 77; reduction policies 88
Anti-Social Family, The (1982) 21
anti-war protest movements 17
Armstrong, Lance 110
Asian Football Confederation (AFC) 59, 171n4
Association of Boxing Commissions (ABC) 132
Athens Summer Olympics (2004) 98
athletes' rights, to both privacy and civil liberties 111

athletic performances and bodies, surveillance of 9, 94, 109–112
Atkinson, Rowland 33

Babel, Ryan 111
Backyard Brawls 124, 137
Bad Sport (crime documentary series) 180
Bare-Knuckle Boxing (BKB) 124, 134; codes of conduct 135; difference with unorganised street fighting 134–135; documentation of 135; events in Great Britain 135; 'London Prize Ring' rules 135; Marquess of Queensberry Rules (1867) 135; organisation of 135; as organised combat sport 136; popularity in global 'North' 135; practice of 135; regulation of 136; standard of 'fair play' 135
Bare-Knuckle Fighting Championship 136
BASE jumping 128–130
Baudrillard, Jean: comparison of hooligan fan behaviour to state terrorism 97; idea of 'hyper reality' 98; Mirror of Terrorism, The 97
BBC Radio 4 15
Beck, Ulrich 128
Belgian Parliamentary Commission of Inquiry 97
Bell, Alasdair 66
Berlin Olympics (1936) 46
"Big Brother" system, of surveillance and control 111
Birmingham School 126

'Black September' Palestinian group 98
Blatter, Joseph 'Sepp' 55–56, 59, 66, 164–165; allegations of white-collar criminality 61; contract with the Caribbean Football Union 64; end of FIFA Presidential era of 62–64; establishment of an ethics committee in FIFA 60; personal connections to Horst Dassler 58; re-election for a fifth term as FIFA president 63
blood doping 110
Bonger, Willem 43
bourgeois criminology, politics of 23
boxing 2, 77, 131–132, 135; bare-knuckle 9, 124, 134–136; kick-boxing 132; Thai-boxing 132; title fights 124; Tottenham Boxing Academy 79–80
'braresembling' devices 110
Brazil Olympic Games (1936) 56
bribery, cases of 8, 53, 55, 61
British Board of Boxing Control (BBBC) 135
British Criminological Association 3
British public schools, modern sports in 79
Broughton, John 'Jack' 135
Brundage, Avery 47
Business for Corporate Responsibility 155, 160–161

capital 54, 80–85, 131, 137–138, 183
carbon dioxide (CO2) emissions 183
Carson, Kit 20
car wash effect 81
Cayman Islands Football Association 62
CCTV cameras: spread of 115; use of 101–103, 106; *see also* surveillance cameras
celebration capitalism 51
chav fan 109
child labour exploitation 145
child poverty 134
Cloward, Richard 14
Club, The 46–48, 51, 56, 66–67
CNBC 58
Coca-Cola 52, 57
Cohen, Albert 14
Cohen, Stan 15, 19–20, 32
combat sports *see* fight sports
Commonwealth Games 54, 102–103
communal belonging 137
community-based programs 29
community-based surveillance 86
Confederation of North, Central America and Caribbean Association Football (CONCACAF) 60; bribery case 63; Gold Cup 62
CONMEBOL (South America) 62
consumer capitalism 3
consumer culture 133–139
Convention on the Protection of the Rights of All Migrant Workers and Members of Their Families (UN) 163
Copa América 62
Copenhagen School 113
corporate crime 180
corporate sponsorships 8, 51
corruption, in sports 4, 64, 68–69
Coulter, Jeff 16
counterterrorism policing campaigns 108
COVID-19 pandemic 8, 10, 181; coronavirus transmission 184; impact on sports 184; public health crisis 170; socially harmful impacts of 134; surveillance technologies 101–102
Covid-criminology 185
crime prevention 2, 83–87, 90, 104, 108, 115; policies for 77; progressive 30; situational and environmental 29; strategies of 86
crime reduction 80, 82–84, 88, 90–91, 180; at regional and national level 77; sport as a tool for 85; strategies for 8
'crimes' committed by athletes/fans 2
crimes of the powerful 8, 41, 160
'crime-sport' nexus 4
criminal behaviour 18, 31, 44, 67–68, 79, 85; causes of 24; within and through sport 8
criminalisation of kids, playing street games 4
criminal justice agencies 14, 78–79
criminal justice system 6, 24, 28, 32–34, 145, 147, 154
criminological imagination 17
criminology: fundamental feature of 127; of sport 1, 3–6, 10, 170, 179, 181, 186
critical criminology: anti-theoretical bias 14; application of 179, 186; branches of 29; British 14; development of 13, 17, 145; emergence of 14–17; first wave of theory 23–28; new criminology and 23–28; second wave of theory 28–32; sociological imagination and 17–23; theory of 14; turn to left realism 28–32; in twenty-first century 32–34; white-collar crime as 43–46
Critical Criminology (1975) 13
Critical Security Studies (CSS) 9, 95–97, 180

critical terrorism studies 95–97
Crystal Palace Expo (1851) 94
cultural capital 80, 85, 131, 137–138
cultural criminology 123–124, 180, 183; edgework, voluntary risk-taking and the joy transgression 127–131; emergence of 125–126; free intellectual space of 127; overview of 125; recognition of emotions and attractions 128; rise of 125–127
Cultural Criminology (1995) 126
cultural interpretations 130

Danish Institute for Sports Studies 65
Dassler, Horst 49–50, 55, 64, 68; connection with Horst Dassler 58; French division of Adidas 47; International Sports and Leisure Marketing (ISL) 48; The Olympic Partners (TOP) contract (1985) 52; and 'The Club' 46–48, 51, 66–67; trade links to East Europe 50
data gathering technologies 107
de Coubertin, Pierre 51–52
Deutscher Fußball-Bund 58
deviant femininity, representations of 183
Deviant Interpretations (1979) 29
D'Hooghe, Michel 62
differential association, theory of 43–44, 67
digital technologies, rise of 112
disloyalty payment 63–65
'disorderly' youth, governance of 87
DLA Piper 165–168
'do-it-yourself' biographies 128
doping tests 115
Downes, David 15, 19–20, 29, 33
Drewry, Arthur 56
drug experimentation 127
Drugtakers, The (1971) 18
drug testing 9, 109–111
drug use, amongst the riders 110

Eastern Bloc 50
edgework: applicability of 130, 140; concept of 124, 127–128, 131; theory of 9
edgeworkers 128–130
elite sports 3, 5, 8, 47, 56, 67, 109, 111, 183
emotionality in criminality, role of 139
emotions, phenomenology of 127
engineered sponsorship 67
Engineers Against Poverty (2014) 155, 160
English Premier League 77, 133

environmental crimes 29, 182–183
Erzik, Senes 62
European Group for the Study of Deviance and Control 16, 33
European Parliament 163
Exeter, Lord 47
'exit-visa' system 166
extreme sports 9, 124, 128, 140

facial recognition software 103, 107
Factory Acts 145–146, 164
Factory Inspectorate 146
'fake' fans 108
fan zones 87, 113, 151
favelas 85
Federal Bureau of Investigation (FBI), US 62
Fédération Internationale de Football Association (FIFA) 4, 34, 41, 66; administrative infrastructure 57; competition to host World Cup finals 59; corruption case 8; dealing with white-collar criminality 70; discourses and regulations 182; European rights to World Cups 57; Executive Committee 62; inter-continental club championships 57; internal ethics committee report 56; operational expenses and services 59; revenues from World Cup 58–59; sponsorship and cash for votes allegations 55–62; whistle-blowers within 59–60; World Cup in Argentina (1978) 57
feminist criminologies of sports 8, 181, 183
fertilizer effect 80
fight sports 124, 131, 132; Bare-Knuckle Boxing (BKB) 134; representations of 134–139; *versus* unorganised street fighting 135; *see also* Bare-Knuckle Boxing (BKB); jiu-jitsu; Mixed Martial Arts (MMA)
financial and economic harm 147
football: commercialisation of 31; free of 'corruption' 55; Heysel Stadium football disaster (1985) 30, 97; Hillsborough disaster (1989) 22; hooliganism in 16, 21–22, 26, 30, 34, 98–99; role in the 'working-class weekend' 22; violence related to 4, 31
Football Supporters' Association (FSA) 169
Football *vs.* Homophobia 169
forced labour 154, 167
Foucault, M. 8, 78, 87, 90, 104
free-market economies, of neocapitalist states 134
free-market principles, in sport 67

Galaxy Football Club 151
'gang' fights 138
Gebrüder Dassler (German shoe company) 46–47
gender determination test 183
'gender-verification' in sport 183
Giulianotti, Richard 1, 4, 5, 21, 80, 86, 88, 91, 93, 96, 98, 101–104, 108, 109, 114–115, 124, 128–129, 153
global capitalism 54
Global North 85, 89, 103, 114–115, 134, 136
global recession 103
Global South 85, 89, 103, 112, 115, 155, 183
Gloves Up 137
Google Scholar 128
Gouldner, Alvin 24, 27
governance 65, 78, 104, 180; at distance 90; and 'fair play' 55; of football 59, 108; levels of 51; mechanisms for monitoring of behaviours 94; modes of 9, 93–94, 111, 115; neoliberal 84; self-governance 87; of sports 41, 46, 93; strategies for 8; taxonomy of 110; of youth 78, 84, 86–88, 90
governing by fun, concept of 78, 86–88
governmentality, concept of 87
'GPSports' tracking devices 110
Gramscian neo-Marxism 15
green criminologies 181–183
guardian angel effect 81
Guardian, The 9, 106, 157, 161, 163–164, 167
Gulf Cooperation Council (GCC) 153–154
Guns Down 137

Hall, Stuart 15–16
Hamad Al Thani, Emir Tamim bin 150
Hammam, Mohammed Bin 59–61
hate crime 34, 147
Havelange, João 55–57, 65–66, 70n3; acceptance of bribe money 61; career in sports administration 56; replacement by Sepp Blatter 58
Heysel Stadium football disaster (1985) 30, 97
higher education 17
high income economy 150
high-risk sports 128
Hill & Knowlton 54, 167
Hillsborough disaster (1989) 21–22, 100, 114, 149

'hippy' culture, rise of 16
HM Revenue & Customs (HMRC) 45
Hodler, Marc 50, 53
homeless populations, displacement of 171
homosexuality, sociology of 21
Homosexual Role, The 21
hooligan databases 103
'hooligan' (fan violence) encounters 22, 97
hooliganism, acts of: football-related 16, 21–22, 26, 30, 34, 98–99
House of Commons 100
How They Stole The Game (1999) 59
human rights abuses 170
Human Rights Watch 154–155, 160–162
human trafficking 154
hyper-masculine competitivism and aggression 123
hyper-surveilled fan zones 87

ice-skating, recreational 148–149
'inauthentic' fans 109
industrial-scientific revolution 135
Infantino, Giovanni (Gianni) 64–66
INGO *Humanity United* 161
inner-city localities 102
Internal Revenue Service Criminal Investigation Division (IRS-CI) 62
international air travelling 183
International Amateur Athletics Federation 47
International Association of Athletics Federations (IAAF) 183
International Centre for Sport Security, The (ICSS) 96, 101
International Centre for Sports Studies, at University of Neuchâtel 64
International Olympic Committee (IOC) 4, 34, 41, 42, 48–55, 66, 70, 154; amendment of the Olympic Charter 101; bid to host games 53; bribery, cases of 52–53, 55; Commission for New Sources of Finance 47; Committee on human rights 154; 'good news' documents 54; ISL's right to act on behalf of 52; overhaul of the bidding process to award cities the Olympic Games 54; 'rules' to protect their own interests 55
international sport 1, 4, 78
International Trade Union Confederation (ITUC) 154–156, 158, 159
inter-personal violence 124, 134, 138
ISL (sports marketing agency) 52, 56, 61, 66, 67

Janette, Christian 57; manipulation of sporting power in USSR 50; role in connecting Samaranch and Dassler 49
Jennings, Andrew 4, 8, 42, 46–61, 63–64, 66–70, 167
jiu-jitsu 132, 138–139
job creation 93
Johansson, Lennart 58
Johnson, David 52
Jones, Wyn 95

'Kafala' system, in Qatari law 144, 157, 160–164; abuse of 166; quest for reform of 165–168; restrictive rules on labour rights 155; sponsorship system 166, 169; story of construction workers' social harm 153–155
Käser, Helmut 58
Kathmandu Post, The 154
Katz, Jack 126
Keller, Stefan 66
Kelly, Laura 78–79, 83–84, 86–89
Kenya Olympics Association 54
King, Anthony 23
Kissinger, Henry 54, 60, 167
'Know the Game Plan – Act' 108

lateral surveillance 94, 107–109, 113
Lauber, Michael 66
Lefkaritis, Marios 62
left realism, theory of 7, 29–34
Lenz, Jűrgen 55, 64, 68
Leoz, Nicolás 61–62
Leoz, Paraguayan 63
Leyton Orient Community Sports Programme 79
liquid modernity 139
Liverpool Football Club (Liverpool F.C.) 22, 97, 100, 116n5
Llona, Angel Maria Villar 62
'London Prize Ring' rules 135
lower-class citizens, criminalisation of 147
Ludvigsen, Lee 101, 113
Lusail City Real Estate Development Company (LCREDC) 161
Lyng, Stephen 127–128

Maduro, Miguel 65
Makudi, Worawi 62
'malestream' criminology 28
Marquess of Queensberry Rules (1867) 135
McIntosh, Mary 15–16, 20–21, 28
Mega Events and Modernity (2000) 94

Midnight Basketball 79
Mills, C. Wright 17, 18
Mirror of Terrorism, The 97
Mitchell, George 55
Mixed Martial Arts (MMA) 9, 124, 128; academic recognition of 131; academic research on 131; cage fighting 131; fighters' motivations and mental health 131; history, representations and consumption 131–134; media and public controversy 133; in North-West England 138; octagon 133; popularity of 132, 134; popular/mediatised depictions of 139; rules of 132; Team Fight Championships (TFC) 134; training activities 139; Ultimate Fighting Championship (UFC) 131–132; in United Kingdom 137; US-based 131–132, 137; *Vale Tudo* (Anything Goes) 132; *see also* Bare-Knuckle Boxing (BKB); jiu-jitsu
Modern Age 134
money laundering 21, 43, 45, 46, 62, 68, 70n2
moral panics 3, 19, 32, 69, 114
Moscow Olympic Games (1980) 50
'most violent' fight sports, representations of 134–139
motorcycle subcultures 16
Muscular Christianity, concept of 79
Myrtle Beach Football Club 151
MySpace.com 123

Nadal, Rafael 111
Nally, Patrick 47–48, 51, 57, 68
National Basketball Association (NBA) 133
National Basketball League (NBA) 113
National Conference of Teaching and Research on Criminology 14
National Deviancy Conference (NDC) 14–15, 16, 33, 145
National Football League (NFL) 105, 133
National Olympic Committee 4, 34, 41–42, 48, 50, 54, 70
Nation, The 171
natural vegetation, destruction of 182
networks 8, 70, 104, 148, 155
New Criminology Revisited, The 32
New Criminology, The (1973) 13, 145
New Right politics 29
New York Times, The 69
non-governmental organisation 55
Norwegian Supporters Alliance (NSA) 169

official criminology, critics of 23
Olympic athletes, health and safety of 182
Olympic Charter 101
Olympic Games 51, 52, 94
Olympic movement 49, 51
Olympic spirit 'Citius, Altius, Fortius' 52
Organization of the Petroleum Exporting Countries (OPEC) 150
organized modern sport 79
organizing of practices 87
Orwell, George 1, 104
Other Price of Britain's Oil, The (1982) 146
Ottoman Empire 150

paramilitary ceasefires, in Northern Ireland 98
Paris School 113
Parker, Paul 108
Parkinson's disease 19
participatory democracy 22
Pattisson, Pete 156, 158–159, 161
pay-per-view television 132–133
pay-to-view outlets 67
Pearson, Geoffrey 28–29
performance-enhancing drugs 52, 81
'perpetrators' as 'terrorists', labelling of 98
personal decision-making 128
personal development 78, 139
petroleum industry 145
physical harms 147, 158
Platini, Michel 63–65
Plummer, Ken 15, 16
political and religious radicalisation, of young people 80
political economy of crime, development of 25
Polletta, F. 14
Positive Futures, in UK 79
power 145
power relations 145
power relations of society,, impact of criminality in 33
Pramanik, Pinki 183
PriceWaterhouseCoopers 66
professionalisation of sports 111
psychedelic culture 27
public disorder, mobile phone footage of 108
public safety and security, surveillance for 105–107
public violence 132

Qatar 66; Abolition of Forced Labor Convention 154; Bahrani rule (1783–1868) 150; bid to host the World Cup 60; DLA Piper 165–168; injustices for migrant construction workers in 146; 'Kafala' system in 144, 153–155, 157, 160–168; Labor Ministry 161, 163; Labour Law 157; labour law reforms 153; mistreatment and death of migrant construction workers 162; National Human Rights Committee 160; national identity card (iqama) 154; National Vision 2030 150; non-payment of wages 159; Ottoman rule (1871–1916) 150; outlook and developments 168–170; power and politics in reforming migrant workers' rights 160–165; Qatar Ladies Open 151; regulating regulation and regulators 165–168; right to host the 2022 FIFA World Cup 64, 96, 144, 149–153; social harms 144, 155–160; sovereign wealth fund 150; Sponsorship Law 160; stadium construction projects 180; Supreme Committee (Q22) 161–162; Tour Championships 151; Tour of Qatar 151; transnational economic power 150; Wahhabi interpretation of Islam 150; World Cup construction projects 158
Qatar Foundation 167
Qatar Holding investment 150
Qatar Investment Authority (QIA) 150
Qatar Tourism and Exhibitions Authority (QTEA) 152

racism and gang warfare 31
radical criminology, idealism of 28–30, 32
Radzinowicz, Leon 15–16
realist criminology, importance of 32
recreational drug, use of 16, 81
relational sociology 9, 144, 147, 170
responsibility, themes of 9, 45, 49, 111, 144, 146–148, 154, 158, 162–166, 169
Rida, Hany Abo 62
risk management 86, 101, 104
risk society 128
Roche, Maurice 94, 101
Rock, Paul 29, 33
Ross, Edward A. 43
Rous, Stanley 55, 57, 69
Russia: Red Army 50; state-sponsored homophobia 149

Salguero, Rafael 62
Salt Lake City games scandal 52
Salt Lake City Olympic Committee (SLCOC) 52–53

Salt Lake City Winter Games (2002) 98
Samaranch, Juan Antonio 50, 51, 66, 167; early life and career in sports journalism 49; Honorary President for Life title 49; as IOC President 48–55; The Olympic Partners (TOP) contract (1985) 52; reform programme at IOC 54
same-sex relations 21
Samoura, Fatma 66
Seaman, David 108
security: governance 104; legacies 9, 93, 100–104, 105, 112; legislation and policing strategies 103; strategies related to 101, 114
Sedgewick, Peter 16
self-gratification, negotiation of 137
self-policing 108
Semenya, Caster 183
Seoul Olympic Games (1988) 51
sex-testing, cases of 183
shared community bonds 80
Shearer, Alan 108
Sheffield Wednesday F.C. 22
Sim, Joe 31
Simmel, Georg 147, 162
skateboards 5
Smart, Carol 23
Smyth, Breen 99
soccer hooliganism 21
Sochi Olympic Games (2014) 152
social capital 80–81, 85
social control 3, 6, 85, 89, 93, 102, 105, 112–113, 180; failures of 125; mechanisms for 86, 88, 90, 181; in 'post-pandemic' world 185; sport for 87; strategies for 86
social exclusion 29, 82, 84
social harms 26, 41, 166, 170–171, 180; construction workers, story of 153–155; and criminal law 145–148; in domain of cultural safety 160; economic dimensions of 158; emotional/psychological 159; financial/economic 159; and migrant workers in World Cup 2022 infrastructure development 155–160; parameters of 146; physical dimensions of 156, 158; in sport 148–149; study of 34; violations of 13
social ills, emergence of 17
social inclusion 79, 82–84; funding-dependent 84; objectives 90
social justice 3, 5–6, 14, 186
socially excluded youth 87

'socially invisible' crime control technology 107
social media, rise of 113
social mobility 80, 82, 84–86
social psychology of social reaction 26
social reaction, political economy of 26
social reproduction 85
social sorting 185
social theory of crime 24, 27
societal obsession 134
societal responsibilities 85
sociology of deviance 2, 16
sociology of sport 1–3
sociopolitical transformation 30
SonntagsBlick 66
South Wales Police 106
South Yorkshire Police 100
sovereign wealth fund 150
Spanish Olympic committee 50
sponsorship rights 52
sponsor transfers 165–166
Sport Based Initiative 90
sport-based interventions (SBIs) 8–9, 77, 88, 181; academic and practitioner-oriented evaluations of 90; as agents of social control 84; assumptions around sport as a 'hook' 78–81; "bottom-up" and "top down" view of 89; 'effectiveness' in improving young people's lives and reducing 'crime' 78; effectiveness of 78, 81–86; employment of 90; justifications for 88; for positive youth development 85; public and private stakeholders 79; relationship to 'at risk' youth 82; as a response to 'troublesome youth' 79; as response to 'youth crime' and 'risks' 78; as social control mechanism 82; social study of 86; strategies for governing youth crime 84; as tools in the reduction of crime 80, 85; as a 'way out' for 'at-risk' individuals 80; working of 88–89; as youth crime reduction tools 180
sport-based program 83–84, 88
sport-based social control 86–88
sport–crime connections 180
Sport for Development and Peace (SDP) 80, 88
sporting violence 124, 137
sport mega-events 9, 59, 87, 113, 181; absence of 'hooligans' and 'terrorists' 97–100; budgets for security at 103; budgets planning and delivery of 96; cultural distinctiveness of 94; economic

aspect of 103; global coverage of 94; 'hooligan' violence 96; housing of 183; impact of COVID-19 pandemic on 184; impact of terrorism on 98; investigation of 94; issue of safety and security at 99; negative impacts on the environment 182; post-9/11 media coverage of 'terrorist threats' at 98; safety issues 93; security enforcement at 100; security legacies 94, 100–104, 164; security-related strategies at 101; surveillance for safety and security 105–107; themes of safety and security 94; unpacking 'safety' and 'security' 97–100; as war zones 98
sport-related programs 89
sports consumption 181
sport–security–surveillance relationship 112–113
sports entertainment 2
sports evangelists 80–81
sports for all 83
sports journalism 49
sports law 179
sports marketing 56, 62
Sports Media LGBT+ 169
Sport Steward Program, in the Netherlands 79, 84
Stadium, Heysel 97
strategic partnerships: security legacies and 102, 114; between security providers at local, national and international levels 103
street crime 14, 31
street fighting 135
structural inequalities 82, 84, 86–88, 90, 136
Sugden, John 8, 41, 50, 56–57, 69, 105, 138–139
Sunday Times, The 59–60
Super Bowl 105–106
surveillance cameras 102, 105
surveillance capitalism 185
'surveillance' of sport: application of 105; of athletic performances and bodies 109–112; "Big Brother" system of surveillance and control 111; contours of 104–112; defined 104; in elite sport 111; governance, mode of 94; intrusive surveillance techniques 107; lateral 107–109; monitoring strategies 105; at post-9/11 mega-events 105; practice of 104; prominence of 104; for safety and security 105–107; social media-related 113; at Super Bowl 105; techniques of 105; typologies of 94, 113

surveillance technologies 101, 103; COVID-19 related 101–102; protest against 107
Sutherland, Edwin 41, 43–44, 56, 67
'sweat shop' industries, sports-related 155
Swiss criminal law 61
Swiss judicial system 70
Sydney Summer Olympics (2000) 96, 182

targeted sport interventions 78
tax haven 70
Taylor, Ian 21–23, 30
Taylor, Laurie 15–16
TEAM 55
Team Fight Championships 124, 137
technological innovations 101
technological progression 104
Teixeira, Ricardo 56, 61
television broadcasting 51
terrorism, acts of 4, 93, 95–99, 105, 113
terrorist threats, media coverage of 98
Tet offensive, in Vietnam 17
Thatcher, Margaret 4, 29, 97
The Olympic Partners (TOP) contract (1985) 52
Tokyo Summer Olympics (2020) 55, 170
Tombs, Steve 31, 34, 43, 70, 144, 148
Tomlinson, Alan 55, 58, 61, 67
Tottenham Boxing Academy, UK 79–80
Tour de France (1998) 110
'tourism development' fund 152
tourists fans 109
'transgression' in sport 180
transgressive identities, formation of 138
transnational fans 109
transnational security industry 103
Transparency of Evil, The (1993) 97
Triesman, David 60

UEFA Champions League 55, 105–106
'underhand' codes of behaving 67
Union of European Football Associations (UEFA): Champions League 105–106; 'Integrity of the UEFA Club Competition: Independence of the Clubs' rule 45
United Nations (UN) 89
United Passions 61
urban crime 104
urban redevelopment 102
urban regeneration 93
Uruguayan Football Association 62

Valcke, Jérôme 60, 63–64
Vencer Program, in Brazil 79

violence, football-related 4
violent fight sports events 137
vote-rigging, in the decision-making processes 46

Walton, Paul 24, 27, 32, 34n1, 145
Warner, Jack 60, 63
wealth and income, redistribution of 147
Webb, Howard 111
Webb, Jeffrey 62
Weber, Jean-Marie 48, 67
Welch, Tom 52
'Welsh School' of security studies 95
Western judicial systems 147
'Western' societies 131, 138
Western super-ego, reorientation of 134–139
'whistle-blowers' within FIFA 59–60, 66
white-collar crime 8, 41–42, 64, 68–69, 146, 151, 180; acts of 70; allegations of 61; Carson's work on 145; club owner's tax evasion 45; concept of 43, 67; corruption and 66–70; as a critical criminology 43–46; defined 43, 45–46; legitimate rackets 46; money laundering 45; Salt Lake City games scandal 52; underreporting of 70
White-Collar Crime (1949) 43
white-collar deviancy 46–47, 51–52, 69
white-collar rule-breaking 45, 69

white-water kayaking 128
Willis, Paul 16
Winlow, Simon 33
Winter Sports Federation 54
wire fraud 62
Women's Tennis Association 150
World Anti-Doping Agency (WADA) 110–111
World Conference on Doping in Sport (1999) 110
World Cup stadiums 6
World Fairs/Expos 94
World Youth Soccer Championships (1997) 70n3
wrestling, professional 2

xenophobia 31, 98

Yallop, David 47, 52, 59
Young, Jock 16–19, 29
young people, profiling of 86
youth crime 78, 80, 82, 88; conceptualisations of 79; issues of 77
youth risk 78

zemiology, theory of 34, 145–148, 170–171
Zen-Ruffinen, Michel 55
Zuboff, Shoshana 185

Taylor & Francis eBooks

www.taylorfrancis.com

A single destination for eBooks from Taylor & Francis with increased functionality and an improved user experience to meet the needs of our customers.

90,000+ eBooks of award-winning academic content in Humanities, Social Science, Science, Technology, Engineering, and Medical written by a global network of editors and authors.

TAYLOR & FRANCIS EBOOKS OFFERS:

- A streamlined experience for our library customers
- A single point of discovery for all of our eBook content
- Improved search and discovery of content at both book and chapter level

REQUEST A FREE TRIAL
support@taylorfrancis.com

Routledge — Taylor & Francis Group

CRC Press — Taylor & Francis Group